# The Shield of Achilles and the Poetics of Ekphrasis

# Greek Studies: Interdisciplinary Approaches
General Editor: Gregory Nagy, Harvard University

# The Shield of Achilles and the Poetics of Ekphrasis

ANDREW SPRAGUE BECKER

ROWMAN & LITTLEFIELD PUBLISHERS, INC.

ROWMAN & LITTLEFIELD PUBLISHERS, INC.

Published in the United States of America
by Rowman & Littlefield Publishers, Inc.
4720 Boston Way, Lanham, Maryland 20706

3 Henrietta Street
London WC2E 8LU, England

British Cataloging in Publication Information Available

**Library of Congress Cataloging-in-Publication Data**

Becker, Andrew Sprague
The shield of Achilles and the poetics of ekphrasis / Andrew
Sprague Becker.
p. cm. — (Greek studies : interdisciplinary approaches)
Includes index.
1. Homer. Iliad. 2. Achilles (Greek mythology) in literature.
3. Art and literature—Greece—History. 4. Trojan War in
literature 5. Description (Rhetoric) 6. Shields in literature.
7. Rhetoric, Ancient. 8. Homer—Technique. 9. Ekphrasis.
10. Poetics. I. Title. II. Series: Greek studies.
PR4037.B39 1994 883' .01—dc20 94–40446 CIP

ISBN 0-8476-7997-7 (cloth : alk. paper)
ISBN 0-8476-7998-5 (pbk. : alk. paper)

Printed in the United States of America

*For Trudy*

# Contents

# Greek Studies: Interdisciplinary Approaches

# Foreword

*by Gregory Nagy, General Editor*

Building on the foundations of scholarship within the disciplines of philology, philosophy, history, and archaeology, this series spans the continuum of Greek traditions extending from the second millennium B.C. to the present, not just the Archaic and Classical periods. The aim is to enhance perspectives by applying various different disciplines to problems that have in the past been treated as the exclusive concern of a single given discipline. Besides the crossing-over of the older disciplines, as in the case of historical and literary studies, the series encourages the applications of such newer ones as linguistics, sociology, anthropology, and comparative literature. It also encourages encounters with current trends in methodology, especially in the realm of literary theory.

*The Shield of Achilles and the Poetics of Ekphrasis*, by Andrew Sprague Becker, is a thorough and definitive guide to the very first attestation of ekphrasis in European literature, the Shield of Achilles in Book XVIII of the Homeric *Iliad*. Even more than that, this book reassesses the basics of ekphrasis itself, the poetic device that allows verbal art to represent visual art. Such a device, as Becker's work demonstrates, not only reflects the esthetic and conceptual world of a given visual art: it also illuminates the very nature of the verbal art that reflects this world. As Hephaestus, the model artisan, proceeds to create that definitive marvel of visual art, the Shield of Achilles, the poet proceeds to turn into words this creation in progress, singing it to his audience. Just as the poet marvels at the divine smith's magnificent work, Becker argues, the audience is meant to marvel at the poet's own song. The poet's response to the ultimate picture is a metaphor, then, for the audience's response to the ultimate song. For Becker, the purpose of the ekphrasis in juxtaposing verbal and visual art is surely not to decide which of the two is the superior medium. It is, rather, to enhance each medium's communicative power by way of the other's.

This book is valuable not only for defining the poetics of ekphrasis. It serves the practical purpose of providing both a commentary on the entire Shield passage of *Iliad* XVIII and a review of literary critical views on ekphrasis, including the ancient sources and the trend-setting 1766 essay *Laokoon*, by Gotthold Ephraim Lessing.

# Acknowledgments

There are many whom I must thank. I start with George Kennedy, who first suggested the writing of this book, and whose gentle but careful guidance could serve as a model of mentorship. I have learned from many fine teachers at the University of Michigan, Cambridge University, and the University of North Carolina at Chapel Hill. But to the following teachers, especially, I owe an unrepayable debt: Gerda Seligson and Glenn Knudsvig, who both brought me to classics; Don Cameron, who first taught me Homer; and Ed Brown and Peter Smith, who taught me much about Greek literature and helped with the early stages of this book. To Gregory Nagy I owe thanks for his consistent support over the last decade and especially his encouragement through the finishing of the book.

I have also been taught less formally by a family in which intellectual exchange and literary discussions were as much a part of daily life as cleaning and cooking. I have discussed much of this book, and learned more than I could acknowledge, from my mother, Judith Becker, both in her writings and in long conversations. Thanks go to my brother, Matthew, who read and criticized a draft of the second chapter; to my sister Margaret, who responded to many of the ideas presented here; and to my cousin David, whose thoughts on classical literature have made me rethink my own. Moreover, there is not a page in this book that is not influenced by my father, Pete Becker; his thoughts and writings about language have been the source and guide for all I do, and his responses to drafts of this book showed me the respect and affection entailed in a close, careful, critical reading.

I would like to thank colleagues past and present here at Virginia Tech, for the kind of environment that helps us all to think and to write and to teach. First, the classicists Glenn Bugh, Nick Smith, Tom Carpenter, Gina Soter, and Terry Papillon. Terry Papillon read through and responded to several chapters of this essay, with characteristic intelligence and good humor; he has taught me a great deal, both as a colleague and a friend. For editing and proofreading, I thank Kendra Yount, a fine student of classics.

Other colleagues have shown me the benefits of a department that includes a variety of languages and literatures. I thank first Chris Eustis, who helped shape the atmosphere of intellectual vigor that I have found here. Richard Shryock organized the Works-in-Progress group, at which I have discussed parts of this book, and he has helped me with several sections of what follows; Lloyd Bishop kept my finger on the pulse of scholarship on ekphrasis in French literature—even where I have not cited it, he has stimulated thought; Alex Mathäs and Dianne Hobbs have helped with German and Spanish; and Steve Baehr's learning and generosity are exemplary, and I thank him for his responses to several parts of this book.

I am grateful to colleagues at other universities, who have commented on parts of what follows, specifically Steven Lonsdale, Mark Edwards, James Heffernan, and James Boyd White. For invitations to test some of these thoughts in lectures, I thank Don Fowler of Oxford University, Salle Ann Schlueter-Gill of Radford University, and Stanley Lombardo of the University of Kansas. I also thank the *American Journal of Philology*, where I first published some of what follows, and audiences at several conferences, where I presented some of the ideas in this book. Penguin, U.K., generously gave permission to use Hammond's translation of the *Iliad* for the extensive quotations in Chapter 4 and Part II.

For two beautiful places to work in the summers, overlooking the Sakonnet River in Portsmouth, Rhode Island, I thank my in-laws, Dr. and Mrs. Harrington; they provided both the "little" house in Island Park as well as the "big" house at the Hummocks, where I wrote several drafts. I also did much writing in the Portsmouth Free Public Library, and thank them for their patience.

Finally, I dedicate this book to Trudy Harrington Becker, *prima inter pares*. She is my touchstone; she has commented on or challenged every page of everything I have written. Her critical eye, her expertise in classics, her wit, and her care have made this book and my life much better than they ever could have been without her.

# PART I

# PROLEGOMENA

The eighteenth book of the *Iliad* ends with a lengthy description of Hephaestus making a new shield for Achilles at the request of Achilles' mother, Thetis (*Iliad* 18.468-608). The description begins with Hephaestus setting to work, gathering and using his tools and metals. The describer then turns to the scenes depicted on this shield. The first is the heavens: the sun, moon, and four constellations (the Pleiades, the Hyades, Orion, and the Bear). There follows a city at peace, divided into two scenes showing social rituals: a wedding procession and the lawful settlement of a blood-feud. After the city at peace comes a city at war; this picture of a walled city besieged by invading armies is the longest of the scenes, and includes plans, battles, an ambush, and the participation of gods in the fray. The next five scenes are of agriculture and husbandry: the ploughing of a field, a harvest, a vineyard with children dancing (accompanied by a boy singing and playing a lyre), a scene depicting the herding of cattle with a vividly described attack by lions, and a brief description of a sheepfold. The final scene is that of a dance floor with young dancers performing an elaborate dance upon it. The entire shield (as the entire earth) is encircled by the river Ocean. The eighteenth book of the *Iliad* then ends with a brief nine lines describing the rest of the weapons and Thetis's departure with the new arms for Achilles.

This description is at the head of a long tradition of ekphrasis, a word I use here to mean the description of a work of visual art. I use the word "ekphrasis" in the modern sense, not in the ancient sense of a description of any kind. The limitation of the term ekphrasis to descriptions of visual art has become widespread, both among classicists and students of other disciplines.[1] Ekphrasis becomes a common feature of Greek and Latin literature, appearing in, e.g., the *Odyssey*, the pseudo-Hesiodic *Shield of Herakles*, Aeschylus *Seven against Thebes*, Euripides *Electra*, *Ion*, and *Phoenissae*, Apollonius *Argonautica*, Theocritus *Idylls*, Moschus *Europa*, Herodas *Mimes*, many poems of the Greek Anthology, Naevius *Bellum Punicum*, Catullus 64, Vergil *Eclogues, Georgics,* and *Aeneid*, Propertius 2.31, Ovid *Metamorphoses*, Statius *Silvae* and *Thebaid*, Petronius *Satyricon*, Silius Italicus *Bellum Punicum*, Valerius Flaccus *Argonautica*, Longus *Daphnis and Chloe*, Achilles Tatius *Leucippe and Clitophon*, Heliodorus *An Ethiopian Story*, Lucian's dialogues, Philostratus the Younger *Imagines*, Quintus of Smyrna *Posthomerica*, Claudian *Panegyrics* and *De raptu Proserpinae*, and Nonnus *Dionysiaca*.

Literary description of art is, of course, not just an ancient phenomenon; it is central to, e.g., Dante *Divine Comedy*, Chaucer *House of*

---

1. See the two major classical dictionaries in English, Hammond and Scullard (1970), p. 377: "*EKPHRASIS*, the rhetorical description of a work of art"; and Howatson (1989), p. 203: "*écphrasis*, type of rhetorical exercise taking the form of a description of a work of art." Cf., e.g., Spitzer (1967), pp. 67-97, especially p. 72; Krieger (1967), p. 110; Kurman (1974), p. 1; Schmeling (1974), p. 80; Bergmann (1979), p. 2; DuBois (1982), p. 3; Goff (1988), p. 42; Dundas (1993), p. 15. The earlier sense of the term is description of any kind, usually as a rhetorical exercise: see Downey (1959). In the *progumnasmata* (ancient Greek rhetorical handbooks), Nikolaus of Myra (fifth century A.D.) is the first to discuss works of art explicitly (Spengel III.492); earlier handbooks mention the making of Achilles' weapons as an example of ekphrasis, but they include it in the category of *tropoi* (customs). The *Imagines* of the Philostrati are well-known examples of rhetorical exercises that describe works of visual art; the term ekphrasis, however, appears only once in the two collections (Philostratus the Younger 390K), and the word itself means only "description." It is made to refer specifically to descriptions of visual art only by a pair of genitive nouns: *graphikês ergôn ekphrasis* (description of works of painting). Of the more than five hundred occurrences of the word *ekphrasis* (in a search on the Ibycus system), nearly two-thirds occur in Eustathius, and very few occur before the third or fourth century A.D. The infinitive *ekphrazein* appears once in Demetrius *On Style* 165 (first century B.C. or A.D.), meaning "to decorate," or "to adorn." The treatise on sublimity attributed to Longinus (probably written in the second century A.D.) does not use the word *ekphrasis*. It is mentioned in the *Rhetoric* that was attributed to Dionysius of Halicarnassus, in a section on mistakes in judicial speeches (10.17). Cf. the similar censure of ekphrasis in Quintilian 2.4.3 and Lucian 59.20. See Harlan (1965). Outside of the field of Classics, the use of the term in its broader, more ancient sense is rare: Preminger and Brogan (1993), pp. 320-321; Krieger (1992), pp. 7-9; Heffernan (1993), pp. 1 and 191 note 2.

*Fame*, Shakespeare *Rape of Lucrece*, as well as the poetry of Shelley, Jorie Graham, John Ashbery, and Eavan Boland. And it occurs in, e.g., Torquato Tasso *Gerusalemme liberata*, Castiglione "Cleopatra," Spenser *Faerie Queen*, Garcilaso de la Vega *Eglogas*, Guillaume de Lorris *Le roman de la rose*, Théophile Gautier *Mademoiselle de Maupin*, Marivaux *Le Télémaque*, Dostoyevsky *The Idiot*, Nathaniel Hawthorne *The House of the Seven Gables*, Hermann Melville *Moby Dick*, Alain Robbe-Grillet *Dans la labyrinthe*, and the poetry of Robert Browning, Rainer Maria Rilke, Robert Lowell, Elizabeth Bishop, Seamus Heaney, Donald Hall, W.H. Auden, e.e. cummings, Jim Bogan, William Carlos Williams, Aimée Hall, Anthony Hecht, Vicki Hearne, Miller Williams, and Joseph Brodsky.

The touchstone for ekphrasis in ancient Greek and Latin literature, and for much later European literature, is the Homeric Shield of Achilles.[2] Part I of this essay is an elaborate setting of the stage in preparation for Part II, which is a detailed commentary on the language of description in the Shield of Achilles. I spend many pages in preparation for the commentary, reading back through the discussion of ekphrasis in ancient rhetorical handbooks, through the later tradition of theory, practice, and reading of ekphrasis (with emphasis on Lessing's *Laokoon*), through the pseudo-Hesiodic *Shield of Herakles*, through descriptions earlier in the *Iliad*, culminating in a scene-by-scene commentary on the Shield. In Part I, I explore how ekphrasis itself has been read, how ekphrasis encourages us to read the poetry that includes it, and how ekphrasis has encouraged aesthetic theories.[3] In the introductory chapters below, I set out a variety of approaches to ekphrasis, each of which provides a different "take" on ekphrasis, and all of which have induced and will prepare for the discussion of the language of description in the Shield of Achilles.

In Part II, I look more specifically at the types of response, attention, and engagement that the Shield of Achilles asks from its audiences. The focus throughout is description itself as a rhetorical move, i.e., the particular ways in which the language of ekphrasis directs our attention.[4] The act of translating visual depictions into poetry provokes many questions, two of which will guide much of what follows. First, what attitude toward

2. In this essay "Shield" refers to the Homeric description of the object, while "shield" refers to the imagined object itself.
3. For a more strictly theoretical view of description, see Hamon (1981), and his influential article "Qu'est-ce qu'une description?" (Hamon 1972); this article is translated in R. Carter and Todorov (1982), pp. 147-178.
4. A still wider application is suggested by G. Miller and Johnson-Laird (1976), pp. 119-120: "The apparent simplicity of descriptive sentences recommends them as the starting points for attempts to construct a theory of linguistic meaning."

representation, visual and verbal, can this ekphrasis encourage? Second, assuming that ekphrasis models a type of response, what kind of audience for the *Iliad* can this ekphrasis encourage us to be?[5]

## Ekphrasis as Metaphor or *Mise en Abîme*

Ekphrasis has often been treated as a metaphor for poetry.[6] In the chapters to follow I treat ekphrasis as such, but specifically as a metaphor for an audience's response to poetry. The relation between the ekphrasis and the (imagined) work of visual art can be read as analogous to that between the reader (or listener) and the poem.[7] To put it in less abstract terms, the bard's response to visual images becomes a model for our response to the epic. I thus treat ekphrasis as a kind of *mise en abîme*, "a miniature replica of a text embedded within that text; a textual part reduplicating, reflecting, or mirroring (one or more than one aspect of) the textual whole."[8] I treat

---

5. There are now many voices asking us to attend to the ways in which Homeric song shapes the responses of a listening or reading audience, even in very specific, subtle, or unconscious ways. See Janko (1992), p. 2; Doherty (1992), pp. 172-177, and Doherty (1991), p. 163: "By dissolving and then re-establishing the distinction between the internal and implied audiences of Odysseus's recital, the narrator is able to model the reception of his own poem. The effect, in other words, is to invert the apparent relations of control over interpretation." (In ancient Greek literature, Plato's *Ion* 535e discusses this control that Homeric epics exert over their own interpretation, through a metaphor of a magnetic stone.) M.W. Edwards (1991), p. 23, referring to "composition by theme," says: "But like so much else in Homer, in his work they are refined into artistic techniques for shaping the hearer's response." Although the conclusions are in many ways contrary to mine, see Ford (1992), p. 5: "I think that any poetry must give or renew for its audience an idea of what it is, if only as a way of telling them how to receive it." On self-consciousness about epic and its language in the *Iliad*, see Stanley (1993), pp. 24 , 290, 313 note 54; Taplin (1992); Slatkin (1991); and, in the *Odyssey*, see Katz (1991) and Peradotto (1990). More generally, on the intricacy and subtlety of effect in individual words and phrases see Nagy (1979), pp. 78-79, 5§19. It is no longer necessary for us to express the surprise of Krieger (1967), p. 105: "It would seem extravagant to suggest that the poem . . . implicitly constitutes its own poetic. I would like here to entertain such an extravagant proposal." Cf. Ricoeur (1981), p. 189.

6. E.g., Manakidou (1993), *passim*, with a convenient summary on p. 270; Meltzer (1987), p. 1; R. Edwards (1989), pp. 3-4, 94, 108, and 166 note 1. Specifically on the Shield of Achilles, see Hurwit (1985), pp. 46-47, 87; Schadewaldt (1966), p. 166; Marg (1957), p. 27; Gregory (1977), p. viii; Burkert (1985), p. 168. Cf. from the ancient Greek commentaries on the *Iliad*, Scholia bT on *Iliad* 3.126-27 (Erbse I, p. 381).

7. On the poetics of the Shield matching the poetics of the rest of the *Iliad*, see Marg (1957); M.W. Edwards (1991), p. 209; Atchity (1978); Stanley (1993).

8. Graff (1987), p. 53.

ekphrasis, however, as a *mise en abîme* of the poetics, not just of the themes of the *Iliad*: in ekphrasis not only does the bard become one of us, an audience, but also the description itself, metonymically, becomes a model for the poem.[9] Description of art in the *Iliad* can serve as a way of training our responses to the epic.

## Analogy and Rivalry

Ekphrasis also has been treated as a symbol of a fundamental goal of poetry: an attempt to represent in words the physical presence, the natural resemblance to its referent, and the still moment of the visual arts.[10] Such a view joins the study of ekphrasis with the study of the analogy and rivalry between the verbal and visual arts. The habit of viewing the visual and verbal arts as sisters or specifically as rivals has a long tradition and has suffused our thinking about art and representation.[11] The earliest example I have

9. On the *mise en abîme* as a trope of the poetics, rather than the content of a work, see Dällenbach (1989), pp. 75-93. Using terms of narratology, my analysis treats ekphrasis as a mirror of the enunciation, rather than the referent(s) of the work. While my focus is the poetics of the Shield of Achilles, there are many fine accounts of the thematic function of the Shield of Achilles within the *Iliad*. A selection should include N. Richardson (1993), p. 17; Stanley (1993), pp. 3-4, 24-25, 189; Byre (1992); Hubbard (1992); Janko (1992), p. 311; M.W. Edwards (1991), pp. 208-209; Nagy (1990b), pp. 250-255; Rabel (1989); M. Lynn-George (1988), pp. 189-190, 193, 197-198; Mueller in Bloom (1986), p. 217; Hardie (1985); Hurwit (1985), p. 71: Kirk (1985), p. 46; Schein (1984), pp. 141-142, cf. p. 93; J.B. White (1984), p. 42; Griffin (1980); Taplin (1980); Nagy (1979), p. 109; Andersen (1976); Gärtner (1976); Shannon (1975); Austin (1966), pp. 295-312; Beye (1966), p. 144; Tashiro (1965), p. 66; Duethorn (1962); Reinhardt (1961), p. 403; Marg (1957), p. 38; Whitman (1958), p. 126; Hampe (1952), p. 21; Schadewaldt (1944), pp. 300, 352-374; Bassett (1938), pp. 98-99; Sheppard (1922), p. 5. M.W. Edwards (1987), pp. 269-286, summarizes the wide range of divergent interpretations of the Shield.

10. Krieger (1992) and (1967); Mitchell (1986), p. 98; Felperin (1985), pp. 166 and 177; Steiner (1982), pp. 1-32.

11. The view of the greater scope and effect of verbal art has been revived through the ages in European and American writings; see, e.g., Thoreau (1983), p. 147: "A written word is the choicest of relics. It is something at once intimate with us and more universal than any other work of art. It is the work of art nearest to life itself. It may be translated into every language, and not only be read but actually breathed from human lips; not be represented in canvas or in marble only, but be carved out of the breath of life itself." Or Dewey (1980), pp. 239-240: "The art of literature thus works with loaded dice; its material is charged with meanings they have absorbed through immemorial time. Its material thus has an intellectual force superior to that of any other art, while it equals the capacity of architecture to present the values of collective life." And 241: "The architectural, pictorial, and sculptural are always unconsciously

discovered of an *explicit* rivalry in extant Greek literature is Pindar *Nemean* 5.1-6 (composed c. 483 B.C., more than two centuries after the Homeric poems are thought to have been recorded). In this poem poetry is said to surpass sculpture, due to poetry's greater ability to spread *kleos* (glory); an explicit comparison between song and sculpture works to the detriment of the latter.[12] For earlier Greek responses to the visual arts we can look to ekphrasis.[13] In such descriptions the relationship between visual images and language is brought into high relief: we can understand these ekphrases as passages that direct the attention of an audience, as it reads or hears a

surrounded and enriched by values that proceed from speech." On the European tradition of comparison between the arts see, e.g., Leonardo da Vinci (1956), p. 18; Sir Philip Sidney (1951), p. 10; Dewey (1980), pp. 187-244; Wallace Stevens (1942), pp. 159-176; Hagstrum (1958); Ong (1967), pp. 111, 117, and 138, and (1977), pp. 122-123 and 125; Praz (1970); Baxandall (1972); W.J.T. Mitchell (1980) and (1986); Maguire (1981); Steiner (1982): E. Cook (1986); Roston (1990); Evett (1991); Heffernan (1979). Some recent critics see a focus on the differences and difficulties of representation as a necessary feature of ekphrasis. A fine book that takes this approach is Heffernan (1993). Cf. Meltzer (1987); M. Shapiro (1990), pp. 97-114; Langer (1957), pp. 75-89. I do not see such a reading as necessary, but merely one of many ways of responding to ekphrasis.

12. See Gentili (1988), pp. 50-60 and 162-165, on the analogy between the verbal and visual arts in Pindar's day. (E.g., p. 164: "He [Pindar] must therefore have conceived of his own work as a craft—as existing, technically, on the same level as one of the figurative arts.") He affirms the likelihood that the two media were considered analogous, and that privilege was given to the verbal arts in representational capability as well as the ability to spread *kleos* (glory). Pindar himself encourages an analogy when he calls his poetry an *agalma* ("statue," "pleasing image," *Nemean* 3.12-13; 8.15-16). (Cf. the similar fourth-century formulation in Isocrates *Evagoras* 73-74.) The Pindaric comparison may have had a predecessor in Simonides' apothegm reported in Plutarch (*De glor. Ath.* 346F). Simonides, Plutarch tells us, said that poetry is silent painting and painting is mute poetry. The context in Plutarch makes it clear that visual arts have something that literature lacks, and literature is improved when it borrows vivid effects from visual representations (347A). (On some of the implications of this particular comparison, see Steiner (1982), pp. 5-7.) Cf. Simonides fragment 190b (Bergk), which uses a term from visual representation: *kata Simônidên ho logos tôn pragmatôn eikôn esti* ("according to Simonides the *logos* is a likeness [*eikôn*] of actions"). And also Solon, reported in Diogenes Laertius I.58: *elege de ton men logon eidôlon einai tôn ergôn* ("he used to say that the *logos* is an image [*eidôlon*] of actions"). Pindar may be working within a tradition of overt analogy between the verbal and visual arts.

13. See Stewart (1966), pp. 554-555: "I don't think we really *know* how the ancients looked at things, or what they expected of visual art, and this is a kind of knowledge that certainly should be sought after. . . . And perhaps a study, not of Greek art *in itself*, but of *writing about* pictures and other forms of representation, might begin to do the job. . . . In general, I see a real need of new studies on *description of art objects in literature*." On the influence of description not only on the response to, but also upon the creation of visual arts in the Renaissance, see Rosand (1990), pp. 61-105. His discussion, *mutatis mutandis*, is a useful model, since he focuses on the artist's responses to descriptions of art in literature, not just artistic responses to literary texts in general.

translation of images into language, to the manner, means, and objects of representation in both visual and verbal media.[14]

The attitude that concerns me here is that of the verbal representation, the ekphrasis, vis-à-vis the (imagined) visual representation. I conclude that the Shield of Achilles is a fulsome and appreciative response to the provocation provided by the visual images; it is a performance or experience of what is seen. The following chapter will outline several readings of the Shield of Achilles to which I wish to respond—those that see it as suggesting the superiority of verbal description over visual depiction, or as a failed attempt to be a clear reflection of visible phenomena, as if the bard were trying to describe a picture but could not help elaborating beyond what could be seen in the (imagined) images. When the Homeric bard describes images in a way that goes far beyond the physical appearance of the (imagined) visible phenomena, the spirit is that of Seamus Heaney's poem "Seeing Things II," which describes a carved stone relief:

> Lines
> Hard and thin and sinuous represent
> The flowing river. . . . Nothing else.
> And yet in that utter visibility
> The stone's alive with what's invisible.[15]

---

14. Such a reading of ancient Greek and Latin ekphrasis has been suggested by Goff (1988), p. 51: "The *ekphrasis* with its more immediately and obviously problematic status, can thus throw into relief the operations we normally perform without such close attention." Cf. Leach (1988), p. 311: "Through their assimilation of visual to verbal artistry such descriptive pauses in poetic narrative may allow us some insight into poetics or else provide by their content a symbolic amplification of theme."

15. Heaney (1991), p. 19.

1

# HOMERIC EKPHRASIS AND "TRUE DESCRIPTION"

*Some of our speech acts can rightly be called illocutionary acts of describing the world. There are, to borrow Wittgenstein's metaphor, language-games of describing. Those games will determine what counts as a good description and what a bad one, internal to the game which is played.*

*- Mason (1989), p. 39*

The Shield of Achilles has been a stimulus for later scholars and theorists to explore the differences between the verbal and visual arts; many have devised schemes for what a description ought to be. I begin with those who find that Homer's practice does not fit their idea of description, then move on to those who find in Homer a paradigm for what description should be.

Paul Friedländer, the author of the only thorough treatment, ancient or modern, of ekphrasis in Greek and Roman literature, assumed that true description is the representation of the surface appearance of a work of visual art.[16] An ekphrasis should try to represent, as faithfully as possible, the *visible* features of a work. Discussing the Shield of Achilles, Friedländer laments that Homer often gets carried away by a "childlike" tendency to fall from true description (*echte Beschreibung*) into storytelling:

---

16. The introduction (pp. 1-103) of Friedländer (1912) is a history of ekphrasis from the Shield of Achilles to the sixth century A.D.

Der Dichter ist einfach nicht imstande, eine bildmäßige
Vorstellung, von der er ausgeht, etwa die belagerte Stadt,
dauernd festzuhalten, sondern er wird von einer durchaus
jugendlichen Freude an belebter Erzählung beherrscht. (p. 2)

The poet is simply not capable of sustaining a picture-like
representation, with which he begins, such as the besieged
city, but he is overcome by a thoroughly youthful pleasure in
animated narration.

According to Friedländer, Homer is still capable, in spite of this weakness, of
actual description, though it is rare:

Hier sollen einige Punkte aufgewiesen werden, an denen
schon bei Homer selbst echte Beschreibung erreicht ist. (p. 3)

Here several points must be shown in which Homer himself
already achieved true description.

Edmund Burke and Gotthold Lessing, to be discussed below, censure the
attempt to describe the surface appearance of a work of visual art, but
Friedländer calls it true description and regrets Homer's translation of
appearance into action. The assumption here illustrated, that description
should name and represent the visible features of a work of art, has led
through the years to a view easily characterized as the "Homer's mistakes"
approach to the Shield. When faced with the vivid and vivifying description
of the depictions in the Shield of Achilles, some critics have seen not a mode
of description, but a deficiency. For example: "The picture is a little
confused, as if Homer himself is deceived by what he is imagining," or "One
is not quite sure whether the pictures on the shield are static or alive; Homer,
in fact, is not quite sure what kind of pictures are made by Hephaestus. . . .
He seems to stand a little bewildered between the realism of the finished
panels, and the limitations of the material."[17] I hope that this study of

---

17. Respectively, Willcock (1984), p. 271, and Whitman (1958), p. 205. Cf. the more
guarded but similar remark of M.W. Edwards (1991), p. 207: "minor confusions in the details of
his account may result from the misinterpretation of a two-dimensional picture." Cf. also
Heffernan (1993), p. 20, who is similarly guarded in his language discussing a passage from the
Shield (*Iliad* 18. 573-86): "In the middle lines the poet seems to forget that he is representing
graphic art; he suppresses all reference to metal as he tells the gruesome story of the lions and the
ox."

ekphrasis will induce us to take another look at what the text is doing. A complex and shifting aesthetic stance does not necessarily mean confusion. Homeric ekphrasis describes an experience of representations, not just their appearance.

Two influential thinkers of the eighteenth century each found in Homeric description a paradigmatic illustration of their divisions between verbal and visual art. Each believed that "true description" did not escape Homer, but rather that Homeric ekphrasis embodied what description ought to be. Edmund Burke used Homeric description as a model in his work of 1757 (revised and expanded in 1759) entitled *A Philosophical Enquiry into the Origins of Our Conception of the Sublime and the Beautiful*, while Gotthold Lessing used it as a pervasive informing archetype for his *Laokoon: oder über die Grenzen der Malerei und Poesie*, published in 1766.[18]

Edmund Burke proposed that a work of literary art should not describe appearance, for then it would be merely an inferior representation. It should, rather, represent the effect (not the visible features) of great beauty; only this will achieve sublimity. He grounds his distinction between the arts in an argument with both Platonic undertones and Aristotelian modifications. The visual arts can affect the audience no more than the object they represent (were it present); on the other hand, the verbal representation, because it is not iconic, can represent the reactions to and feelings about the object, and so elicit a stronger emotional response (p. 60). Poetry, in fact, causes Burke to visualize very little (pp. 167, 170, 171), as it concentrates instead on the significant yet invisible aspects of phenomena.[19] This observation then becomes prescriptive and evaluative as the discussion continues. He contends that sublimity is a higher goal than beauty and that poetry gives access to sublimity, while the visual arts depict only beauty, the lesser of the two. Fundamental to Burke's distinctions between the two media is the

---

18. E. Burke (1968); Lessing (1988; 1984). I must here say that I shall use but not endorse the views of Edmund Burke and Lessing. They are sources of provocation and stimulation, but I find much that is hard to accept in both, not least of which are the desire to find fixed boundaries between the arts, the desire to rank them, and the consequent devaluation of the range and force of visual representations. For similar reservations, see W.J.T. Mitchell (1986), p. 98 and Dewey (1980), pp. 189 and 226. For a modern view of ekphrasis that sees pervasive rivalry and contest, see Heffernan (1993).

19. An American ekphrasis that shows the same propensity would be the long description that opens chapter 3 of Melville's *Moby Dick* (1992), pp. 15-16: we are asked, and asked explicitly, to share an experience of viewing, not to assume that we see without the mediation of the describer's words.

representation of effect. For example, after considering Homeric description, Burke writes:

> In reality poetry and rhetoric do not succeed in exact
> description so well as painting does; their business is to
> affect rather by sympathy than imitation; to display rather the
> effect of things on the mind of the speaker, or of others, than
> to present a clear idea of the things themselves. This is their
> most extensive province and that in which they succeed the
> best. (p. 172)

Burke is responding to a belief that painting is the more powerful form of representation; he reacts specifically against a view that clarity is the paramount virtue in the arts, and that the visual arts are more successful in this vein than the verbal.[20] Burke disagrees to such an extent that the province allowed to the visual arts, clarity and precision, is relegated to a secondary status, to the realm of "mere" beauty. Poetry, on the other hand, can represent and elicit the sublime, according to Burke, because it represents thoughts, emotions, and reactions to beauty.[21] It represents effect, and here effect *is* essence. If one achieves clarity, one loses power and sublimity; but if one represents the emotions and thoughts elicited by visible phenomena, then one achieves a sublimity greater than that of the phenomena themselves. Burke prepares the ground for his devaluation of visual art by saying:

> Certain it is that the influence of most things on our passions
> is not so much from the things themselves, as from our
> opinions concerning them; and these again depend very

---

20. The passage I have quoted was added by Burke to his second edition, perhaps after further consideration of Abbé du Bos (first published under this name in 1755, but published anonymously in 1719), with which Burke had become familiar through an English translation published in 1748. Abbé du Bos says that painting has primacy over language, even in affecting the passions, because of its clarity. Such writings, which give privilege to visual arts over verbal, are not as common as those that give the palm to language. Perhaps the most famous is Leonardo da Vinci (1956), p. 18: "If you call painting mute poetry, poetry can also be called blind painting. Now think, which is the more damaging affliction, that of the blind man or that of the mute? . . . If the poet serves the senses by way of the ear, the painter does so by way of the eye, a worthier sense." Cf. the modern example in Nemerov (1972-73): "It is because / Language first arises from the speechless world / That the painterly intelligence / Can say correctly that he makes his world." See also Rosand (1990), especially pp. 69 and 96, and Rudolf Arnheim, "A Plea for Visual Thinking," in W.J.T. Mitchell (1980), pp. 171-179.

21. Burke's elaborations on the primacy of verbal art were stimulated in part by "Longinus" *On Sublimity* (e.g., 15.2 or 36.3). It had become popular through Boileau's translation of 1674, which Burke read early in his life.

much on the opinions of other men, conveyable for the most
part by words only. (p. 173)

He makes his case explicit, when discussing examples of ekphrasis:

> In painting we can represent any fine figure we please; but
> we can never give it those enlivening touches which it may
> receive from words. . . . It is true, I have here no clear idea,
> but these words affect the mind more than the sensible image
> did, which is all I contend for. (p. 174)

This is due to the ability of words to give us effect, which brings the desired
sublimity.[22] When considered in light of Burke, the particular focus of an
ekphrasis can imply that there are significant differences in the abilities of the
sister arts to represent the world, and these differences give rise to a view that
the verbal arts are more powerful in representation than the visual.[23]

## Lessing's *Laokoon* and the Shield of Achilles

Here is an interpretive model developed explicitly in response to the
Shield of Achilles. Lessing's oft-cited interpretation of the Shield of Achilles
is found in chapters XVI-XIX of *Laokoon: oder über die Grenzen der
Malerei und Poesie.*[24] Its influence is pervasive, even among those who take
issue with his conclusions; André Gide echoed the sentiments of many when
he remarked: "Le Laocoon de Lessing est oeuvre qu'il est bon tous les trente
ans de redire ou de contredire."[25] Though Lessing claims that his essay is not
to be understood as a systematic analysis, he does begin his discussion of
Homer "from first principles" (*aus ihren ersten Gründen,* p. 104) of the
distinction between the arts: the visual arts can enter into a "suitable relation"
(*bequemes Verhältnis*) only with bodies in space, while the verbal arts can do

---

22. In the reaction of the elders to Helen (3.156-59), the *Iliad* provides an apt example of
affecting the audience through the representation of effect, not appearance. Burke uses this
passage as support for his argument (pp. 171-172).

23. See A.S. Becker (1993a) for an experimental reading that uses Edmund Burke (and
Lessing) to try to discover an implicit rivalry between the arts in Hesiod's descriptions of
Pandora.

24. The text used is Lessing (1988). The translations are from Lessing (1984).

25. Gide (1947), p. 36. "The *Laocoon* of Lessing is a work that it is good to restate or to
contradict every thirty years."

so only with actions in time. Painting, which stands for the visual arts in Lessing's analysis, can attempt to imitate actions, but it can do so only by suggestion; it cannot enter into a suitable relation with actions. Poetry, on the other hand, can attempt to imitate appearance, but again only by suggestion, and to do so is seen as a waste of talent. Homer is then produced as authority:

> Ich würde in diese trockene Schlußkette weniger Vertrauen setzen, wenn ich sie nicht durch die Praxis des Homers vollkommen bestätigt fände, oder wenn es nicht vielmehr die Praxis des Homers selbst wäre, die mich darauf gebracht hätte. (p. 105)

> I should put little faith in this dry chain of reasoning did I not find it completely confirmed by the procedure of Homer, or rather if it had not been just this procedure that led me to my conclusions. (p. 79)

Lessing claims that Homer represents progressive actions, with bodies and objects included only as necessary for the representation. Homer's detailed picture of an action is one

> aus welchem der Maler fünf, sechs besondere Gemälde machen müßte, wenn er es ganz auf seine Leinwand bringen wollte. (p. 106)

> which the artist would have to break up into five or six individual pictures if he wanted to put the whole of it on canvas. (p. 79)

His examples of Homer's translation of object into action are the chariot of Hera (*Iliad* 5.720-32), the dressing of Agamemnon (*Iliad* 2.43-47), and the bow of Pandarus (*Iliad* 4.105-11). When, at *Iliad* 2.101-8, Agamemnon's scepter is described, Lessing says: "Statt einer Abbildung gibt er uns die Geschichte des Zepters" (p. 108; "Instead of an illustration he gives us the story of the scepter," p. 81).[26] Lessing then generalizes the local observation:

> Doch nicht bloß da, wo Homer mit seinen Beschreibungen dergleichen weitere Absichten verbindet, sondern auch da, wo es ihm um das bloße Bild zu tun ist, wird er dieses Bild in eine Art von Geschichte des Gegenstandes verstreuen, um

---

26. Similar is the description of the scepter at *Iliad* 1.234-39. This passage, and the others used by Lessing, will be discussed below in Chapter 4.

die Teile desselben, die wir in der Natur nebeneinander
sehen, in seinem Gemälde ebenso natürlich aufeinander
folgen, und mit dem Flusse der Rede gleichsam Schritt
halten zu lassen. (p. 111)

But it is not only where Homer combines such further aims
with his descriptions that he disperses the image of his object
over a kind of history of it; he does this also where his sole
object is to show us the picture, in order that its parts which
in nature we find side by side may follow one another in his
description just as naturally, and keep pace, as it were, with
the progress of the narrative. (p. 83)

Drawing his inspiration from his reading of Homer, he lays a foundation for
the theory of the limits of painting and poetry; actions in time are the proper
province of poetry, because language is a medium perceived through time. In
this way the medium enters into a *bequemes Verhältnis* with its referent.

In chapter XVII Lessing fills out this proposition; the discussion
turns to arbitrary signs, and to the Shield of Achilles. The words of poetry,
says Lessing, can indeed try to represent bodies in space; their lack of
physical or natural connection to the referent frees them from the limitations
of the visual arts. Because they are arbitrary (symbolic) signs, they can appeal
to ideas rather than images.[27] In attempting to represent phenomena,
however, the verbal medium should be made transparent. If a poet does
describe, then he will try to ensure illusion:

Sondern er will die Ideen, die er in uns erwecket, so lebhaft
machen, daß wir in der Geschwindigkeit die wahren
sinnlichen Eindrücke ihrer Gegenstände zu empfinden
glauben, und in diesem Augenblicke der Täuschung uns der
Mittel, die er dazu anwendet, seiner Worte bewußt zu sein
aufhören. (p. 113)

He wants rather to make the ideas he awakens in us so vivid
that at that moment we believe we feel the real impressions
which the objects of these ideas would produce on us. In this
moment of illusion we should cease to be conscious of the
means which the poet uses for this purpose, that is, his
words. (p. 85)

---

27. Cf. Charles Sanders Peirce's symbolic signs, discussed below, p. 33 note 60.

Lessing's hope is for total enchantment (*thelxis*), to turn listeners into viewers. There remains, however, the problem of the portrayal of bodies in space in a literary medium; Lessing sees it as an insurmountable difficulty for language to achieve such an illusion, such a forgetting of the distance between word and visible object. The literary description, when it tries to portray visual characteristics, cannot become transparent:

> Und dieses Täuschende, sage ich, muß ihnen darum
> gebrechen, weil das Koexistierende des Körpers mit dem
> Konsekutiven der Rede dabei in Kollision kömmt (p. 116)

> And this illusion, I say, must be wanting because the
> coexistent nature of a body comes into conflict with the
> consecutive nature of language. (p. 88)

According to Lessing, despite the advantages of arbitrary signs the word still cannot enter into a sufficiently suitable relation with bodies in space; the verbal medium itself remains too apparent to allow poetry to represent appearance. It is for this reason that he censures the description of bodies in space. Conversely, the same is true for the visual arts in representing an action. A basic assumption is that such illusion, such transparency of the medium that transports the hearer, is the goal of poetry. There follows, however, in Lessing's account, a curious distinction: when illusion is not the goal, and when the writer appeals merely to the reader's intellect, description is acceptable. But this is not poetry: for example, didactic verse describes phenomena, but it is not considered poetry.[28] The descriptions in Vergil's *Georgics* are Lessing's examples of how unpoetic Vergil can be. Lessing admires Homer since he, in the Shield of Achilles, avoids description and turns image into action.

Chapter XVIII then returns to the premise of XVI:

---

28. "Überall, wo es daher auf das Täuschende nicht ankömmt, wo man nur mit dem Verstande seiner Leser zu tun hat, und nur auf deutliche und soviel möglich vollständige Begriffe gehet: können diese aus der Poesie ausgeschlossene Schilderungen der Körper gar wohl Platz haben, und nicht allein der Prosaist, sondern auch der dogmatische Dichter (denn da wo er dogmatisieret, ist er kein Dichter), können sich ihrer mit vielem Nutzen bedienen" (p. 116). "In every case, therefore, where illusion is not the object and where the writer appeals only to the understanding of the reader and aims only at conveying distinct and, insofar as this is possible, complete ideas, these descriptions of bodies, excluded from poetry, are quite in place; and not only the prose writer, but also the didactic poet (for where he becomes didactic he ceases to be a poet) can use them to great advantage" (p. 88).

Es bleibt dabei: die Zeitfolge ist das Gebiete des Dichters, so
wie der Raum das Gebiete des Malers. (p. 119)

It remains true that succession of time is the province of the
poet just as space is that of the painter. (p. 91)

The attempt by either the verbal or the visual arts to transgress this boundary
is seen as an intrusion, as a "squandering of the imagination to no purpose."[29]
Raphael, however, is commended for suggesting the previous position of a
depicted figure, and so suggesting action, by means of the fall of drapery (p.
120). The boundaries (*die Grenzen*) are loosening a bit. Homer is then
forgiven for occasionally holding one's gaze on an object; e.g., Καμπύλα
κύκλα, χάλκεα, ὀκτάκνημα ("curved wheels, bronze, eight-spoked," *Iliad*
5.722-23) and, ἀσπίδα πάντοσ᾽ ἐΐσην, καλήν, χαλκείην, ἐξήλατον ("a
shield balanced all around, beautiful, bronze, hammered out," *Iliad* 12.294-
95).[30] Lessing says:

Wer wird ihn darum tadeln? Wer wird ihm diese kleine
Üppigkeit nicht vielmehr Dank wissen, wenn er empfindet,
welche gute Wirkung sie an wenigen schicklichen Stellen
haben kann? (p. 122)

Who would censure him for this? Who would not rather
thank him for this little extravagance when he feels what a
good effect it can have in some few suitable passages?
(p. 93)

These exceptions remind the reader of Lessing's earlier warning that this is
not to be taken as a systematic analysis. In any case, the boundaries (*die
Grenzen*) continue to fade. It will become apparent later in Part II of this
essay that dwelling on visual appearance is much more common in the *Iliad*
than Lessing acknowledges.

The Shield of Achilles remains Lessing's focus as he notes that
Homer has been called a teacher of painting, "ein Lehrer der Malerei" (p.
123), in a life of Homer attributed to Dionysius of Halicarnassus. Lessing
disputes this claim: the Shield is represented in the *Iliad* as a process, as an

---

29. "der Dichter viel Imagination ohne allen Nutzen verschwendet" (p. 120).

30. In Monro and Allen's Oxford text (1920) the phrase reads: αὐτίκα δ᾽ ἀσπίδα μὲν
πρόσθ᾽ ἔσχετο πάντοσ᾽ ἐΐσην. / καλὴν χαλκείην ἐξήλατον (quickly in front [of him] he
[Sarpedon] held his shield, balanced all around, beautiful, bronze, hammered out). In fact, the
text describes this shield at some length, focusing our attention on the appearance and
manufacture of Sarpedon's shield for nearly three more lines.

action in time; hence it is foreign to the concerns of painting. A comparison is made with the Shield of Aeneas (Vergil *Aeneid* 8.626-728), much to the benefit of Homer:

> Homer läßt den Vulkan Zieraten künsteln, weil und indem er ein Schild machen soll, das seiner würdig ist. Virgil hingegen scheinet ihn das Schild wegen der Zieraten machen zu lassen, da er die Zieraten für wichtig genug hält, um sie besonders zu beschreiben, nachdem das Schild lange fertig ist. (p. 127)

> Homer has Vulcan produce skillful ornaments because he has to produce and does produce a shield worthy of him. Virgil, on the other hand, appears to have him produce the shield for the sake of its decorations, since he considers them important enough to be specially described long after the shield is finished. (p. 97)

So closes Chapter XVIII.

Chapter XIX dismisses those who censure Homer's Shield of Achilles, and begins to affirm more boldly the mimetic primacy of poetry over painting. The first objection to the Shield, that there is an implausible multiplication of scenes, is rejected by Lessing. He proposes that the concave side, as well as the front, was decorated. As evidence of this possibility he cites Pliny *Natural Histories* 36.4, which speaks of the decorations on both the inner and outer face of Phidias's shield of Athena.[31] It is a curious defense of Homer, since Lessing is shortly to affirm that there is a separate literary aesthetic, which allows the poem to range more freely than a painting over its subject.

Jean Boivin defended Homer's representation of the shield, but Lessing claims that Boivin failed to recognize the verbal aesthetic, and so multiplied the images excessively.[32] For example, Lessing sees the whole scene of the public lawsuit (497-508) as one depiction, but one that is elaborated poetically. When a poet wishes to describe a suggestive picture he

---

31. "in quo Amazonum proelium caelavit intumescente ambitu parmae; eiusdem concava parte Deorum et Gigantum dimicationem" (on which he engraved the battle of the Amazons in the convex circle of the round shield; on the concave part of it [he engraved] the fight between the Gods and the Giants).

32. See Boivin (1970, first published 1715), pp. 234-241.

must use the advantages (*die Vorteile*) available to his own medium.[33] These advantages are then elaborated:

Die Freiheit, sich sowohl über das Vergangene als über das
Folgende des einzigen Augenblickes in dem Kunstwerke
auszubreiten, und das Vermögen, sonach uns nicht allein das
zu zeigen, was uns der Künstler zeiget, sondern auch das,
was uns dieser nur kann erraten lassen. (p. 129)

The liberty to extend his description over that which
preceded and that which followed the single moment
represented in the work of art; and the power of showing not
only what the artist shows, but also that which the artist must
leave to the imagination. (p. 99)

The poet's power is the explicit representation of the inferences and interpretations suggested by the work of art; this is an extension of the earlier discussion of arbitrary signs and their access to ideas. Lessing puts it in terms of the describer's freedom to explicate what is implied in the image:

Doch was, um mich mit der Schule auszudrücken, nicht *actu*
in dem Gemälde enthalten war, das lag *virtute* darin, und die
einzige wahre Art, ein materielles Gemälde mit Worten
nachzuschildern, ist die, daß man das letztere mit dem
wirklich Sichtbaren verbindet, und sich nicht in den
Schranken der Kunst hält, innerhalb welchen der Dichter
zwar die Data zu einem Gemälde herzählen, aber
nimmermehr ein Gemälde selbst hervorbringen kann.
(pp. 129-130)

However, to use the language of scholastic philosophy, what
is not contained in the picture *actu* is there *virtute*; and the
only true way to express an actual picture in words is to
combine *virtute*, i.e., what is implied in the picture, with

---

33. In the course of the *Laokoon* Lessing claims that the verbal arts are more comprehensive in their mimetic capabilities; *die Grenzen* are modified and the visual arts are an inferior type of representational art, as the word gains unconditional primacy. The verbal arts have been privileged throughout, despite the claim here to draw them equal. See, e.g., p. 77, or p. 109, where Lessing, after quoting Homer's description of the scepter of Agamemnon (*Iliad* 2.100-109), says: "So kenne ich endlich dieses Zepter besser, als mir es der Maler vor Augen legen, oder ein zweiter Vulkan in die Hände liefern könnte" ("And so finally I know this scepter better than if a painter were to place it before my eyes or a second Vulcan in my very hands," p. 81). See W.J.T. Mitchell (1986), pp. 95-115, for a harsh and persuasive critique of this view.

what is actually visible, and not to confine oneself to the
limits of the art, within which the poet can reckon the data
for a painting, to be sure, but can never create a painting.
(p. 100)

In the Shield of Achilles, then, Lessing sees a new image not whenever the
description presents a new action or aspect of a scene, but only when the
description returns to Hephaestus's workshop to open a new vignette (*Iliad*
18.483, 490, 541, 550, 561, 573, 587, 590, 607).

After these chapters dealing with the Shield, Chapters XX and XXI
treat Homer's refusal to describe great beauty; Lessing says that Homer
recognized that language would necessarily fail in such an endeavor. What
then should the poet do when a beautiful image or person is called for?
Lessing again looks to Homer. Responding to the same passage that caught
Edmund Burke's attention (*Iliad* 3.156-59), Lessing admires Homer, who
describes Helen through her effect on those who see her:

Was Homer nicht nach seinen Bestandteilen beschreiben
konnte, läßt er uns in seiner Wirkung erkennen. Malet uns,
Dichter, das Wohlgefallen, die Zuneigung, die Liebe, das
Entzücken, welches die Schönheit verursachet, und ihr habt
die Schönheit selbst gemalet. (p. 144)

What Homer could not describe in all its various parts he
makes us recognize by its effect. Paint for us, you poets, the
pleasure, the affection, the love and delight which beauty
brings, and you have painted beauty itself. (p. 111)

Lessing asserts the primacy of verbal mimesis in response to what he sees as
a false privilege given to the visual arts; the *Laokoon* consistently responds to
an opposing view that the visual arts are more vivid in representation, and
that the verbal arts are pale imitations of phenomena. For example, in the
following passage Lessing explicitly challenges the perceived primacy of the
visual arts and defends literary mimesis. Give us charm, says Lessing, for that
is beauty in action:

Ein andrer Weg, auf welchem die Poesie die Kunst in
Schilderung körperlicher Schönheit wiederum einholet, ist
dieser, daß sie Schönheit in Reiz verwandelt. Reiz ist
Schönheit in Bewegung, und eben darum dem Maler weniger
bequem als dem Dichter. (p. 145)

Another way in which poetry can draw even with art in the description of physical beauty is by changing beauty into charm. Charm is beauty in motion and for that reason less suitable to the painter than the poet. (p. 112)

Lessing says he is drawing the verbal arts even with the visual, but he does so in the very area in which visual art was earlier given primacy: the depiction of physical beauty. Representing charm, an effect of beauty, turns out to be more worthy than representing beauty. In this way he gives the palm to the verbal arts. According to Lessing, a describer can emphasize the primacy of verbal representation and demonstrate its greater range and mimetic force by describing aspects of beauty that have a more suitable relation (*bequemes Verhältnis*) to poetry than to painting, such as *Reiz, kharis,* "charm."[34]

Lessing's method is to be admired: he asks that we examine how the text fixes our attention. Such a method makes him alert to the poetics of the *Iliad*. His basic outline of the arts will be used in what follows to organize the commentary on Homeric representation. His claim, that the translation of image into story is the characteristic feature of Homeric ekphrasis, is, for the most part, true. But his further claim, that the translation of image into action is the proper way for poetry to represent, is more difficult to accept. Even his model, the *Iliad*, transgresses the "limits" (*die Grenzen*) more often than he acknowledges. In attitude as well as practice, the *Iliad* belies Lessing's analysis. As I discuss in Part II, the Shield of Achilles treats visual images as opportunities for elaboration, responding with admiration and engagement; the tone is thus foreign to the kind of rivalry between the arts that is basic to Lessing's analysis.[35] As we shall see shortly, the *Iliad* shows more than one way of adapting a work of visual art to words, and so does not fit so cleanly into Lessing's scheme.[36]

Ekphrasis in the *Iliad* will not fit into the strictures of proper poetic description outlined in this chapter. The Shield of Achilles is not proper description, as in Friedländer, because it strays far from the visible surface of

---

34. That Lessing associates this charm with the ancient Greek *kharis* is made clear by his quotation in this passage of lines from the *Carmina Anacreontea* (16.26-28 West), which include the *Kharites*.

35. Cf. Heffernan (1993), pp. 10-22, which is a careful discussion by one who, unlike myself, does see a rivalry between the arts in the Shield.

36. The lasting appeal of Lessing's *Laokoon*, however, lies in its compelling conceptual framework rather than his attention to particulars. On just this question, of Lessing's ideas carrying more weight than his observation of detail, Coleridge writes in a letter that Lessing is "acute; yet acute not in the observation of actual Life, but in the arrangements and management of the Ideal World" (Coleridge 1956), p. 437.

a work of art. It does not focus merely on effect, as Edmund Burke would have it, because it actually does describe the physical appearance of the images. Finally, and similarly, it will not stay within Lessing's limits, because it carefully and appreciatively interrupts the narrative to dwell upon objects in space. All these views of descriptive propriety can find support in Homeric practice; but each sets rules and boundaries and limitations that ignore much of the poetic practice of the *Iliad*. Each, however, focuses our attention on some aspect of Homeric description, and I shall borrow from each of these critics, and others, in order to describe better what happens in a Homeric ekphrasis.[37]

---

37. Cf. the caveat of Schelling's *Philosophie der Mythologie*, quoted in Zuckerkandl (1956), p. v: "First and above all, an explanation must do justice to the thing that is to be explained, must not devaluate it, interpret it away, belittle it, or garble it, in order to make it easier to understand. The question is not 'At what view of the phenomenon must we arrive in order to explain it in accordance with one or another philosophy?' but precisely the reverse: 'What philosophy is requisite if we are to live up to the subject, be on a level with it?' The question is not how the phenomenon must be turned, twisted, narrowed, crippled, so as to be explicable, at all costs, upon principles that we have once and for all resolved not to go beyond. The question is: 'To what point must we enlarge our thought so that it shall be in proportion to the phenomenon.'"

# 2

# ANCIENT GREEK RHETORICIANS ON EKPHRASIS: HERMENEUTICS AND THE *SHIELD OF HERAKLES*

Ancient Greek literary criticism of the Hellenistic and Roman periods is concerned primarily with the teaching of oratory. As such, we often find it difficult to use in our reading of poetry. Nevertheless, this criticism offers not only particular insights but also ways of reading that can affirm, illuminate, add to, deepen, correct, alter, overturn, or otherwise defamiliarize our own response to literature. In this chapter, through an analysis of criticism dealing with ekphrasis found in Greek handbooks of rhetorical exercises (*progumnasmata*), I begin to develop a way of reading and responding to ekphrasis that I shall use with the Shield of Achilles. To illustrate the method, I use the *Shield of Herakles*, a descriptive fragment of 480 lines attributed in antiquity to Hesiod, but now thought to be of the early sixth century B.C.[38] The conclusion of this chapter will relate both the ancient Greek rhetorical theory and poetic practice of ekphrasis to the hermeneutics of Paul Ricoeur, in order to consider the larger questions involved in reading ekphrasis. From the critical and poetic practices, illustrated by the *progumnasmata* and the *Shield of Herakles*, I shall propose a double movement of literary representation in ekphrasis: acceptance of the illusion

---

38. On the date of this text, see R.M. Cook (1937), pp. 204-214; C.F. Russo (1950), p. 34; M.L. West (1985), p. 136; and Janko (1986), pp. 38-59, which provides a good bibliography.

proposed by the ekphrasis is accompanied by a complementary breaking of that illusion.[39] The phrase "breaking the illusion" carries, here, a rather mild sense; it indicates that a certain self-consciousness expressed in the description adds another dimension, perhaps unsettling the illusion, or balancing it, or bracketing it. The illusion is still in play, but it is held a bit more lightly and with an acknowledgment of its irony.

## The Rhetorical Criticism of Ekphrasis

Four collections of rhetorical exercises, all from the first through the fifth centuries A.D., have come down to us under the names of Aelius Theon, Hermogenes of Tarsus, Aphthonius of Antioch, and Nikolaus of Myra.[40] Despite the popularity of ekphrasis in ancient Greek poetry and prose, it is rarely mentioned in ancient Greek criticism, and these handbooks provide the first relatively full discussions. These handbooks treat description both as a simple window to visible phenomena and as a transformation of that phenomena through the language and the experience of the describer.[41] I begin with the simpler view of literary representation, then move on to the qualifications of this view.

### Description as Window

The earliest extant handbook is that of Aelius Theon, probably composed in the first century A.D. One of his ten exercises is ekphrasis,[42] which he defines as

---

39. Literary works and literary criticism frequently encourage both of these stances in relation to representations. Iser (1974), p. 288, describes this double movement as oscillation. In contrast, Howard Nemerov, in W.J.T. Mitchell (1980), p. 10, emphasizes the balance or equilibrium attained in this double movement. For the now canonical formulation of the "willing suspension of disbelief," which corresponds to what I have called "acceptance of illusion," see Coleridge (1965), volume 2, p. 6.

40. Kennedy (1983), pp. 54-73, gives a good overview of the rhetorical handbooks.

41. For discussion of the common contrasting views of language as either a window to be looked through or an object to be looked at, see Toni Morrison (1992), p. 17; Ruthven (1979), pp. 13-15; Lanham (1976), pp. 1-35. A poem that illustrates this contrast vividly and gracefully is "Spring and All VI," by William Carlos Williams (1986), pp. 191-192.

42. The ten exercises are fable, narrative, anecdote, commonplace, praise and invective, comparison, speech of a mythological or historical character, ekphrasis, argument, and law (Spengel II.72-130).

λόγος περιηγηματικός, ἐναργῶς ὑπ' ὄψιν ἄγων τὸ
δηλούμενον. (Spengel II.118)

Descriptive language bringing that which is being made
manifest vividly before the sight.[43]

This definition is repeated with only minor changes in the three other extant
handbooks.[44] It suggests that a goal of ekphrasis is to make language a
window, through which the audience is to view the described phenomena.
The audience is not to attend to the levels of mediation between it and the
world represented, but is, rather, to accept the illusion that it is actually seeing
what is described.

The two virtues of ekphrasis given in the handbooks, *saphêneia*
(clarity) and *enargeia* (vividness), also suggest this goal of unmediated access
to visible phenomena.[45] A writer achieves clarity and vividness by using a
style that does not distract the audience, one that does not call attention to
itself or remind the audience that words are creating what it sees. Aphthonius
expresses this desire when he calls for the language of description "to imitate
completely the things being described":

---

43. Translations of passages from the handbooks are my own. I translate *periêgêmatikos* as
"descriptive" for lack of a better alternative; it characterizes a type of discourse that shows its
audience around, that gives it a tour.

44. In the handbook attributed to Hermogenes (second century A.D.), the definition reads:
λόγος περιηγηματικός, ὡς φασι, ἐναργὴς καὶ ὑπ' ὄψιν ἄγων τὸ δηλούμενον (Spengel
II.118, "descriptive language, as they say, vivid and bringing that being made manifest before the
sight"). Aphthonius (fourth or early fifth century A.D.) defines it as λόγος περιηγηματικὸς ὑπ'
ὄψιν ἄγων ἐναργῶς τὸ δηλούμενον (Spengel II.46, "descriptive language bringing the thing
being made manifest vividly before the sight"). And Nikolaus of Myra (fifth century A.D.) writes:
λόγος ἀφηγηματικός . . . ὑπ' ὄψιν ἐναργῶς ἄγων τὸ δηλούμενον (Spengel III.491,
"digressive language . . . bringing the thing being made manifest vividly before the sight").

45. Spengel II.16 and II.119. The association of clarity and vividness has a long history in
ancient Greek texts. See Plato *Timaeus* 72b8-c1 and *Laws* 645c1; Demosthenes 14.4, 19.263, and
26.92; Plutarch *Moralia* 583b10-c1 and 1070c7-8; Lucian *Assembly of the Gods* 19. The two
virtues also occur together in much Greek criticism. See Dionysius of Halicarnassus *Isocrates* 2
and 11, *Isaeus* 3, *Demosthenes* 58, *Letter to Pompeius* 3 and 4, and *On Imitation* fragment 6.3
(Usener-Radermacher); Hermogenes *On Types of Style* 291 and 319 (Rabe). Demetrius *On Style*
treats both clarity (191-203) and vividness (208-20) as aspects of the plain style. These virtues
are not so joined in Aristotle's *Rhetoric*, although one could derive their association from his
discussion of *saphêneia* (clarity) at 1404b.

ὅλως ἀπομιμεῖσθαι τὰ ἐκφραζόμενα πράγματα.
(Spengel II.47)

Similarly, Nikolaus remarks:

πρὸς γὰρ τὴν ὑποκειμένην ὑπόθεσιν ἁρμόζειν δεῖ καὶ
τὸ τῆς ἀπαγγελίας εἶδος. (Spengel III.493)

To the proposed subject one should also fit the form of the
narrative.

And Theon, with a fine musical metaphor:

τὸ δὲ ὅλον συνεξομοιοῦσθαι χρὴ τοῖς ὑποκειμένοις τὴν
ἀπαγγελίαν . . . μηδὲ τὰ τῆς ἑρμηνείας ἀπᾴδειν τῆς
φύσεως αὐτῶν. (Spengel II.119-20)

It is necessary that the narrative [apaggelian] be entirely
likened to the underlying things [the subjects], . . . and that
the style not be out of tune with their nature.[46]

Ancient Greek criticism commonly calls for style to fit subject matter.[47] But
in this context such a call reinforces the view that the language of description
is to go unnoticed, to act as a window to phenomena.

Aphthonius then notes more specifically the style that ekphrasis
should use to achieve this goal, saying that "those writing ekphrases should
exhibit the relaxed style."

ἐκφράζοντας δὲ δεῖ τόν τε χαρακτῆρα ἀνειμένον
ἐκφέρειν. (Spengel II.47)

---

46. Cf. Hermogenes: ἔτι μέντοι συνεξομοιοῦσθαι τὰ τῆς φράσεως ὀφείλει τοῖς
πράγμασιν (Spengel II.16, "Still one ought to liken the [characteristics] of the expression to the
subject matter").

47. E.g., Aristotle Rhetoric 1404b, 1408a-b (especially 1408a11); Demetrius On Style 120;
Dionysius of Halicarnassus Demosthenes 18, Lysias 13, Letter to Pompeius 3, On Literary
Composition 11, 13, 20. Cf. Cicero Orator 79, De oratore 1.130, 3.37, 3.210-12, and Partitiones
oratoriae 19; Quintilian 11.1-4, especially 11.3.30 and 11.3.61.

This is a style that calls minimal attention to itself, thereby giving a relatively clear, unhindered view of the described phenomena.[48] Contributing to this desired transparency of language, according to Aelius Theon, is the lack of explicit interpretation in ekphrasis. In a commonplace (*topos*), a writer relates his own opinion, saying whether the things discussed are noble or disgraceful or the like; whereas in ekphrasis,

ψιλὴ τῶν πραγμάτων ἐστὶν ἡ ἀπαγγελία.
(Spengel II.119)

the narration of the subject matter [facts] is bare.

The describer encourages the audience to accept the illusion and, in so doing, diminishes attention to the medium (language) and the mediator's experience.

In the passages I have quoted, ekphrasis is to induce the audience to imagine that they are actually seeing the phenomena being described. The handbooks thus propose a type of faithful and unproblematic representation in description. Though this transparency of language seems to be the goal of ekphrasis, there are hints of another concern.

### Description as Interpretation

The rhetorical handbooks first emphasize the access to visible phenomena gained through language, then attend to both the act of describing and the language of ekphrasis itself. The rhetoricians thus qualify their claim that description turns listeners into viewers. Aelius Theon elaborates his account of vividness (*enargeia*) by saying:

ἐνάργεια τοῦ σχεδὸν ὁρᾶσθαι τὰ ἀπαγγελόμενα.
(Spengel II.119)

the vividness of *almost* seeing the things narrated.

Hermogenes similarly says:

δεῖ γὰρ τὴν ἑρμηνείαν διὰ τῆς ἀκοῆς σχεδὸν τὴν ὄψιν
μηχανᾶσθαι. (Spengel II.16)

---

48. The relaxed style (*kharaktêr aneimenos*) is that of dialogue (Demetrius, *On Style* 21); it is also conversational and loose (*kata tên anesin*), according to Dionysius of Halicarnassus, *On Literary Composition* 21.

It is necessary that the style *almost* produce sight through hearing.

And Nikolaus writes of a speech:

ὑπ' ὄψιν ἡμῖν ἄγοντα ταῦτα, περὶ ὧν εἰσιν οἱ λόγοι,
καὶ *μόνον οὐ* θεατὰς εἶναι παρασκευάζοντα.
(Spengel III.492)

bringing these things before our sight, [these things] which the speeches are about, and *all but* making us spectators.

We are almost or all but to be made viewers.[49] The illusion in ekphrasis is not full enchantment; the audience is not to give itself over completely to the world represented by the description. What ensures that we will not begin pecking away at the grapes of Zeuxis, that we will not really forget the describer and the language that creates the illusion? The handbooks suggest an answer: the reaction of the viewer, the describer's experience or interpretation of phenomena, is to be part of the description after all. Any description is necessarily an interpretation; a describer selects and organizes an infinite variety of aspects of phenomena. But some texts downplay the mediating presence of the describer and the language of description, some call our attention to them, and some do both.

Ekphrasis here is not to describe just the visible appearance of the work and the world it represents, but to include the judgments and emotions of the describer. Aelius Theon, who has just told us to keep the narrative clear of the narrator's thoughts, also suggests that a student of rhetoric follow the lead of Homer and express reactions, beginning, he says,

ἐκ τοῦ καλοῦ καὶ ἐκ τοῦ χρησίμου καὶ ἐκ τοῦ ἡδέος,
οἷον "Ομηρος ἐπὶ τῶν 'Αχιλλέως ὅπλων ἐποίησεν,
εἰπὼν ὅτι καὶ καλὰ ἦν καὶ ἰσχυρὰ καὶ ἰδεῖν τοῖς μὲν
συμμάχοις ἐκπληκτικά, τοῖς δὲ πολεμίοις φοβερά.
(Spengel II.119)

---

49. Ekphrastic vividness is similarly qualified in other criticism from the first few centuries A.D. E.g., Georgios Khoiroboskos (Spengel III.251); Zonias (Spengel III. 163-64); "Longinus" 15.2. The Scholia to the *Iliad*, which frequently apply rhetorical theories to poetry, also qualify discussions of visual vividness by including *skhedon* (nearly) and the like: e.g., Scholia bT on 16.294a (Erbse IV, p. 231); bT to 23.362-72 (Erbse V, p. 427). In Roman criticism, cf. *Ad Herennium* 4.55.68; Quintilian 4.2.123 and 6.2.32; C. Iulius Victor and Priscian, in Halm (1964), pp. 436 and 558.

from the fine and the useful and the pleasurable, as Homer
did in the arms of Achilles, saying that (they were) fine and
strong and astounding to see for his allies, but fearsome for
the enemies.

The focus is not just the visual appearance of the work of art, but also the
relations between the describer and that work. In other words, an awareness
of the scene and context and agent of the description is brought to our
attention. An ekphrasis is thus to be both a clear representation of visible
phenomena, and also, in Clifford Geertz's fine phrase, "thick description."[50]

Although the handbooks suggest that one include several types of
evaluations and judgments in a description, the most forceful of these, and
that most appropriate to literary ekphrasis, is *thauma* (marvel, wonder,
astonishment, or amazement). In his discussion of ekphrasis, Aphthonius
gives an example of a description, in which he writes:

καὶ τὸ θαῦμα γέγονεν ἄπιστον. (Spengel II.49)

and the wonder was incredible.

Such an expression of wonder brings the focus back to the context of the
description: Who speaks? Where? Why? To whom? These are the questions
that remind the audience of its own mediated access to the described
phenomena. By including wonder in the description, the writer ensures that
we not ignore two types of interaction that create what we see: that between
the describer and the referent and that between the describer and the
audience.

Attention to the interpreter between the audience and the world
described would seem to diminish the force of the illusion, but, according to
the handbooks, the interpreter's expressions of emotion contribute to clarity
and vividness. The illusion is not actually broken, but rather colored, by
explicitly including a human experience of the observed phenomena in the
description. Reactions of the describer serve to guide our own, and can

---

50. This phrase is discussed in the first chapter ("Thick Description: Toward an Interpretive
Theory of Culture") of Geertz ( (1973), especially pp. 6-10. See also Geertz (1988), p. 28.
Boulding (1956), pp. 16-17, eloquently addresses the question of the viewer being part of the
viewed.

enhance our (imagined) image.[51] A more complex picture of ekphrasis emerges from the handbooks, but it does not belie the initial emphasis on (almost) turning listeners into viewers.

Aphthonius further associates wonder with another way of emphasizing the describer's reactions:

τὸ μὲν δὴ κάλλος κρεῖττον ἢ λέγειν· εἰ δέ τι παρεῖται, ἐν παρενθήκῃ γεγένηται θαύματος. (Spengel II.49)

The beauty is greater than one could express. If it is passed over, it comes about in an aside of wonder.[52]

To say that something is inexpressible reminds the audience subtly but forcefully that it is not seeing what is described. Such a concession to ineffability reveals the relationship between the describer, the phenomena being described, and the language of description, which cannot completely represent the visible world. Aphthonius has thus associated an expression of wonder, emphasizing the mediator (describer), with an expression of inexpressibility, calling attention to the medium (language). The use of "almost" and "all but" in the handbooks becomes appropriate and effective, as we see that in a description the medium and the mediator are not to go unnoticed. There is, rather, a double movement of creating an illusion while acknowledging the process by which one shapes the (actual and potential) audience's response to what is described.

According to the handbooks, a description should, on the one hand, encourage us to enter the world described and its ways of making sense. On the other hand, the description should encourage us to remain aware of our relationship to the describer and the language of the description; we are to bring that world into our own context of interpretation, our own ways of making sense. These rather cursory accounts of ekphrasis, written for

---

51. As Nikolaus says of Demosthenic ekphrasis: πάθος ὑπ' ὄψιν ἄγειν πειρᾶται διὰ τοῦ λόγου (Spengel III.493, "He tries to bring emotion before the sight through language [the speech]"). Cf. Quintilian 8.3.70.

52. The phrasing in Aphthonius is close to that of Xenophon *Memorabilia* 3.11.1, in which the beauty of a woman named Theodotê, while often painted, is beyond description: *kreitton eiê logou to kallos* ([saying that her] beauty is greater than *logos*). Cf. Ralph Waldo Emerson (1951), p. 271 ("The Poet"): "A beauty not explicable is dearer than a beauty which we can see the end of." This sentiment, that inexpressibility enhances wonder, appears also in ancient Greek literature: e.g., Demosthenes 21.72 and Plutarch *Moralia* 383a. On the inexpressibility *topos*, see de Jong (1987), pp. 47-48.

students of grammar and rhetoric in the first few centuries A.D., turn out to be quite appropriate to description in early Greek poetry. The pseudo-Hesiodic *Shield of Herakles*, composed more than half a millennium before the *progumnasmata*, is a useful example.[53]

## The Rhetorical Handbooks and a Distant Text

The *Shield of Herakles* creates just such a double response, both an acquiescence in and a critical appreciation of the illusion produced by the ekphrasis.[54] While describing the shield, the language of description effaces its role (as a translation of visual images into words), and so draws us into the illusion that we are viewers; but the description also calls attention to its role (as a transformation of visual images into words), and so breaks the illusion. The passage draws us into the illusion in two ways. First, it makes us viewers of the depictions on the shield, by calling attention to color, texture, and spatial arrangement. Second, it takes us through the depictions and into the world represented by those images: to do so the ekphrasis includes the thoughts and motives of the depicted figures, narrates consecutive actions they perform, and describes the sound and voice of the pictures. Emphasis either on the depictions or the referent of the depictions diminishes the

---

53. On literary ekphrasis influenced by rhetorical handbooks, see Bartsch (1989), p. 13 (e.g.): "the novels undeniably reflect the rhetorical and literary conventions of the day." See also M. Roberts (1989), pp. 38-65. Onians (1980), pp. 1-23, boldly and carefully develops the relationship between art and description in the second through sixth centuries A.D., and the influence of rhetorical training on a viewer's experience of art. Cf. Heath (1989), pp. 102-103, on the Homeric Scholia: "The critical tools which these commentators used were derived primarily from rhetoric, and the rhetorical analysis of poetry meets with some resistance today; moreover the problem of anachronism is particularly acute when one is examining Hellenistic exegesis of pre-Classical texts. Nevertheless, I believe that . . . we shall find that rhetorical theory was able to furnish Hellenistic critics with a flexible interpretive model and one rather well adapted to their object of study."

54. For other literary aspects of the *Shield of Herakles*, see van Groningen (1958), pp. 109-123; for its influence on ancient art, see H.A. Shapiro (1984), pp. 523-529. This poem has been much maligned; e.g., R.M. Cook (1937), p. 205: "It appears the work of a hack poet, who dispenses to a great extent with the processes of original invention." Similar censure appears in Easterling and Knox (1985), p. 103; Thalmann (1984), p. 162; Hurwit (1985), p. 230; Fränkel (1975), p. 111. Although my focus is the *Iliad*, and the *Shield of Herakles* serves here only as an example, an ulterior motive of these pages is to find ways to appreciate what the *Shield of Herakles* does.

audience's concern for the describer and the language of description; our gaze is trained on the visual images and the phenomena they represent. I here examine the way the poem, by focusing on the depictions themselves, creates illusion; then discuss the way the poem draws our attention to the referent of the depictions; and finally I turn to the emphasis on the describer and the description, which complements that illusion.

The *Shield of Herakles* regularly draws attention to the physical appearance of the work of art.[55] As the ekphrasis opens, the poet describes the striking visible aspects of the shield:

πᾶν μὲν γὰρ κύκλῳ τιτάνῳ λευκῷ τ' ἐλέφαντι
ἠλέκτρῳ θ' ὑπολαμπὲς ἔην χρυσῷ τε φαεινῷ
λαμπόμενον, κυάνου δὲ διὰ πτύχες ἠλήλαντο. (141-43)

for its whole orb was a-shimmer with enamel and white
ivory and electrum, and it glowed with shining gold; and
there were zones of cyanus drawn upon it.

In these lines, the emphasis on material begins to turn listeners into viewers of the physical surface of the shield.[56] The poet also calls attention to visible appearance, throughout the description, by noting the placement and spatial arrangement of these materials on the shield.[57] Unlike the mention of material, however, most of the indications of spatial arrangement call attention to the referent as well: the arrangement of the depiction mirrors the arrangement of what is depicted.[58] The same is also true of the frequent reference to color and number: these are visible features shared by the depictions and the depicted phenomena.[59] As such, they draw attention to the close, iconic relationship between the visual images and what they

---

55. Translations of single words or phrases from the *Shield of Herakles* are my own; for quotations of a whole line or more, I use Evelyn-White (1914).

56. The material surface of the shield is also mentioned in lines 144, 167, 183, 188, 192, 199, 203, 208, 212, 220, 222, 225, 226, 231, 236, 243, 249, 271, 295-96, and 313. This regular mention of material ensures that the surface appearance of the worked metal remains in the forefront throughout this ekphrasis.

57. Lines 144, 154-56, 161, 168, 178, 191-92, 197, 201, 207, and 216.

58. For such a relationship between the depiction and what is depicted, see 147, 179, 183, 185, 195, 208, 220, 221, 224, 233, 253, 261, 270, 285, 296, 305, and 314.

59. Color: 146, 153, 159, 167, 186, 194, 221, 249, 252, 265, 294, and 300. Number: 162, 173, 211, 234, and 272.

represent.[60] The illusion encouraged thereby is one of seeing pictures that faithfully and unproblematically capture their subject.

The ekphrasis frequently leaves the depicted surface behind and takes us to the next level of illusion, that of the referent (the world represented by the pictures). One way of calling attention to the world depicted, rather than to the depiction itself, is to include the thoughts and motives of figures depicted on the shield:

τοὶ δ' ἔτι μᾶλλον ἐγειρέσθην κοτέοντε μάχεσθαι. (176)

And both sides were roused still more to fight because they were angry.[61]

The description of movements and sounds made by the depicted figures also emphasizes the referent:

τὰ δ' ἐπικροτέοντα πέτοντο
ἄρματα κολλήεντ', ἐπὶ δὲ πλῆμναι μέγ' ἀύτευν. (308-9)

the jointed cars flew along clattering and the naves of the wheels shrieked loudly.[62]

These aspects of the description draw us through the image itself and into the world represented by that image.

The features I have been discussing to this point diminish our concern for the describer. But other aspects of the ekphrasis call attention to the describer and the description, both of which lie between us and the visible

---

60. I use the term "iconic," as well as "indexical" and "symbolic," in the sense of Charles Sanders Peirce (1931-58). An icon is "a sign which refers to the object it denotes merely by virtue of characters of its own" (volume 2, p. 247). An index is "a sign which refers to the object it denotes by virtue of being really affected by that object" (volume 2, p. 248). A symbol is "a sign which is constituted as a sign merely or mainly by the fact that it is used and understood as such" (volume 2, p. 307). Although these categories are not discrete—a given sign will fit different categories depending upon the way it is understood and the use to which it is put—these relationships of resemblance, contiguity, and convention prove useful for organizing our observations.

61. Cf. 169-71, 239-40, 251, and 304.

62. Cf. 164, 257, 274, 278, 280, and 316. Lines 231-33 would seem to belong in this list, as they say that the represented figures make noise even though they are depictions: footsteps of running Gorgons ring on the surface of the shield. But this does not ask us to imagine that we are seeing the referent unmediated, as do the other references to sound and motion; it emphasizes, rather, the magical relationship of visual image to referent.

phenomena. When calling attention to the interpretation of the describer, this ekphrasis qualifies the illusion that we are viewers, as is recommended by the rhetorical handbooks. Several times the *Shield of Herakles* explicitly reminds the audience that the images resemble what they represent. For example, the ekphrasis says of depicted Centaurs:

καί τε συναΐγδην ὡς εἰ ζωοί περ ἐόντες. (189)

and they were rushing together *as though* they were alive.

And of Ares:

αἵματι φοινικόεις ὡς εἰ ζωοὺς ἐναρίζων. (194)

he was red with blood *as if* he were slaying living men.[63]

In the passages quoted earlier, the mention of physical features of the shield that seem to resemble their referents (color, shape, arrangement) kept our focus on the depictions and their subject matter. But here an explicit expression of similarity reminds us of the describer: a simile openly interprets, and so brings the visual representation into the describer's own understanding of the world. It reminds us that we are "seeing" a human response to depicted phenomena, not the phenomena themselves.

A simile is, however, a rather subtle way of reminding us of the describer. There are more explicit ways, more like those proposed in the rhetorical handbooks. Several times in the course of the description the poet steps back from the attempt to represent visible features and expresses *thauma* (wonder).[64] As the ekphrasis opens, the entire shield is called a *thauma idesthai* (140, "a wonder to behold"); then when the ekphrasis is drawing to a close the same sentiment is recalled, but intensified:

---

63. Other explicit expressions of the similarity between the image and what it represents occur at lines 198, 214-15, 228, 244, and 314.

64. As R.M. Cook (1937), p. 205, says of *thauma*: "The author lets the reader know what his emotions should be." On wonder in early Greek literature, see the provocative study of Prier (1989), reviewed by A.S. Becker (1991). See also A.S. Becker (1993a), pp. 283-284. A familiar ekphrasis that stresses the reactions of the viewer is the description of Hepzibah looking at a miniature likeness of a young man in the second chapter ("The Little Shopwindow") of Nathaniel Hawthorne's *The House of the Seven Gables* (1981), p. 22.

θαῦμα ἰδεῖν καὶ Ζηνὶ βαρυκτύπῳ. (318)

A wonderful thing to see—even for Zeus the loud-thunderer.

If only expressed at the beginning and the end of the ekphrasis, we could see wonder as a transitional feature, part of the ring-composition of this work; the illusion would then be broken as the poem moves from the larger narrative into the description and back again. But in the midst of the description we are twice told of the interpreter's amazement: *thaumata erga* (165, "wondrous works") and *thauma idesthai* (224, "a wonder to behold").[65] The *Shield of Herakles* does not ask us to attend to different levels of representation at different times; it shifts the focus in the course of the ekphrasis, in single passages, and even within single lines. In this way, the ekphrasis encourages both acceptance of the illusion that we are viewers *and* awareness of the describer who creates that illusion. Hence we sustain a more complex picture of representation. As I shall elaborate in the final section of this chapter, the two perspectives are complementary, not competing.

An expression of *thauma* (wonder) takes on new significance when joined with a verb of speaking and thinking, instead of the expected verb of seeing. As the poet describes the image of Perseus, which seems to float above the surface of the shield, he says:

θαῦμα μέγα φράσσασθ', ἐπεὶ οὐδαμῇ ἐστήρικτο. (218)

very marvellous to mention, since he was not supported anywhere.

The phrase "marvellous to see" brings the describer into the picture, but the phrase "marvellous to mention, note, remark, say, or consider" refers to the relationship of the describer to both the picture and the audience.[66] Since words provide the audience's only access to the entire matrix of

---

65. The *Shield of Herakles* also emphasizes reactions, both to images and to what they represent, by calling attention to *deinotēs* (terribleness) and other emotional qualities: lines 147, 148, 149, 160, 161, 166, 192, 200, 202, 206, 216, 223, 226, 227, 233, 236, 242, 243, 250, 262, 266, 268, 272, 278, 280, and 285.

66. Commenting on line 218, C.F. Russo (1950), p. 132, sees the infinitive indicating perception rather than expression: "ἐννοῆσαι, a osservarsi (*oculis considerare*), e perciò a capirsi (*mente concipere*). È piú forte della solita espressione θαῦμα ἰδέσθαι." Athanassakis (1983), p. 133, on the other hand, translates the phrase as "a marvel too great for words." On the association of the middle voice of *phrazō* with both perception and expression, see Chantraine (1980), p. 1224. Cf. *Homeric Hymn to Apollo* 415: *phrassasthai mega thauma kai ophthalmoisin idesthai* (a great marvel to mention/consider and to see with the eyes).

representation, the phrase "marvellous to mention" highlights the layer of verbal mediation: the language that gives us phenomena experienced by the describer (or perhaps creates these phenomena).

In several scenes the focus turns even more patently to the language of description, the describer, the act of describing, and hence the audience that receives and creates images through the ekphrasis. The poet calls the image of Phobos *ou ti phateios* (144, "not in any way expressible"). Similarly, the depicted heads of snakes are said to be *ou ti phateiôn* (161, "not in any way expressible"). Finally, the Gorgons are *ou phatai* (230, "not expressible"). In these acknowledgments that some phenomena are indescribable, the description directs the audience's attention to the poet's attempt to turn visible images into words. These expressions of inexpressibility suggest not only the mediator (describer), as do expressions of wonder, but also the medium (language). Recall the discussion of Aphthonius, who associated wonder with indescribable beauty; his phrase *kreitton ê legein* (greater than one can express) calls attention to what the speaker deems the limits of language. The phrase refers to the difficult act of trying to turn listeners into viewers through the medium of words—the problems of translating a visual image into a verbal representation. This same feature in the *Shield of Herakles* indicates, and induces in the audience, a self-consciousness about the mimetic capability of language. But, as in the handbooks, inexpressibility enhances the vividness of the (imagined) images, and our admiration of them.

The *Shield of Herakles* draws explicit attention to the relationship between the audience and the describer, the describer and the language of description, the description and the visual representation, and finally the visual representation and its referent.[67] In order to recapitulate and illustrate this range of representation, I shall work through the opening lines of the ekphrasis. Parts of the passage have already been discussed, but responding to the lines as they come in the poem will demonstrate how the various types of attention are blended in this work. The description of the shield begins thus:

Χερσί γε μὴν σάκος εἷλε παναίολον, οὐδέ τις αὐτὸ
οὔτ' ἔρρηξε βαλὼν οὔτ' ἔθλασε, θαῦμα ἰδέσθαι.    140

---

67. Although my focus is the poetics of this ekphrasis, much of the significance of the passage still lies in the subject matter depicted by the visual images. On the thematic import of the ekphrasis in the poem as we have it, see Thalmann (1984), p. 63: "Cumulatively, then, the pictures on the shield make an implicit statement about war. It is monstrous, irrational, an activity proper to beasts in which man also engages." McClatchy has written a poem entitled "The Shield of Herakles" (1990), which is a moving verse response to the images on this shield; he treats them as a warning of the perils of (even defensive) force.

πᾶν μὲν γὰρ κύκλῳ τιτάνῳ λευκῷ τ' ἐλέφαντι
ἠλέκτρῳ θ' ὑπολαμπὲς ἔην χρυσῷ τε φαεινῷ
λαμπόμενον, κυάνου δὲ διὰ πτύχες ἠλήλαντο.
ἐν μέσσῳ δ' ἀδάμαντος ἔην Φόβος οὔ τι φατειός.
(139-44)

In his hands he took his shield, all glittering: no one ever
broke it with a blow or crushed it. And a wonder it was to
see; for its whole orb was a-shimmer with white ivory and
electrum, and it glowed with shining gold; and there were
zones of cyanus upon it. In the centre was Fear worked in
adamant, unspeakable.

The shield first appears as a shining and useful object. The familiar phrase
*thauma idesthai* (a wonder to behold) then sets the matrix of representation in
motion: this reaction reminds us that we are not seeing the object, but the
poet's experience. The subsequent lines (141-43) name the materials of the
shield and remark again on its sheen. Unlike an expression of wonder, the
naming of these physical features keeps our attention on the object itself,
without recalling the interpreter. In line 144 the remaining levels of
representation are brought out. The opening phrase, *en messôi* (in the
middle), gives spatial orientation, while *adamantos* (of adamant) gives us the
material of this image. The focus remains on the object itself with the verb
*eên* (there was); this verb does not shift attention to Hephaestus (as would,
e.g., "he made"), or to the describer (as would, e.g., "one could see"). The
naming of Phobos in the middle of line 144 is, then, the first sign that now a
relationship between the visual image and its referent is being represented.
From the opening lines to this point, the ekphrasis has described the visible
object, the reaction of the poet to the object, and what is depicted upon the
object. Then the final phrase, *ou ti phateios* (not in any way expressible),
completes the ekphrastic picture. This expression of inexpressibility recalls to
our attention the interaction between the language of description, the
describer, and the visual representation. Also, like the expression of wonder,
it recalls the audience's relation to the entire ekphrasis. From this point until
the opening line of the next section (154), the description elaborates the
referent, Phobos, without further regard for verbal and visual mediation.

This complex mixture of interpretation, mediation, and mimesis can
make an ekphrasis, both in poetic practice and rhetorical theory, a lesson in
two movements in a text: the audience's acceptance of illusion is
accompanied by an awareness of the source, the work, the context, and the
production of that illusion. Ekphrasis encourages us to think of representation

as a function of these two complementary processes. The consonance of much earlier poetic practice with the views of ekphrasis found in the rhetorical handbooks suggests that such a double movement of illusion and disillusion is widespread and can be useful in reading works from disparate ages and genres.

When read in this way, ekphrasis invites us to consider responses to visual representation, then also, by analogy, to consider our response to literary representation. The next, and final, section of this chapter introduces a way in which ekphrasis can encourage us to think about poetry.

## Ekphrasis and Reading

*Ekphrasis would entail not just translating a statue's language into our own, finding a place for its imagined words in the given world. It would also involve letting the words which the statue speaks unsettle or recreate the words we already seem to know.*
*- Gross (1989), p. 24.*

Ekphrasis has been read as a metaphor for poetry.[68] If we do read it so, then what effect could this have on our own responses to literary works?[69] A step toward an answer would be to reaffirm that ekphrasis focuses attention not only on the subject matter of a work, but also on the ways in which a work does what it does to its audience. In an ekphrasis, the response of a describer to a work of visual art can thus become a metaphor for the response of an audience to the description itself, and to other texts as well. In both the theories of the rhetorical handbooks and the poetic practice of the *Shield of Herakles*, ekphrasis responds to visual art by a complementary engagement with and detachment from the phenomena described. By describing the referent of visual images, the ekphrasis accepts the illusion suggested by a

---

68. See Prolegomena to this book, p. 4, note 6.

69. Cf. Fish (1972), p. 386: "Whatever is persuasive and illuminating about this analysis (and it is by no means exhaustive) is the result of my substituting for one question—What does this sentence mean?—another, more operational question—What does this sentence do?" (See pp. xi-xii for Fish's analogous approach to a whole work.) Cf. also Tyler (1978), p. 177, for a similar view in an analysis not of literature but of language: "In this discussion I am substituting 'What do we do when we refer?' 'Why do we refer?' 'How do we refer?' and 'When do we refer?' for the philosopher's 'To what does this word refer?.'"

work of art. By describing the surface appearance and the materials of the images, it asks us to imagine that we see the visual representation. But, by repeatedly calling attention to the act of describing and the language of description, the ekphrasis reminds us that it represents a human experience, a translation of visible phenomena into language. The description directs us neither to be enchanted alone nor dispassionate alone. We are encouraged, on the one hand, to accept the illusion the ekphrasis proposes, to try on the world of the text and to enter into its ways of making sense; but we are also encouraged to remain self-conscious about our response to representations, to bring the text into our own world and our own ways of making sense.

Ekphrastic reading, as developed here, is similar to the response to literature outlined in Paul Ricoeur's essay, "Appropriation."[70] He proposes that we enter a given text with a degree of suspension and acquiescence, as in play (an act he calls "divestiture"); but then we are to bring the new, perhaps enlarged understanding gained thereby into our own world (a process called "appropriation"). The two perspectives may be set out as follows:

| *Divestiture* | *Appropriation* |
|---|---|
| - Acceptance of illusion | - Attention to the working of illusion |
| - Enchantment | - Self-consciousness |
| - Literature as escape or diversion | - Literature as "equipment for living"[71] |
| - Context of creation | - Context of reception |
| - Literature as experience of foreignness, difference | - Literature as experience of ourselves, recognition. |

In Ricoeur's hermeneutics, neither side alone will do. While we read, we are making constant adjustments between them. The result is to bring together the audience, the work, and the world proposed by the work: "the aim of all hermeneutics is to struggle against cultural distance."[72] Such an aim suggests an ethical, as well as an aesthetic dimension to our reading.[73] The struggle is

---

70. Ricoeur (1981), pp. 182-193. For a related discussion of metaphor, which similarly focuses on both engagement and detachment, see Moran (1989).

71. I borrow this phrase from Kenneth Burke's essay, "Literature as Equipment for Living," in K. Burke (1973), pp. 253-262.

72. Ricoeur (1981), p. 185. One could add: "or any kind of distance."

73. See A.L. Becker (1982), p. 124: ". . . how does one describe a language in order not to exclude esthetic—one might even say moral—values." Also particularly appropriate is A.L. Becker (1988), p. 32: "And why describe languages—that is, languaging in different societies? I think the answer, as Geertz often puts it, is to learn to converse with those we have difficulty

not to meet one's own mind in a distant text, i.e., to believe, reductively, that what is foreign is, underneath it all, just like us. Nor does Ricoeur encourage the other extreme, the alienating belief that distant texts cannot speak to one's own life and thought (a kind of historicism gone wild). Ricoeur's hermeneutics does not limit us to interpreting the text in its original context, nor to reading only for application in our own. Through a fertile engagement in similarity and difference, he asks us to adopt the new ways of thinking proposed by a text but also, having done so, to adapt those new ways to our own experiences and intentions and desires.[74]

The movement between these two perspectives reflects the movement in an ekphrasis. Visual appearance is respectfully represented, but also transformed by language into a human experience, a reaction to what is seen. Ekphrasis can thus provoke us both to divest and to appropriate. Using the rhetorical handbooks in conjunction with the *Shield of Herakles* results in a way of reading the language of description in ekphrasis that makes the texts both enchanting and pertinent, revealing and relevant. We are encouraged, by both ancient criticism and poetic practice of ekphrasis, to try to read more generally in this fashion. I shall argue that the Shield of Achilles has just this effect, encouraging both appropriation and divestiture. To return to the question that opened this section of the essay, the extension of this kind of response to other texts is a result of reading ekphrasis as a metaphor for reading poetry.

---

conversing with. Whether they are our own neighbors and family or people halfway around the world, the same kinds of differences are involved, I think, and learning about one teaches about the other. Recognizing the dramatic differences I confront in speaking to a Balinese prepares me to recognize the more subtle differences I confront in speaking to my wife and children, and it teaches me to respect them, not out of some abstract moral principle, but as the practical first step in having my own differences respected."

74. See Poirier (1992), p. 167: "Reading is nothing if not personal. It ought to get down ultimately to a struggle between what you want to make of a text and what it wants to make of itself and you." Cf., with a somewhat different tone, Furbank (1991), pp. 8-9: "But what, further, we find is that Diderot is reenacting not just the creative process but the critical one also. Good criticism, it is implied, has to be a two-stage enterprise: first a wholehearted and generous, even credulous, response; and then a reappraisal in colder blood." Ekphrasis reenacts this process as well, but suggests that the two stages occur simultaneously.

# 3

# LEVELS OF REPRESENTATION IN EKPHRASIS

*In essence, a formal model is nothing but a restatement of the facts
at a tighter level of generalization. . . . It is thus an indispensible
methodological preliminary to the real task at hand, explanation.
There is one thing, however, that a formal model can never do: It
cannot explain a single thing.*

*- Givón (1979), pp. 5-6*

From reading ekphrases, especially the Shield of Achilles, I have derived a paradigm that separates the different levels of response to which the description calls attention. Ekphrases describe not only the referent of the image, but also the relationship of that referent to the medium of worked metal, to the manufacture of the image, to the artisan and artistry, and the effect of all this on the viewer of the image (usually the bard); the bard, in turn, acts as our guide as we imagine the images. Like Lessing, I claim to be describing Homeric practice; my scheme, however, is designed to be only a guide, and does not carry presumptions of propriety. The forms of attention, separated in analysis but blended as we hear or read the *Iliad*, can be schematized as follows.

## The Four Levels

*Res Ipsae* — Referent.[75] A focus on the events and characters that constitute the subject matter of the picture. This level of mimesis is based upon the recognition and elaboration of what is depicted by the image. The subject matter is often turned into a small story; as such this category can fit the strictures of Edmund Burke and Lessing. This category can be further subdivided into naming, interpreting (thought, speech, motion, etc.), and dramatizing (making a story by describing the same figure engaged in consecutive actions). The rhetorical distinction between naming, interpreting, and dramatizing lies in the distance our imagination is drawn through an imagined image and into an imagined event. Naming supplements the image with the associations of the word, but it does not necessarily take the attention far from the surface of the work. Interpreting more explicitly, i.e., including details inferred from or known about the referent but not appearing in the image, draws the audience into the illusion that it is observing the referent. When an image is dramatized, finally, the suggested referent of the image has taken hold to such a degree that the medium of worked metal is no longer part of the description.[76] Dramatization of an image marks full engagement in the illusion of the representation; the surface of the work becomes a transparent window to the scene evoked therein.[77]

*Opus Ipsum* — A focus on the physical medium. In ekphrasis this is the surface appearance of the work of visual art. It serves to defamiliarize by calling attention not to the world, but to the window through which we see it. By "defamiliarization" I mean no more than explicit attention to the medium rather than the referent—attention to the way in which we come to imagine,

---

75. I use Latin names for these categories not just for pleasure or show, but also to focus attention on the levels of descriptive response proposed in this essay, and to add a certain vividness and memorability.

76. Dramatization is rare in the Shield of Achilles (*Iliad* 18.506, 520-32, and 578-86), but some later ekphrases use a work of visual art as a springboard, which the narrative leaves behind and dramatizes without further attention to the visual medium: e.g., Catullus 64 (with the exception of, perhaps, the phrase *parte ex alia* in line 251); Longus *Daphnis and Chloe*; Petronius *Satyricon* 89.

77. This is seen as a defining feature of Homeric poetry by Ford (1992). On p. 6, e.g., he speaks of a Homeric "notion of past actions as the substance on which poetry offers us a transparent window"; or p. 7: "The poetry of the past fulfilled its design as long as audiences forgot the performing poet, and themselves, and everything but the vivid and painless presence of heroic action of old." Cf. also Walsh (1984), pp. 13-14. My discussion of Homeric ekphrasis will suggest a more self-conscious audience, and a Homeric poetry more reflective of its own genesis and its medium. Such self-consciousness is closer to the Homeric poetics argued in, e.g., Peradotto (1990), Katz (1991), Slatkin (1991), and Stanley (1993).

see, or know whatever it is we come to imagine, see, or know.[78] Attention is paid to color, shape, texture, arrangement, size, and, at times, material. This is Paul Friedländer's *echte Beschreibung* (true description).

*Artifex* and *Ars* — A focus on the creator and creation of the work of art, and their relation to the medium and the referent. Attention is here drawn to the making of the work of art. This focus is praised by Lessing. In ekphrasis, this level represents the relationship between the artist, the work, and the referent. There are three explicit types of focus on the *artifex* and *ars*: direct mention of the artisan, mention of workmanship or material of the work, and attention to the process of manufacture (another way of making a story). It will become apparent that the third type, describing the manufacture, is parallel to the common description of the history of a work of visual art. In such cases, the genesis of the work is not narrated, but rather its reception, use, and function through time.

*Animadversor* — A focus on the effect of or reaction to the work of visual art, praised by Edmund Burke and Lessing. In the Shield, this is the reaction of the bard to the images described, which then guides the reaction of the audience. It calls attention to the interpreter between the audience and the work, and the verbal medium into which these images are translated; it represents the relationship between the audience, the bard, the artistry, the object, and the referent. This is another way of making a story, as the describer's experience and response are described.

The spirit of this typology is that of Kenneth Burke's "terministic screen": "Pick some particular nomenclature, some one terministic screen . . . that you may proceed to track down the kinds of observation implicit in the terminology you have chosen."[79] Responding to ekphrasis using these levels of attention, using this particular terministic screen, counterbalances the type of criticism that assumes the Shield of Achilles is an unsuccessful attempt to represent the surface appearance of a work of visual art, or a purely poetic piece without concern for the visual medium.[80] It is, rather, a description of a more complex experience of images, not just their physical appearance.

---

78. In contemporary criticism the term "defamiliarization" often refers to our response to the referent; it means that art "makes the stone more stony." Similar to this is a poem's attention to the devices wherebye it represents, and that is the sense in which I use the term here. It means that the description is making the representation more "representation-y." On defamiliarization, see Holub (1984), pp. 18-21.

79. K. Burke (1966), p. 47. Cf. K. Burke (1969), p. 472: "a given terminology coaches us to look for certain kinds of things rather than others. . . . Some terminologies contain much richer modes of observation than others."

80. See discussion of Homer's "mistakes," above in Chapter 1.

Rarely does a line or word or phrase have a simple focus: the poetics of description, in practice, is one of subtle changes of emphasis, not exclusivity of focus. The levels of attention in ekphrasis, as outlined here, are a way of organizing the at times elusive movement of the language of description. The combination and adaptation of these types of description in the poem creates an ekphrasis that does not merely act as a copy of a preexisting, extra-linguistic reality. The description, rather, reflects, recapitulates, and perhaps creates a relationship between that reality and the various transformations it undergoes before and when the audience perceives it. Using these levels and the relations between them, I shall explore the ways in which the poem guides the audience, creates it in its role, and so establishes its own poetics.

There are still wider implications of a close reading of the Shield of Achilles: not only does it provide a paradigm with which we can approach other ekphrases, but a close reading of Homeric ekphrasis will show that there is no separate type of "visual" poetry. Ekphrasis is not a unique kind of poetry, distinguished in its poetics; as such, the types of response encouraged by ekphrasis can more easily be generalized into ways of responding to the *Iliad*. As an example of the use of these levels of representation, I turn first to the lines that prepare us to respond to the entire *Iliad*, then to similes, which are often compared to the Shield of Achilles.

## The Proem of the *Iliad* and Ekphrasis

The opening lines of the *Iliad* contain intimations of the poetics explored later in the Shield of Achilles. The narrator, the act of narrating, and the medium are made explicit to the reader; the lines draw attention to more than the events and characters of the tale, i.e., more than the story itself (the referent). The proem also represents the act of storytelling, the storyteller, the imagined audience, and how they all relate to that story.

### The First Three Words of the Iliad

The opening line of the *Iliad* reads:

Μῆνιν ἄειδε, θεά, Πηληϊάδεω 'Αχιλῆος. (1.1)

Sing the wrath, goddess, of the son of Peleus, Achilles.[81]

The first word directs attention not to the medium of song, nor to the act of singing, nor to their effects, but to the message, matter, world beyond the poem, theme, referent (what I am calling *"res ipsae"*).[82] *Mênin* (wrath), being the emphatic first word, suggests the priority of the referent in this epic; this priority is confirmed by the scarcity of explicit attention to song and of first-person address by the narrator.[83]

This first word, *mênin*, is in the accusative case, and so it sets up a syntactic expectation of a transitive verb. As such it also suggests that the subject matter of the poem, the referent, is to be acted upon—that it is part of a larger action. The second word, *aeide* (sing), fulfills this syntactic expectation, and creates a complex poetic and rhetorical effect. On the one hand it draws attention to the medium that will present and produce the referent. It alerts us that we will not experience "wrath," but an artistic rendering of wrath in song: the mediating qualities of epic song in relation to the subject matter are part of the picture. But more than song itself is part of the picture: the noun *aoidê* (song) would emphasize the medium, but the verb of creation, *aeide* (sing), draws attention to the process as well as the final product. It tells the audience that the work of verbal art is not to be imagined as a completed, preexisting product; it is a process, and it will be created as one listens.

The person and mood of the verb *aeide*, especially when coupled with the following noun *theâ* ("goddess," in the vocative case), add another level to the poetics of Homeric representation. If the verb were third-person singular in the indicative mood, and the goddess were named in the nominative case, then the phrase would read "the goddess sings the wrath." Attention would be drawn to the referent (wrath) by the direct object of the verb, to the medium and its creation (song and singing) by the verb, and to the source or singer (the goddess) by the noun in the nominative case. The bard would remain in the background. However, as it stands in our texts, the phrase can be rendered: "Sing the wrath, goddess." The verb, second-person singular in the imperative mood, and the noun in the vocative case still point

81. Translations from the *Iliad* in this chapter are my own.
82. In Homeric Greek the bard can either sing a song or the theme of a song. At *Iliad* 2.484-87 and *Odyssey* 8.538 the theme is sung. Song or words are sung at *Iliad* 1.473; *Odyssey* 1.339; *Odyssey* 8.90-91; *Odyssey* 17.519. The medium of song is emphasized in *Iliad* 1.607 and *Odyssey* 10.221. *Iliad* 9.189 and *Odyssey* 8.73 are ambiguous.
83. See de Jong (1987) for implicit attention to song and narration.

to the source (the goddess), but also bring the bard to the audience's attention: the imperative mood and the vocative case explicitly enact a scene in which the bard addressing the Muse is part of the picture. The first three words of the *Iliad* have included the referent, the medium, the act of creating that medium, the source of the song, as well as the bard, who is both source (for the audience) and audience (for the Muse's performance).

Compare the opening phrase of the *Odyssey*:

ἄνδρα μοι ἔννεπε, Μοῦσα.

Tell me [of] the man, Muse.

The initial word *andra* (man) names the referent, the subject matter of the song, again in the accusative case; the verb *ennepe* (tell) is also in the imperative mood and the noun *Mousa* (Muse) in the vocative case.[84] The pronoun *moi* (to me) names the speaker and so makes explicit the presence of the bard, which was implied in the opening line of the *Iliad*.[85] The inclusion of the bard, as the one who addresses the Muse, draws the audience into the picture as well. The bard does not ask her to make *him* sing, but to sing herself; the bard is not the source of the song, but rather the initial listener. The bard is one of us; his reactions are those of an audience, and so those reactions can be taken as a guide for our own, in a synechdochic manner.[86] This is the gentle rhetoric of the proem (and the poem); it is a rhetoric of inclusion. Attention to the mediator between us and the Muse's song emphasizes the intimacy of the bard not only with the source, but also with the audience. This explicit attention to the levels of mediation does not call the representation into question; such attention, by establishing intimacy and authority, enhances our trust in the bard and in the fidelity of the representation. I hope to show that the Shield of Achilles has a similar effect.

---

84. On *ennepe* (tell) vs. *aeide* (sing) see M.L. West (1981), p. 113, who sees no significant distinction, and Thalmann (1984), p. 121, who sees a marked difference (i.e., *aeide* draws attention to the medium, while *ennepe* does not).

85. Cf. the address to the Muses at *Iliad* 2.484: *Espete nun moi* (Tell, now, to me).

86. As the proem to the *Odyssey* closes (1.10), the first-person pronoun is made plural to include the audience: *thea, thugater Dios, eipe kai hêmin* (goddess, daughter of Zeus, tell also to us). See Heubeck, West, and Hainsworth (1988), p. 73: "*hêmin*: the poet and his audience." (Within this note they also consider the possible senses of *kai*, which I have rendered "also.") The bard no longer leaves us to infer that we are hearing the song as he does. In the *Iliad* the expansion from the bard as auditor to the bard as part of the larger audience remains implicit. Cf. the synechdochic response to a rhapsode's performance of Homeric epic in Plato *Ion* 533d1-e3; see also A.S. Becker (1993b).

After the first three words of the *Iliad*, there are already several levels of literary mimesis. The opening phrase of this epic asks that the reader attend not to the referent alone, but also to the relationships between referent, song, singing, and audience.

## The Fourth Word, the Fifth, and Beyond

The second half of the first line of the *Iliad* begins to elaborate the referent *mênin*. The genitives name and provide a patronymic for Achilles: *Pêlêiadeô Akhilêos* (of Achilles son of Peleus). These words draw attention away from the dramatic setting of *aeide thea* and, by naming, focus on the subject matter of the poem. The patronymic evokes Achilles' history, as we move into the tale. As the second line begins, attention remains on the referent, but now the relationship between the bard and that referent is expressed:

οὐλομένην, ἣ μυρί' Ἀχαιοῖς ἄλγε' ἔθηκε.

destructive [wrath], which brought upon the Achaeans
countless pains.

The initial word of the line is a reaction to, impression of, or interpretation of the referent of the poem: the word describes a response of the bard (or the epic tradition) to the referent.[87] Following this participle, a clause begins to narrate the effects of Achilles' wrath on the Achaeans; a story begins to take shape. The proem of the *Iliad* does not then return to song or the act of singing after the opening line. Once the focus turns from the medium to the referent, there it remains until the opening line of the next section

τίς τ' ἄρ σφωε θεῶν ἔριδι ξυνέηκε μάχεσθαι; (1.8)

and which one of the gods set these two fighting in strife.

The interrogative mood, like the imperative, is a reminder of the source and the mediator, the Muse and the bard.[88]

---

87. See M.W. Edwards (1991), pp. 5-6, on *oulomenên* expressing the narrator's regret, and hence being an index of the bard. Cf. de Jong (1987), pp. 143-144.

88. Redfield (1979), p. 96, argues that in line 6 *ex hou* (from which [time]) is to be taken with *eteleieto* (was coming to completion) in line 5, not with *aeide* (sing). Attention would not thereby

*Implications*

While these lines are in mind, consider the first lines of the first earthly scene of the Shield:

'Εν δὲ δύω ποίησε πόλεις μερόπων ἀνθρώπων
καλάς. ἐν τῇ μέν ῥα γάμοι τ' ἔσαν εἰλαπίναι τε.
(18.490-1)

On [the shield] he made two cities of mortal men,
beautiful [cities]. In one there were weddings and feasts.

The first line contains a verb of fashioning (*poiêse*, "he made"), showing the visual medium not as product but as process (cf. *aeide*); the referent (*poleis*, "cities") is named in the accusative case (cf. *mênin*, "wrath"). This referent is modified by a genitive phrase (*meropôn anthrôpôn*, "of mortal men"), the first an adjective and the second a noun (cf. *Pêleiadeô Akhilêos*, "of the son of Peleus, Achilles"). The second line begins with a term (*kalas*, "beautiful") that indicates a response to (reaction to, effect of) the referent (cf. *oulomenên*, "destructive"). This is followed by a clause (*en têi men rha gamoi t' esan eilapinai te*, "in one there were weddings and feasts") further elaborating the referent, and beginning to tell its story (cf. *hê muri' Akhaiois alge' ethêke*, "which brought upon the Achaeans countless pains"). In the lines that follow there is no explicit mention of the medium, the shield itself, until the opening line of the following scene (541, cf. *Iliad* 1.8). Like the proem of the *Iliad*, the language of description in the Shield of Achilles represents a relationship between the referent of the image (the events and characters portrayed therein, *res ipsae*), the material (visible surface of the image, *opus ipsum*), the maker and making of the image (*ars et artifex*), and the reactions of the bard (*animadversor*). The specific descriptive technique, as well as the more abstract forms of attention, link the proem to the Shield; given this concinnity, the ability of a visual medium to represent significant aspects of the world is not called into question. Imagined scenes of life and imagined depictions on the Shield are represented in the poem through the same descriptive language, the same types of stories.

---

turn back to the singing before line 8. Cf. Kirk (1985), p. 53, note to 1.6-7, for cautious support of the opposite view.

## Simile and Ekphrasis

The Shield of Achilles also recalls Homeric similes; their poetics, like that of the proem, corresponds to the poetics of the Shield.[89] There are three bases for the comparison: the referent, effect on the reader, and poetic technique. The scenes of animals, agriculture, and peaceful city life are said to contrast with, to figure, and to comment upon the martial world of the epic (referent); there is an emphatic slowing of the narrative effected by both simile and ekphrasis (effect); similes and the Shield both translate images into small stories (technique).[90] It is in this translation of the referent of the images into narrative that the mode of description in the similes corresponds to that of the Shield. The stories elaborated in similes include specific detail, cause and effect, prior and subsequent events, reactions of characters and the bard, and movement.[91] Most of the extended similes have these characteristics in various combinations. The opening of the third book of the *Iliad* serves as a useful example:

---

89. In a section on similes M.W. Edwards (1991), pp. 24-41, mentions the arms of Achilles four times (pp. 35, 36, 37, 41). On p. 39 Edwards says that "the Homeric simile for a moment unites narrrator and audience" (cf.p. 1); so too ekphrasis. See also Kirk (1985), p. 46: "the extraordinary description of the Shield of Akhilleus—a symbolic representation, simile-like but on a larger scale, of the scenes and values of peace and war." See Lonsdale (1990a) for more on simile and ekphrasis.

90. On similes as contrast see Fränkel (1921), p. 103; Schein (1984), p. 141. As delay see A. Cook (1984), p. 42; Coffey (1957), pp. 113-132. As stories (which also slow the narrative) see D. Marshall, in Bloom (1986), pp. 234-235. Likening the effect of simile and description, M.W. Edwards (1987), p. 109 says: "Fundamentally, a simile, like a detailed description of an artifact or an artifact's history, is a technique of expansion, a means of creating a pause in the forward movement of the narrative. Cf. also Myres (1930), p. 509; M.W. Edwards (1987), p. 271; Kirk (1985), pp. 77-78; Lonsdale (1990b). W.C. Scott (1974), pp. 190-205, has a convenient list of similes.

91. Energy and movement are seen as a characteristic of Homeric song. Cf. Aristotle's comment on Homer at *Rhetoric* 1412a10: *kinoumena gar kai zônta poiei panta, hê d' energeia kinêsis* (for he makes all things moving and living, and [their] energy is movement); Demetrius *On Style* 81-82; Havelock (1986), p. 76; Whitman (1958), p. 117; Bowra (1972), p. 141; Hampe (1952), pp. 39-40. Pope, in the preface to his *Iliad* (1796), volume 1, pp. v-vi, says: "What he writes is of the most animated nature imaginable; everything moves, everything lives, and is put into action." The Scholia to the *Iliad* see vividness (*enargeia*) as a general quality of Homeric description; the source of *enargeia* is the specific, detailed elaboration found in both simile and ekphrasis. E.g., Scholia T to 5.664 (Erbse II, p. 90); bT to 15.381-84 and 506 (Erbse IV, pp. 91, 112); bT to 16.762-63 (Erbse IV, p. 298); bT to 22.61-65 (Erbse V, p. 277). On simile and visualization, see bT to 4.141c (Erbse I, p. 475) and bT to 23.692-94 (Erbse V, p. 475). For a useful outline of the criticism in the scholia, see Kirk (1985), pp. 38-43; for a fuller discussion, see Meijering (1987).

Αὐτὰρ ἐπεὶ κόσμηθεν ἅμ' ἡγεμόνεσσιν ἕκαστοι,
Τρῶες μὲν κλαγγῇ τ' ἐνοπῇ τ' ἴσαν, ὄρνιθες ὥς,
ἠΰτε περ κλαγγὴ γεράνων πέλει οὐρανόθι πρό,
αἵ τ' ἐπεὶ οὖν χειμῶνα φύγον καὶ ἀθέσφατον ὄμβρον,
κλαγγῇ ταί γε πέτονται ἐπ' Ὠκεανοῖο ῥοάων,         5
ἀνδράσι Πυγμαίοισι φόνον καὶ κῆρα φέρουσαι·
ἠέριαι δ' ἄρα ταί γε κακὴν ἔριδα προφέρονται. (3.1-7)

When the troops on each side were arrayed with their
leaders, the Trojans went forth with a piercing cry and shout,
like birds, just as the piercing cry of cranes comes forth in
the sky, when they flee the winter and the endless rain, with
piercing cry they fly to the streams of Ocean, bringing
bloodshed and death to the Pygmy people; early in the
morning they engage in their harmful battle.[92]

The bare phrase *"ornithes hôs"* (as birds) is made more specific by the naming of the birds in the subsequent line (*geranôn*, "of cranes"). The clause comprising the fourth line adds cause and prior action, giving the reason for their flight. A picture of the cranes in flight and their goal follows. The final line of the vignette notes the effect of their migration. Similarly in the Shield of Achilles the scene of the lawsuit (18.497-508, discussed below in Part II) begins with a crowd gathered in the square; the cause of this gathering is then given. The motives of the litigants are expressed and their actions are narrated. The scene ends with a picture of two gold talents, and their use in the result of this suit is noted. The simile and the scene from the Shield show a similar poetics, both elaborating with the same type of detail.[93]

It is not surprising that images of everyday life on the shield elicit the same poetic response as images of everyday life in similes. This consonance, however, diminishes the audience's concern for the mediating quality of the visual arts; the techniques of visual mimesis are noted, appreciated, and accepted, while the description elaborates the referent. The description will supplement the visual image, going beyond what could be seen, but this is neither a statement of mimetic primacy nor a questioning of the representational capabilities of the visual arts. The description creates, in our experience of the poem, a consonance between life and depicted life.

92. On the war between the Pygmies and the Cranes, see Kirk (1985), p. 265, note to lines 5-6. In his note on line 7 (ibid.), Kirk prefers to render *êeriai* as "through the air," rather than "early in the morning" as I have done.

93. Elaboration of this type is also found in the descriptions of warriors. Naming leads to a story (e.g., 4.473-79; 5.707-10; 13.171-81, 363-73; 16.179-95; 21.34-48).

# 4

# PATTERN AND DEVIATION: DESCRIPTION

# OF ART IN THE ILIAD

*Criticism should engage itself not with rendered experience but with the experience of rendering; it must always go back to acts of rendition, to language, which is one reason why there are so many quotations in this book and so much verbal analysis of them.*
*- Poirier (1987), p. 111*

One learns to read an ekphrasis just as one learns to respond to any work of art, visual or verbal.[94] Descriptions of artwork elsewhere in the *Iliad* establish the patterns and expectations for ekphrasis in this epic: having read or heard the descriptions in the *Iliad* as a whole, we can better appreciate the particular poetics of the Shield of Achilles. In this chapter I have chosen passages from the *Iliad* that illustrate the characteristic techniques of Homeric description.[95] With the exception of the Arms of Agamemnon, postponed to

---

94. Cf. Geertz (1983), pp. 94-120, especially pp. 102-108. Also Baxandall (1972), p. 152: "An old picture is a record of visual activity. One has to learn to read it, just as one has to learn to read a text from a different culture, even when one knows, in a limited sense, the language: both language and pictorial representation are conventional activities."

95. Ekphrases not discussed include 7.219-24; 10.260-71, 439-41; 12.294-98; 13.21-26; 14.178-80, 214-18; 18.369-71, 373-81, 389-90, 400-2; 23.740-49.

the end of the chapter, these ekphrases are discussed in the order in which they appear in the *Iliad*.

## The Scepter of Agamemnon

In the first book, Achilles swears his oath, and uses the scepter, a work of manual art, as a symbol:

ναὶ μὰ τόδε σκῆπτρον, τὸ μὲν οὔ ποτε φύλλα καὶ
                                                    ὄζους
φύσει, ἐπεὶ δὴ πρῶτα τομὴν ἐν ὄρεσσι λέλοιπεν,      235
οὐδ' ἀναθηλήσει· περὶ γάρ ῥά ἑ χαλκὸς ἔλεψε
φύλλα τε καὶ φλοιόν· νῦν αὖτέ μιν υἷες 'Αχαιῶν
ἐν παλάμῃς φορέουσι δικασπόλοι, οἵ τε θέμιστας
πρὸς Διὸς εἰρύαται· ὁ δέ τοι μέγας ἔσσεται ὅρκος.
(1.234-39)[96]

I swear by this staff, which will never again put out leaves and branches, from the moment it parted from its stump in the mountains, and it will sprout no more, since the bronze stripped it of its leaves and bark all round. Now the sons of the Achaians carry it in their hands when they give judgments, those who guard the ways of justice under Zeus: an oath by this staff has power to bind. (Hammond, p. 56)[97]

The scepter is described not as it appears, but through its genesis; its prior state, the way it was altered, the use to which it is put—all are ways of describing significant aspects of an object without describing its visual appearance. This is a type of representation that is characteristic of Homeric ekphrasis (and simile). In describing a visible object, in translating an image

---

96. For discussion of *Iliad* 1.234-39, see Schein (1984), pp. 96-97; M. Lynn-George (1988), pp. 47-49; Easterling (1989). On the scepter as it relates to a contrast between gold-immortality-culture vs. vegetation-mortality-nature, see Nagy (1979), pp. 179-80, 10§8; 188, 10§17; 109, 10§18. For the similarity between this description and Homeric similes, see Kirk (1985), p. 77, note to 234-39. On this scene and the description of the scepter in the second book of the *Iliad*, see Lowenstam (1993b), p. 67.

97. In this chapter and throughout Part II, translations of quotations from the *Iliad* are those of Hammond (1987). Translations of individual words and lines in the text are my own.

into words, the poem here chooses to emphasize actions in time rather than visible features of an object in space. In this way the poem emphasizes those significant aspects of an object that are more conventionally accessible to its own verbal mode of representation than is visible form. The appearance of the scepter (i.e., *opus ipsum*) is, indeed, noted at the end of Achilles' oath, as he throws the scepter to the ground; but this appearance is represented as the result of actions in time: *khruseiois hêloisi peparmenon* (1.246, "pierced with golden studs"). This participial phrase assures that the action of the *artifex* is part of the picture.

In the second book Agamemnon, awakened by the deceptive dream, rises and dresses (2.42-45), then takes up his scepter:

εἵλετο δὲ σκῆπτρον πατρώϊον, ἄφθιτον αἰεί·
σὺν τῷ ἔβη κατὰ νῆας 'Αχαιῶν χαλκοχιτώνων.
(2.46-47)

And he took up the sceptre of his fathers, imperishable for all time, and with this in his hands he went down to the ships of the bronze-clad Achaians. (Hammond, p. 66)

The first line notes its history and function with the adjective *patrôion* (of the fathers). The phrase *aphthiton aiei* (unperishing ever) is another reminder of the narrator (who is the *animadversor*); this is a characteristic of the scepter known and made meaningful through language, through what can be said about the scepter, not from observation of it. The description responds to, rather than merely envisions, the appearance of the object in space. These are lines of which Lessing would approve: objects in space are included as part of actions in time.

This scepter appears again in the second book, and is there described in a fashion that further elaborates its history:

... ἀνὰ δὲ κρείων 'Αγαμέμνων    100
ἔστη σκῆπτρον ἔχων, τὸ μὲν "Ηφαιστος κάμε τεύχων.
"Ηφαιστος μὲν δῶκε Διὶ Κρονίωνι ἄνακτι,
αὐτὰρ ἄρα Ζεὺς δῶκε διακτόρῳ ἀργεϊφόντῃ·
'Ερμείας δὲ ἄναξ δῶκεν Πέλοπι πληξίππῳ,
αὐτὰρ ὁ αὖτε Πέλοψ δῶκ' 'Ατρέϊ, ποιμένι λαῶν·    105
'Ατρεὺς δὲ θνῄσκων ἔλιπεν πολύαρνι Θυέστῃ,
αὐτὰρ ὁ αὖτε Θυέστ' 'Αγαμέμνονι λεῖπε φορῆναι,
πολλῇσιν νήσοισι καὶ "Αργεϊ παντὶ ἀνάσσειν.

τῷ ὅ γ' ἐρεισάμενος ἔπε' Ἀργείοισι μετηύδα.
(2.100-109)

Then lord Agamemnon rose, holding his sceptre, the work of
Hephaistos' labour. Hephaistos gave it to lord Zeus the son of
Kronos: and Zeus gave it to Hermes the guide, the slayer of
Argos: and lord Hermes gave it to Pelops the charioteer, then
Pelops in turn gave it to Atreus, shepherd of the people.
Atreus as he was dying left it to Thyestes, rich in flocks, then
in turn Thyestes left it to Agamemnon to carry, to be king
over many islands and all of Argos. Leaning on this sceptre
Agamemnon spoke to the Argives. (Hammond, p. 67)

As with most significant objects in the *Iliad* (and the wrath of Achilles that
opens the epic), the scepter is introduced in the accusative case as the direct
object (in this case of a participle, *ekhôn* "holding"). The end of the
description is also marked by an action of Agamemnon: *tôi g' ereisamenos*
(leaning upon it). Between these indications of the larger action in which the
object is used, the description briefly notes its manufacture by Hephaestus—
*ars et artifex*—then moves to the history of the object. Again description is
not of appearance.[98]

The three descriptions of scepters show three ways to turn a work of
art into a story: the bard may describe its manufacture, its use, or its history.
In each of these descriptions of the scepter, there are no pictures to describe,
but the bard nevertheless translates objects in space into actions in time.

# The Tapestry of Helen

The tapestry of Helen is the first work of representational art to be
described in the *Iliad*; it invites comparison to the song of the bard, as each

---

98. See S. Richardson (1990), p. 63: "This story of the scepter's transmission from Zeus to
Agamemnon, a genealogy of sorts, stands in the place of a description of its physical appearance.
. . . [T]he length, color, or polish of the scepter is irrelevant, so the narrator does not waste time
with a physical description. But the scepter is a sign of authority, which is pertinent to this
episode, and he decides that it is worth a brief pause to imbue the scepter with symbolic
significance by giving it a history." Cf. *Iliad* 23.744-49. Such inclusion of history is common in
the description of heroes as well (e.g., 13.171-81, 361-69; 21.34-48).

represents the figures and actions of the war.[99] Its history cannot be narrated, since it is a work that we experience as it is being made, as the Shield of Achilles or a performance of epic song itself. But, as in the descriptions of the scepter, the appearance of the tapestry is noted only cursorily:

᾿Ιρις δ' αὖθ' ῾Ελένῃ λυεκωλένῳ ἄγγελος ἦλθεν,
εἰδομένη γαλόῳ, ᾿Αντηνορίδαο δάμαρτι,
τὴν ᾿Αντηνορίδης εἶχε κρείων ῾Ελικάων,
Λαοδίκην, Πριάμοιο θυγατρῶν εἶδος ἀρίστην.
τὴν δ' εὖρ' ἐν μεγάρῳ· ἡ δὲ μέγαν ἱστὸν ὕφαινε,    125
δίπλακα πορφυρέην, πολέας δ' ἐνέπασσεν ἀέθλους
Τρώων θ' ἱπποδάμων καὶ ᾿Αχαιῶν χαλκοχιτώνων·
οὓς ἕθεν εἵνεκ' ἔπασχον ὑπ' ῎Αρηος παλαμάων.
(3.121-28)

Now Iris came bringing the news to white-armed Helen, in the form of her sister-in-law, the wife of Antenor's son, married to lord Helikaon son of Antenor—she was Laodike, the most beautiful of Priam's daughters. Iris found Helen in her room, working at a great web of purple cloth for a double cloak, and in it she was weaving many scenes of the conflict between the horse-taming Trojans and the bronze-clad Achaians, which they were enduring for her sake at the hands of Ares. (Hammond, pp. 88-89)

Before the tapestry itself is mentioned, the narrative emphasizes visual aspects of the scene: *leukolênôi* ("white armed," of Helen), *eidomenê galoôi*, *eidos aristên* ("resembling her sister-in-law," "noble appearance," of Iris disguised as Laodice). But the rest of the description of Laodice emphasizes history rather than appearance: *Antênoridao damarti, tên Antênoridês eikhe kreiôn Helikaôn* ("wife of the son of Antenor, whom Antenor's son, lord Helicaon, held," 122-23). Description of a person, in its combination of appearance and history, is parallel to the description of scepters and other works of art in the *Iliad*, to be discussed below. Such a consonance suggests

99. Scholia bT on *Iliad* 3.126-27 (Erbse I, p. 381) call the tapestry an archetype for the bard's *poiêsis*: ἀξιόχρεων ἀρχέτυπον ἀνέπλασεν ὁ ποιητὴς τῆς ἰδίας ποιήσεως. (the poet shaped a worthy model [*arkhetupon*] of his own poetry). The bibliography on this passage is extensive. I mention here works that discuss the passage in terms of the analogy and rivalry between the arts: Kennedy (1986), pp. 5-14; Bergren (1979-80), pp. 19-34; Snyder (1981), pp. 193-196; Schein (1984), p. 23; Thalmann (1984), pp. 27, 153, and 166; Austin (1975), pp. 127-128; Whitman (1958), pp. 117-118; M. Lynn-George (1988), p. 29.

again that works of visual art are described in a fashion having as much to do with the poetics of the *Iliad* as with the nature of the referent. This supports the supposition that, when description goes beyond what is actually on the imagined surface of the depiction, this is not a sign that the description is surpassing the visual image, nor a sign of a fault in the description; it is a way of describing, whether objects or characters, within the epic.[100]

After Iris's arrival, Helen's weaving is described (125-28). The passage begins by focusing on the larger action of which the tapestry is part: the work is first mentioned in the accusative case, as the direct object of a verb of manufacture, describing the artist and her work (i.e., *artifex et ars*). Attention turns to the object itself (i.e., *opus ipsum*) with the noun that names it (*histon*, "loom") and the adjective that describes it (*megan*, "large"). Visual appearance is then developed by the two adjectives that open the following line (*diplaka porphureên*, "two layered, shining purple"); they focus on features of the work itself, as perceived by the eye. Adjectives that describe size, color, and shape draw minimal attention to the perceiver; they focus attention on the surface of the tapestry. This single phrase, however, is the only description of the physical and material surface of the tapestry.

The lines then take us through to the represented world (126-28), i.e., *res ipsae*. But even as we are drawn into that world, the verb *enepassen* ([she] was weaving in) prevents us from losing sight of the artist's action and the medium in which the images are woven (both *artifex* and *opus*).[101] *Enepassen* ensures that the composition of the visual medium is part of the picture: it notes that the battles (*aethlous*, 126) are representations, and so does not permit full illusion. This description, like most in the *Iliad*, does not come to rest in any one level of representation, but rather includes the relations among the world (*res ipsae*), the work of art (*opus ipsum*), the artist (*artifex*), and the words of the describer (*animadversor*).

In the next two lines (127-28), the battle of Trojans and Achaeans becomes the focus of the description. The formulaic line 127 directs attention to *res ipsae* and not to *opus ipsum*, the woven representations. The recurrence of this same line only four lines later (131) shows a concinnity between the language used to describe a depiction of these contests (127) and that which describes the contests themselves (131). Epic formulaic language here discourages a differentiation between the representational capabilities of the

---

100. See Mason (1989), p. 39—quoted as an epigraph for Chapter 1—on the different language-games of description, which direct the choices made in an ekphrasis.

101. The verb is used again only once in the *Iliad* : at 20.440-41 Andromache weaves images of flowers on a robe.

verbal and the visual media, and encourages a conflation of the two.[102] The next line (128) leaves the woven images behind and describes the world as known through the words of the poem: *hous hethen heinek' epaskhon ep' Arêos palamaôn* (which they suffered for her sake at the hands of Ares). The description notes the underlying, invisible, yet significant aspects of the scene. After this line, which responds to but does not describe the tapestry, attention returns to the larger narrative (129).

The description of Helen's tapestry begins, as do most ekphrases in the *Iliad*, with the object as part of a larger action. Our attention is directed first to the artist manufacturing the work (*artifex*), then to the object itself (*opus*), and then through to the referent of the representation (*res ipsae*). The same progression of focus marks the opening passages of the Shield of Achilles. For example, *Iliad* 18.468-77 focus on the work in Hephaestus's workshop (*ars et artifex*), then 478-82 focus on the physical object (*opus ipsum*), subsequently 483-89 move into the represented world (*res ipsae*). Helen's tapestry, then, with its specific affinity to the Shield of Achilles in both content and poetics, prepares us more directly to respond to the later, larger ekphrasis. Verbal and visual arts work in similar ways, the description tells us; this encourages an analogy between the arts, though it is never made explicit in the *Iliad*. Such an analogy between visual and verbal representation gives us more confidence in reading an ekphrasis as a *mise en abîme* for the poetics of the *Iliad*: the narrator becomes an audience, and the narrator's reactions, while in that role, can guide those of his own audience, the listeners and readers of the *Iliad*.

## The Bow of Pandarus

At *Iliad* 4.105-13 comes a description of the bow[103] belonging to Pandarus, the archer who, at Athena's instigation, shoots Menelaus and thus breaks the truce between the Trojans and Achaeans:

---

102. Kirk (1985), p. 281: "The repetition may . . . underline the correspondence between Helen's work and the world outside." (The line appears twice more in the *Iliad*, at 3.251 and 8.71.) Cf. Marg (1957), p. 25. See Kennedy (1986) for a reading of this scene that sees a privilege for the bard's own mimesis over that of Helen.

103. On the composition of the bow, see Lorimer (1950), p. 290 and Kirk (1985), p. 341, note to 4.110.

αὐτίκ᾽ ἐσύλα τόξον ἐΰξοον ἰξάλου αἰγὸς                              105
ἀγρίου, ὅν ῥά ποτ᾽ αὐτὸς ὑπὸ στέρνοιο τυχήσας
πέτρης ἐκβαίνοντα δεδεγμένος ἐν προδοκῇσι
βεβλήκει πρὸς στῆθος· ὁ δ᾽ ὕπτιος ἔμπεσε πέτρῃ.
τοῦ κέρα ἐκ κεφαλῆς ἐκκαιδεκάδωρα πεφύκει·
καὶ τὰ μὲν ἀσκήσας κεραοξόος ἤραρε τέκτων,          110
πᾶν δ᾽ εὖ λειήνας χρυσέην ἐπέθηκε κορώνην.
καὶ τὸ μὲν εὖ κατέθηκε τανυσσάμενος ποτὶ γαίῃ
ἀγκλίνας. (4.105-13)

At once he took out his polished bow, made of horn from a
leaping wild goat that he himself had once shot under the
chest as it sprang down from a rock: he had lain in wait in a
hide, and hit the goat in the chest, so it crashed on its back on
the rock below. The horns growing from its head were
sixteen palms long. These a bowyer skilled in hornwork had
prepared and fitted into a bow, then smoothed the whole to a
fine polish and capped it with a tip of gold. Pandaros bent
back this bow, strung it, and laid it carefully on the ground.
(Hammond, p. 98)

The bow is introduced in the accusative case, as part of an action; it is
modified by an adjective that helps the audience to visualize the bow, but that
also calls attention to the skill of the *artifex*: euxoon (well polished) refers to
the activity of the craftsman in a way that, e.g., *megan* (large) would not. The
mention of the material out of which the bow is made then leads to a
description of how Pandarus caught the goat, and how the craftsman
fashioned its horns into the bow. The physical object serves as a stimulus for
a story, which need not be concerned with the appearance of the object.

Three actions are part of the description of the bow. The framing
action is Pandarus's removal of the bow from its case (105). Then the bard
tells how Pandarus captured the goat from whose horns the bow is made
(106-8). Finally, we learn how a craftsman fashioned the bow from these
horns (109-11). The description moves from the context, to the object, to the
story elicited by the object, to the artist and his artistry, then back to the
narrative context again (112). Describing an object through the stories it
elicits is, at this point in the *Iliad*, already being established as a manner of
description, a mode that will be exaggerated in the Shield of Achilles.[104]

---

104. An outward and visible sign becomes a similar stimulus for a story in the well-known
description of the scar of Odysseus (*Odyssey* 19.386-475). See the dated but justly famous essay

More specifically, the type of elaboration in this description anticipates the levels of attention outlined above. The object is introduced in the accusative case as part of an action in the larger narrative; there is an emphasis on the artistry and the artist, supplementing attention to its appearance. There are no representations on the bow, so the level of *res ipsae* is absent; but the narration of history and manufacture plays much the same role, as it is a story elicited by the object. While an emphasis on the *animadversor* seems to be missing, it is included in the adverb *eu* ("well," 111), used also as a prefix to the adjective *euxoon* (105): *eu* implies the judgment of the narrator, who lies between us (the audience of the description) and the described object, and gives us our only access to that object.

The Shield of Achilles seems, at times, implausible, but descriptions such as this one make it more likely that the description of Achilles' shield is not merely a poetic piece using the visual image as a pretext. Like earlier ekphrases, the Shield directs us, repeatedly throughout the description, to imagine a work of art. Even when it is made into a tale, even when the description leaves the visible for the verbal, the Shield is similar to unproblematic ekphrases elsewhere in the *Iliad*. It is, then, probable that an archaic Greek audience, when hearing the Shield of Achilles, would not be led by its poetics to think that it does anything other than describe a magnificent work of art.[105]

## The Chariot of Hera and the *Aegis* of Athena

While ekphrases tend not to cluster in the *Iliad*, at the end of the fifth book two appear together.[106] The chariot of Hera is described first:

ἡ μὲν ἐποιχομένη χρυσάμπυκας ἔντυεν ἵππους      720
"Ηρη, πρέσβα θεά, θυγάτηρ μεγάλοιο Κρόνοιο·
"Ηβη, δ' ἀμφ' ὀχέεσσι θοῶς βάλε καμπύλα κύκλα,
χάλκεα ὀκτάκνημα, σιδηρέῳ ἄξονι ἀμφίς.

in Auerbach (1953), pp. 1-19, and now see Rutherford (1992), pp. 182-84 for discussion and further bibliography on the narrative qualities of the description of the scar.

105. J. Carter (1972), pp. 25-58, notes that the Shield is extraordinary, but similar enough to archaic Greek art to make it imaginable for a Homeric audience.

106. On the related clustering of similes (e.g., *Iliad* 2.455-73) and their effect, see M.W. Edwards (1991), p. 39.

τῶν ἤτοι χρυσέη ἴτυς ἄφθιτος, αὐτὰρ ὕπερθε
χάλκε᾽ ἐπίσσωτρα προσαρηρότα, θαῦμα ἰδέσθαι·  725
πλῆμναι δ᾽ ἀργύρου εἰσὶ περίδρομοι ἀμφοτέρωθεν·
δίφρος δὲ χρυσέοισι καὶ ἀργυρέοισιν ἱμᾶσιν
ἐντέταται, δοιαὶ δὲ περίδρομοι ἄντυγές εἰσι.
τοῦ δ᾽ ἐξ ἀργύρεος ῥυμὸς πέλεν· αὐτὰρ ἐπ᾽ ἄκρῳ
δῆσε χρύσειον καλὸν ζυγόν, ἐν δὲ λέπαδνα     730
κάλ᾽ ἔβαλε χρύσει·· ὑπὸ δὲ ζυγὸν ἤγαγεν Ἥρη
ἵππους ὠκύποδας, μεμαυῖ᾽ ἔριδος καὶ ἀυτῆς. (5.720-32)

Hera, then, queenly goddess, daughter of great Kronos,
busied about the harnessing of the horses with their golden
head-pieces. And Hebe quickly fitted the curved wheels to
the chariot-frame, bronze wheels with eight spokes, at each
end of the axle made of iron. Their felloes are of
imperishable gold, and all round them are fixed tyres of
bronze, a wonderful sight. The naves that revolve on either
side are of silver: and the platform is made of gold and silver
straps stretched tight, and twin rails run round it. From it
there extends a pole of silver: at the end of this Hebe lashed a
beautiful yoke of gold, and fitted it with lovely golden yoke-
straps. And Hera brought the swift-footed horses under the
yoke, eager for the clash and shout of battle.
(Hammond, p. 125)

The passage begins by narrating the action of which the object is part; bodies
in space are part of actions in time. A novelty in this ekphrasis is the
sustained attention to materials. The horses are *khrusampukas* ("with golden
crown," 720); the eight-spoked wheels are *khalkea* (bronze); the rest of the
description includes *sidêreôi* (of iron), *khruseê* (golden), *argurou* (of silver),
*khruseoisi* (golden), *argureoisin* and *argureos* (of silver), *khruseion kalon*
(golden, beautiful), and *kal' khrusei'* (beautiful, golden).[107] However, even in
this passage dominated by attention to the appearance of the object, the
process of making of the chariot is kept in the foreground. If compared to a
term such as "yellow," the words "gold," "silver," and "iron" carry an
intimation of the manufacture of the object: they name the materials out of
which the object was made, and hence mark not just *opus ipsum* but also *ars*
and even *artifex*. This ekphrasis also includes the reaction of the perceiver,
not only in the the adjective *kalon* (beautiful), but more forcefully with the

---

107. The description of Poseidon's arrival at his palace (*Iliad* 13.21-26) has a similar
emphasis on material.

phrase *thauma idesthai* ("a wonder to behold," 725). This phrase marks a reaction to an object; it expresses a relationship between *animadversor* and *opus*.[108] The adjective *aphthitos* ("imperishable," 724) is a similar reflection of the *animadversor*, as it marks what is known or said about the golden wheel-rim, rather than its surface appearance.[109]

While the chariot is introduced in the accusative case, as part of an action, that action soon slows and the gaze dwells on specific parts of the object. The transitive verb *bale* ("threw," 722) gives way to *eisi* ("there were," 726), *pelen* ("there was," 729), or no verb at all (with the copula implied, 724-25). In the ekphrases to come, the use of such existential verbs is a way for a description to suspend the narrative movement and hold attention on a visible surface: there is no story here.[110] Typically, however, the description does not describe an object for long without including a story of an action in time: in the midst of this focus upon the chariot there occur reminders of actions: *entetatai* ("was stretched tight," 728) and *prosarêrota* ("having been fit," 725). As this ekphrasis draws to a close, the narrative returns in full force with a temporal adverb and verbs of action: *autar ep' akrôi / dêse* ("then upon the top she bound," 729-30), *ebale* (she threw), and *êgagen* ("she led," 731).

This passage fits the now expected pattern of introducing a significant object as part of a larger action, drawing attention to some aspect of that object for several lines, then returning to the action that introduced the digression. The description of the chariot of Hera calls attention primarily to the work itself (*opus ipsum*) and its relation to the observer (*animadversor*), while the actions of the *artifex* are subtly included in the midst of the description. It differs from other similar passages in the emphasis on visual appearance: it gives us beauty, not charm. In this respect, it does not meet the strictures of Lessing, but fits Friedländer's idea of "true" description (*echte Beschreibung*). However, there is more variety in Homeric description than either allows.

Immediately following the description of Hera's chariot, Athena, about to dress for battle, takes off her robe, which is described with emphasis on Athena as *artifex* :

---

108. The phrase *thauma idesthai*, which is common in Iliadic ekphrasis, will be discussed at length in Part II. Cf. the use of *thauma* in the handbooks and the *Shield of Herakles*, as discussed in Chapter 2.

109. This adjective was used of Agamemnon's scepter, discussed above in this chapter.

110. See the use of the copula to this effect in the *Shield of Herakles* (discussed in Chapter 2).

αὐτὰρ Ἀθηναίη, κούρη Διὸς αἰγιόχοιο,
πέπλον μὲν κατέχευεν ἑανὸν πατρὸς ἐπ' οὔδει,
ποικίλον, ὅν ῥ' αὐτὴ ποιήσατο καὶ κάμε χερσίν.
(5.733-35)

And Athene, daughter of Zeus who holds the aegis, let slip to
the floor of her father's house her soft embroidered robe,
which she herself had made and worked with her hands.
(Hammond, p. 125)

The robe is introduced in the accusative case, again as part of a larger action.
It is described by a tactile and a visual adjective: *heanon* ("soft" or "pliant")
and *poikilon* (intricately embroidered);[111] the bard here elaborates the
description by referring to the skill of the *artifex*. Athena then begins to arm
herself :

ἡ δὲ χιτῶν' ἐνδῦσα Διὸς νεφεληγερέταο
τεύχεσιν ἐς πόλεμον θωρήσσετο δακρυόεντα.
ἀμφὶ δ' ἄρ' ὤμοισιν βάλετ' αἰγίδα θυσσανόεσσαν
δεινήν, ἣν περὶ μὲν πάντη Φόβος ἐστεφάνωται,
ἐν δ' Ἔρις, ἐν δ' Ἀλκή, ἐν δὲ κρυόεσσα Ἰωκή,        740
ἐν δέ τε Γοργείη κεφαλὴ δεινοῖο πελώρου,
δεινή τε σμερδνή τε, Διὸς τέρας αἰγιόχοιο.
κρατὶ δ' ἐπ' ἀμφίφαλον κυνέην θέτο τετραφάληρον
χρυσείην, ἑκατὸν πολίων πρυλέεσσ' ἀραρυῖαν.
(5.736-42)

And she put on Zeus the cloud-gatherer's own tunic in its
place, then dressed in her armour for the misery of war.
Round her shoulders she hung the tasselled aegis, a fearful
weapon, set with Panic all around it in a circle: and on it
there is Strife, and Power, and chilling Rout, and set there
too is the head of the fearful monster Gorgon, a thing of
fright and terror, a potent sign from Zeus who holds the
aegis. And on her head she placed a golden helmet, set round
with horns, four-bossed, and decorated with a hundred cities'
men-at-arms. (Hammond, p. 125)

The *aegis* is introduced as part of an action (again in the accusative case), and
is modified by an adjective that appeals to the eye (*thussanoessan*, "tasseled,"

---

111. On the aesthetic of *poikilos*, see B.H. Fowler (1984), pp. 119-149.

738).[112] Although any adjective, on some level, implies a describer, some emphasize qualities of the object itself, while others draw attention to the observer who interprets and responds to the object. The adjective that begins line 739, *deinên* (terrifying), is one of the latter; it draws attention to the relationship between the object and the observer. Much like the noun *thauma* (wonder), this adjective notes the effect of the observed phenomena (*opus ipsum*) on the observer (*animadversor*).[113] This description opens with the role of this object in the narrative, then briefly describes *opus ipsum*, and, as the second line opens with *deinên*, turns to the describer who responds to the *aegis*.

The clause that follows (*hên peri men pantêi Phobos estephanôtai*, "all around it [the *aegis*], Fear was set as a rim") simultaneously directs attention to an image portrayed upon the *aegis* and the visual medium in which it is portrayed.[114] The referent is named in the nominative (*Phobos*, "Fear"), which could encourage us to imagine an actual figure, not a depiction; but the verb *estephanôtai* (was set as a rim) and the prepositional phrase *hên peri* (around it) keep our attention on the pictured surface. In the following lines (740-41), the visual medium is apparently not part of the picture and the focus remains on the referent. Yet the anaphoric *en de* (and on [it]) ensures that our attention does not stray far from the surface upon which the images are portrayed. This *en de* is a reminder of the verb *estephanôtai*, which in turn reminds us of the metallic surface that holds these pictures.[115]

---

112. It is difficult to say just what the *aegis* is. See Kirk (1985), pp. 161-162, note to *Iliad* 2.446-51, where the options of shield or shawl are discussed. The *aegis* appears in *Iliad* 2.447-49, where it is described as tasseled, specifically with tassels of tightly woven gold, and it is further characterized as "ageless" (*agêrôn*) and "deathless" (*athanatên*).

113. On *deinos*, see the discussion of the *Shield of Herakles* in Chapter 2. The style of this description of the *aegis* is much like that of the *Shield of Herakles*, although on a much smaller scale: both mark sections by repeating *en de* (and on it), like the Shield of Achilles, but with the copula *ên* (there was) expressed or implied, unlike the Shield of Achilles.

114. Depictions of shields from ancient Greece show such apotropaeic personified abstractions. See Johansen (1967), pp. 92-126; Lorimer (1950), pp. 132-194. Similar images adorn the shield of Agamemnon (*Iliad* 11.32-37) and Herakles's shield (*Shield of Herakles* 144, 148, 155-56, 195-96, 223-25, 227, 236-37, 248-51, 264-68). Five of the shields in Aeschylus's *Seven against Thebes* (385-90, 432-34, 465-69, 491-96, 538-44) have such frightening images. See Zeitlin (1982) on these shields. Such personified abstractions appear in a perhaps spurious section of the Shield of Achilles (18.535-38), discussed in Part II, but are rare elsewhere in the *Iliad* (4.440; 5.518, 593; 11.3, 73; 20.48).

115. In the Shield the same two words (*en de*) introduce each new image: *Iliad* 18.483, 490, 541, 550, 561, 573, 587, 590, 607. There is also a further anaphoric repetition of these words in 483-85. This assures the audience's continued awareness of the metallic medium. Cf. The ekphrasis at *Iliad* 14.214-18, with a similar repetition of *en*.

The preposition and the particle are enough to keep the surface of the shield, *opus ipsum*, in the audience's imagination.

In the description of the Gorgon head there is a telling consonance between the image and the phenomenon represented by that image. The adjectives used are *deinoio* ("terrifying," modifying *pelôrou*, "monster") and the paired *deinê te smerdnê te* (both terrifying and dreadful). Both refer to reactions of an *animadversor*, but either of these adjectives could describe the reaction of a viewer to the referent itself, or to a depiction of that referent: the adjective *deinos* refers both to the medium of the representation (739) and the referent of that representation (741-42). Through this use of *deinos*, a striking correspondence is established between *opus ipsum* (medium) and *res ipsae* (referent). An effect of this correspondence is respect for the mimetic capabilities of the visual art, for its ability to draw together medium and referent. In this way, the passage is similar to the description of Helen's web, with its admiration for visual mimesis.

An aesthetic such as this, an aesthetic that explicitly admires the successes of representation without concern for the possible cost of the representation, prepares us for the aesthetic of the Shield of Achilles. I borrow the phrase "cost of representation" from W.J.T. Mitchell: "Every representation exacts some cost, in the form of lost immediacy, presence, or truth, in the form of a gap between intention and realization, original and copy."[116] Part of my argument in this essay is that, even if one assumes such a gap, the Shield of Achilles encourages us to see and admire how it is bridged by the artist and the bard.[117] There the description represents and supplements the imagined visual images in a way that does not suggest a rivalry or the presumed primacy of the verbal representation. The describer acts, rather, as a congenial audience, willing to respond to the images both with engagement and with a more detached appreciation. If one sees in the Shield of Achilles a *mise en abîme* for the poetics of the *Iliad*, as I argue, then

---

116. In Lentricchia and McLaughlin (1990), p. 21:

117. Cf. Poirier (1992), p. 150: "One virtue of the sound I am describing is, then, that it can create spaces or gaps in ascertained structures of meaning and that it can do so in such a way as simultaneously to create trust and reassurance instead of human separation." The Homeric attitude toward "cost" is much like that of Frost, Stevens, and Emerson, as characterized in Poirier (1992), p. 149: "A deconstructionist argues that when a word is used as the sign of a thing it creates a sense of the thing's absence more than of its presence. This means . . . that the word is not the thing it represents. Language, so the argument goes, can create an abyss—a Frostean gap with a vengeance—and writing is constructed on that abyss. Emersonian pragmatists like Frost or Stevens scarcely deny this, but for them the evidence of a gap or an abyss is an invitation simply to get moving and keep moving, to make a transition." See also the discussion of the golden handmaids of Hephaestus in Chapter 5.

this description of the *aegis* of Athena helps make a case for a rhetoric of ekphrasis: we are encouraged to be the kind of engaged and appreciative and accepting audience for the *Iliad* that the narrator of the *Iliad* is for visual depictions.

## The Cup of Nestor

In *Iliad* 11 there is a short ekphrastic passage with a wide range of aesthetic response:

ἥ σφωϊν πρῶτον μὲν ἐπιπροΐηλε τράπεζαν
καλὴν κυανόπεζαν ἐΰξοον, αὐτὰρ ἐπ' αὐτῆς
χάλκειον κάνεον, ἐπὶ δὲ κρόμυον ποτῷ ὄψον,      630
ἠδὲ μέλι χλωρόν, παρὰ δ' ἀλφίτου ἱεροῦ ἀκτήν,
πὰρ δὲ δέπας περικαλλές, ὃ οἴκοθεν ἦγ' ὁ γεραιός,
χρυσείοις ἥλοισι πεπαρμένον· οὔατα δ' αὐτοῦ
τέσσαρ' ἔσαν, δοιαὶ δὲ πελειάδες ἀμφὶς ἕκαστον
χρύσειαι νεμέθοντο, δύω δ' ὑπὸ πυθμένες ἦσαν.      635
(11.628-35)

She first moved up a table for them, a beautiful polished
table with feet of dark blue enamel, and on it she placed a
bronze dish with an onion as accompaniment for the drink,
and fresh honey, and beside it bread of sacred barley-meal.
Next a most beautiful cup, which the old man had brought
from home—it was studded with rivets of gold, and there
were four handles to it: on each handle a pair of golden
doves was feeding, one on either side: and there were two
supports below. (Hammond, p. 209)

The stage is set for the Cup of Nestor by a series of vivid images. The first adjective *kalên* ("beautiful," 629) notes the reaction of the *animadversor* to the appearance of the table; *kuanopezan* ("having legs of dark blue enamel," 629) draws attention to a physical feature of the table. The third adjective *euxoon* ("well polished," 629) is a judgment of the table by the *animadversor*; but this adjective attributes the table's appearance to the work of an *artifex*. The relations between three levels of representation—*opus, artifex,* and *animadversor*—are included in this adjective. The basket is then described as brazen and the honey as yellow; both describe appearance, though *khalkeon* (brazen) hints at an *artifex* by naming the material.[118] In this context of visual splendor comes the ekphrasis of the Cup of Nestor.[119]

In line 632 the cup (*depas*) is first mentioned in the accusative case as another direct object of *epiproiêle* (she brought forward). Lessing is right: in the *Iliad* objects are usually described as part of actions. Nevertheless, with the adverb *par* (beside) and the adjective *perikalles* ("very beautiful," 632) the description is careful to note arrangement in space (of which Friedländer would approve) and the describer's reaction (which would be praised by Edmund Burke, as well as Lessing). Quickly, then, the ekphrasis turns to the history of the cup: *ho oikothen êg' ho geraios* ("which the old man brought from home," 632). The opening phrase of the next line draws attention to its manufacture: the participial phrase *khruseiois hêloisi peparmenon* ("pierced with golden studs," 633) describes its outward and visible state as the result of the activity of an *artifex*, in a way that (e.g.) "there were studs upon it" would not. The next phrase gives the number of handles on the cup: *ouata d' autou / tessar' esan* ("and there were four handles of it," 633-34). This phrase merely describes the state of the object, using the copula, a noun, a numerical adjective, and an adverb indicating spatial arrangement. This clause describes the cup without drawing attention to the *artifex*. In these two and one-half lines the cup has been presented as part of an action in the larger narrative, as it appears to the eye, through the history of its presence in the Greek camp, and through its workmanship. Now the focus turns to the images represented upon it:

δοιαὶ δὲ πελειάδες ἀμφὶς ἕκαστον
χρύσειαι νεμέθοντο, δύω δ' ὑπὸ πυθμένες ἦσαν.
(11.634-35)

on each handle a pair of golden doves was
feeding, one on either side: and there were two supports
below. (Hammond, p. 209)

The noun phrase (*doiai peleiades*, "two doves") names the referent, the prepositional phrase (*amphis hekaston*, "on both sides [of] each") locates the images on the object, and the adjective *khruseiai* (golden) gives appearance and material. The focus is on *opus ipsum* with an eye to *ars et artifex*. After

---

118. For a well-known ekphrasis of a metal basket, see Moschus's *Europa* 37-62.

119. For bibliography on this cup, and its relation to actual cups from early Greece, see Hainsworth (1993), p. 292, note to 11. 632-35.

the phrases "two doves around each handle, golden" one would expect "were fashioned" to complete the sentence. But ekphrasis in the *Iliad* freely combines different levels of aesthetic response: the doves are not fashioned, but feeding (*nemethonto*). This verb momentarily draws us through to the referent and describes *res ipsae*, actual doves doing what actual doves do. The second half of this line then returns to the appearance of the cup, naming a feature, using the copula, and modifying with a numerical adjective and a spatial adverb. The description thus returns to a less complex representation of *opus ipsum*.

*Opus* and *res ipsae* come together in the description and are intertwined with attention to both *artifex* and *animadversor*. The inclusion of so many levels of representation in such a few lines is revealing: it tells us that the levels are not separate modes of description, but rather complementary aspects of a full description in the *Iliad*.[120]

# The Arms of Agamemnon

*Often . . . a short form of a type-scene (or other structural pattern) precedes a fuller version, as if to familiarize the hearer with the concept before its most significant occurrence.*
*- M.W. Edwards (1991), p. 19*

The Shield of Achilles is unique in the *Iliad*; no other work of art is described at such length or with such elaboration. Only this description of the arming of Agamemnon is comparable, yet it is merely thirty lines long (11.16-46) and describes several pieces of armor. Nevertheless, since it is the only other extended description of representational art, and since it can

---

120. The separation of these categories is be a useful task for us as we try to understand the movement of Homeric description; but ultimately such distinctions must be left behind. Cf. Tannen (1988), p. 91: "Like all atomistic schemes, the separation of these aspects of language into discrete categories is a falsification for heuristic purposes. All aspects work together."

function as a preparatory scene for the Shield of Achilles, it calls for a more detailed analysis.[121] The description begins:

ἐν δ' αὐτὸς ἐδύσετο νώροπα χαλκόν.
κνημῖδας μὲν πρῶτα περὶ κνήμῃσιν ἔθηκε
καλάς, ἀργυρέοισιν ἐπισφυρίοις ἀραρυίας. (11.16-18)

and among them he himself armed in gleaming bronze. First he placed greaves on his legs, a fine pair, fitted with silver ankle-pieces. (Hammond, p. 195)

The armor is first described in the accusative case (*nôropa khalkon*, "gleaming bronze") as the direct object of *eduseto* (he put on). The narrative action in which the described objects are used continues to be the focus of the ekphrasis for four lines, beginning with *eduseto* and continuing with *ethêke* (he placed), and, in line 19, *edune* (he was putting on). Each verb has Agamemnon as its subject and a part of the armor as its object. These opening lines follow the now familiar pattern of introducing significant objects as part of an encompassing action.

Despite the emphasis on action, the visual appearance of these objects is an important part of the description. It is most apparent in the adjectives *nôropa* (gleaming) and *argureoisin* (silver); yet, as expected, these are not unambiguous signals attending to appearance alone—the former suggests the perceiver, while the latter suggests the making of the arms. The description also appeals to the eye simply by naming the object: *knêmidas* ("greaves," 17), *episphuriois* ("ankle clasps," 18). A name is enough to elicit a visual image.[122]

The adjective *kalas* ("beautiful" or "fine," 18) further emphasizes the appearance of the object through the response of the viewer. As above, it does not tell us what the object looks like, but guides our imagined image by giving us the judgment of the describer. This postponed adjective also induces a pause; the glance lingers at the opening of a new line on the surface

---

121. Relatively full arming scenes, without this emphasis on representation, occur at 3.330-38, 16.131-39, and 19.369-91; such scenes are discussed in Shannon (1975). On the relation of Agamemnon's armor to what we know of early Greek armor, see Hainsworth (1993), pp. 215-223.

122. See Foucault (1970), p. 9: "And the proper name . . . gives us a finger to point with, in other words, to pass surreptitiously from the space where one speaks to the space where one looks; in other words, to fold one over the other as if they were equivalents."

of the imagined objects.[123] The narrative is slowed while attention is drawn to the *animadversor*'s relation to the object. As line 18 continues, the phrase *argureoisin episphuriois araruias* (fit with silver ankle clasps) represents the material used in the objects and the act of making them. The latter is implied by the participle *araruias* (fit), which in this context connotes human action (that of the *artifex*, not of Agamemnon). To this point, within the larger action of Agamemnon's arming, the armor is represented through its surface appearance, its material, its manufacture, and its effect on the viewer.

The second line of this ekphrasis (line 17) is of further interest, considered in the terms of signs used in representation. Such greaves were formed not only to fit, but also to resemble the shins they protected.[124] The language used in this description, although its signs are symbolic and not iconic, replicates this relationship of physical similarity: the same stem appears in the word for "greaves" (*knêmidas*) and the word for "shins" (*knêmêisin*). Although the word *knêmidas* does not physically resemble greaves, and although the word *knêmêisin* itself does not physically resemble shins, the relationship between the two words (aural and, for us, visual) is iconic. Language has made a connection of actual physical similarity between the words used to denote phenomena that are similar in appearance. This poetic version of iconicity makes the language seem a more powerful mimetic medium; language seems to enter into the kind of representation usually reserved for the visual arts, symbolically creating Lessing's *bequemes Verhältnis*, imitating the visible correspondence between a soldier's shins and his greaves.[125]

After the opening lines of this ekphrasis, the description turns to a particularly Homeric mode of representation, which is by now familiar. The corselet is described as follows:

δεύτερον αὖ θώρηκα περὶ στήθεσσιν ἔδυνε,
τόν ποτέ οἱ Κινύρης δῶκε ξεινήϊον εἶναι.            20
πεύθετο γὰρ Κύπρονδε μέγα κλέος. οὕνεκ' Ἀχαιοὶ
ἐς Τροίην νήεσσιν ἀναπλεύσεσθαι ἔμελλον·
τοὔνεκά οἱ τὸν δῶκε χαριζόμενος βασιλῆϊ. (11.19-23)

Next he put a corselet around his chest, which Kinyres once

---

123. On enjambement, see M.W. Edwards (1991), pp. 42-44 and (1966), pp. 115-179; Higbie (1990); Barnes (1979), pp. 1-10; Kirk (1966), pp. 75-152. On postponed adjectives in the *Iliad*, see the remarks of Redfield (1979), p. 100.

124. On Homeric greaves, see Catling (1977), pp. 143-161, and figures XIV-XVI.

125. Cf. Chapter 2, p. 33, note 60, for Peirce's iconic, indexical, and symbolic signs. See also the discussions of *Iliad* 18.470 and 476, in Part II.

gave him as a gift of friendship. The great news had come to
him in Cyprus that the Achaians were to sail a fleet against
Troy: and so he made Agamemnon a gift of the corselet, to
please the king. (Hammond p. 195)

The corselet is introduced in the accusative case, as part of the narrative of
Agamemnon's action, but the bard turns immediately to a story it elicits. This
description shows the same tendency as that of Nestor's cup, Pandarus's bow,
Agamemnon's scepter, and the descriptions of people, such as Laodice (*Iliad*
3.122-24) or Glaucus (*Iliad* 6.149-211): the tendency is to treat phenomena of
the world as stimuli for stories.

After the history of the corselet, the ekphrasis does not keep the
same emphasis on story: as later in the Shield of Achilles, there is here a
blending of perspectives. The description now gives an account of its
appearance:

τοῦ δ᾽ ἤτοι δέκα οἶμοι ἔσαν μέλανος κυάνοιο,
δώδεκα δὲ χρυσοῖο καὶ εἴκοσι κασσιτέροιο·            25
κυάνεοι δὲ δράκοντες ὀρωρέχατο προτὶ δειρὴν
τρεῖς ἑκάτερθ᾽, ἴρισσιν ἐοικότες, ἅς τε Κρονίων
ἐν νέφεϊ στήριξε, τέρας μερόπων ἀνθρώπων. (11.24-8)

It had ten bands of dark blue enamel, and twelve of gold, and
twenty of tin: and enamel snakes reached up to the neck,
three on each side, like rainbows which the son of Kronos
fixes in the cloud as a sign for humankind.
(Hammond, p. 195)

These *oimoi* (strips, lines, layers) are described as they appear and are not
turned into a story: they are introduced in the nominative case, not the
accusative, and the verb is simply the copula *esan* (there were). This switch
from accusative to nominative, and to the copula from transitive verbs, directs
attention away from the action and to the object itself. There is no reminder
of Agamemnon's action: just a description of the *opus*, and a hint of the
*artifex* in the naming of the material. The subsequent line (25) gives us
number and a different material; then the figures appear (26-28). The
movement of line 28 reflects the rhythm of many ekphrases: the line begins
with the material out of which the image is made (*kuaneoi*, "of enamel"),[126]
then it names what the image represents (*drakontes*, "snakes") and so begins

---

126. On *kuaneos*, see Irwin (1974), pp. 79-110, who sees the word as meaning merely "dark,"
rather than "made of blue enamel."

to draw attention through the medium and into the referent. The verb *orôrekhato* (had stretched themselves up) suggests not representations of serpents but living serpents; it leaves the surface of the work for the referent. The final prepositional phrase, however, brings us back to the immediate frame (the work itself) on which the serpents are fashioned. These three lines include a matrix of *opus*, *animadversor*, and *res ipsae*. The serpents may be images made of blue enamel, but they are also stretching and writhing beasts; they are described as representations, but also as alive. The description simultaneously represents the visual medium and the world which that medium depicts: illusion and defamiliarization are unproblematically included in the description. The bard can see images as images and still react to the referent as though it were unmediated.

An ekphrasis could emphasize the visual medium and the referent in such a way that the distance between the images made of enamel and actual serpents is brought to the surface. On the other hand, in a single line (26) the description combines illusion with attention to the medium that creates that illusion. It combines them with such ease that, in the audience's experience of the ekphrasis, the distance between image and referent diminishes. The bard's words treat the image as a lens, allowing us to imagine the referent without losing sight of its status as an image. The effect is then to encourage the audience's trust in the visual representation; admiration here lies not in the illusion that art is life, but in such explicitly expressed and experienced and admired similarity between image and life.

The following lines (27-28) focus on the reaction and interpretation of the narrator; the similetic comparison of the serpents to rainbows (*irissin eoikotes*, "resembling rainbows") is a sign of the thoughts of an *animadversor* viewing the images. Like the adjectives *kalos* (beautiful, fine) and *deinos* (terrible), a simile is a way for the description to shape the audience's reactions to an imaginary work of art by representing not just appearance but also response.[127] Within the simile itself, the effect of the images is further emphasized: *teras meropôn anthrôpôn* (an omen/sign for mortal men).[128]

---

127. See the discussion of a similar emphasis in the description of Hephaestus's golden handmaids in Chapter 5.

128. Contrast the phrase *Dios teras aigiokhoio* (sign of *aegis*-bearing Zeus) in the description of the *aegis* (*Iliad* 5.742, discussed above in this chapter). While the phrase in book 5 has *teras* with a genitive, the subjective genitive naming Zeus does not point to us, the audience, as does the objective genitive naming mortal men here in 11.28. Note also that the word *teras* has just occurred in line 4 of book 11, as a sign of war carried by Eris (Strife). Hainsworth (1993), p. 214, note to 11.4, says of *teras*: "what Eris held in her hands it is impossible to say, and perhaps was never precisely conceived." And on p. 219, note to 11.27-28, he describes *teras* as "a divine interference with the course of nature such as to cause encouragement or dismay."

Such explicit inclusion of the reaction of the viewer guides the reaction of the audience to these imagined images. Significance here lies in the relationships among the world, the material work of visual art, and the reaction of the viewer.[129]

The subsequent description of the *xiphos* (sword) is reminiscent of the lines on the greaves:

ἀμφὶ δ' ἄρ' ὤμοισιν βάλετο ξίφος· ἐν δέ οἱ ἧλοι
χρύσειοι πάμφαινον, ἀτὰρ περὶ κουλεὸν ἦεν          30
ἀργύρεον, χρυσέοισιν ἀορτήρεσσιν ἀρηρός. (11.29-31)

Over his shoulders he slung his sword: there were gold nails shining on it, and the scabbard sheathing it was of silver, attached to a baldric of gold. (Hammond, p. 195)

It begins with spatial arrangement, but it is the arrangement of an action (*baleto*, "he threw"), and the sword is the accusative direct object. Then the representation turns to the materials, their appearance and placement, and the *artifex*. The preposition *en* (on) begins to direct attention to the object itself; the noun that follows (*hêloi*, "studs") draws this focus still closer. The next line opens not with a new item, but with a lingering look at the material of the studs (*khruseoi*, "golden"). An intransitive verb (*pamphainon*, "were shining") holds attention on the visible surface of the work; this verb denotes a quality of the surface of the metal and the play of light upon it. Unlike terms such as *daidaleos* (finely wrought) and *araruias* (fit), *pamphainon* does not call attention to the *artifex*; *pamphainon* does not call as much attention to the *animadversor* as terms such as *thauma* (wonder) and *deinos* (terrifying). It directs the audience to physical features of the object itself. The stress given this word by the prefix (*pam* < *pan*, "thoroughly") may, however, be a hint of the *animadversor*: the question is one of emphasis, of what the poem asks the reader to imagine by the use of particular descriptive language. With *pamphainon*, the focus is more on a characteristic of the object, than on the reaction of the interpreter.

These lines continue to focus not on an activity or on a story but on the appearance of the arms. The next phrase indicates spatial arrangement by the adverb *peri* (around), while the verb *êen* (there was), as *esan* (there were) in line 24, is a signal that the action has been replaced by the image. The scabbard is named (*kouleon*) and modified by an adjective that notes its

---

129. The poetics of this simile is similar to that of an ekphrasis: it gives history, and effect, and it is put into action in the last clause. On the likeness of simile and ekphrasis, see Chapter 3.

material (*argureon*, "silver"). As above, naming the material of an object can remind us of *ars et artifex*, though such a reminder is subtle; here the name merely continues the emphasis on objects in space. However, the perfect participle *arêros* (fit), as *araruias* in line 18, is a stronger reminder of the *artifex*: a present state is described as the result of a completed action.[130] In these three lines describing the sword, the ekphrasis concentrates on representing the appearance of the object, with a glance at the two actions involved, the arming of Agamemnon and the manufacture of the armor.

As expected, the description of his shield opens with a return to the action of Agamemnon (it is introduced in the accusative case), but this does not prevent the describer from dwelling on the object, with four adjectives and a modifying clause:

ἂν δ' ἕλετ' ἀμφιβρότην πολυδαίδαλον ἀσπίδα θοῦριν,
καλήν, ἣν πέρι μὲν κύκλοι δέκα χάλκεοι ἦσαν,
ἐν δέ οἱ ὀμφαλοὶ ἦσαν ἐείκοσι κασσιτέροιο
λευκοί, ἐν δὲ μέσοισιν ἔην μέλανος κυάνοιο.          35
τῇ δ' ἐπὶ μὲν Γοργὼ βλοσυρῶπις ἐστεφάνωτο
δεινὸν δερκομένη, περὶ δὲ Δεῖμός τε Φόβος τε.
(11.32-37)

And he took up his mighty covering shield, a beautiful piece
of intricate work which was plated with ten circles of bronze,
and there were twenty bosses round it, white with tin, and at
the centre of the plates one boss of dark blue enamel.
Crowning the shield was the grim mask of Gorgo, glaring
fearfully, with terror and Panic on either side.
(Hammond, p. 195)

The first adjective *amphibrotên* (covering the whole person), tells the size and shape of the shield (*opus ipsum*).[131] The adjective *poludaidalon* (very elaborately adorned) points to the work of an *artifex*. The next adjective (*thourin*, "impetuous" or "eager") is an epithet transferred from Agamemnon to the shield: this hypallage is a verbal level of representation, creating meaning through the observer's use of language. It represents an impression of the *animadversor* that, in this case, serves to conflate object and reaction.[132] The next line opens with *kalên* ("fine" or "beautiful"), postponed as it is so frequently in the *Iliad*; this adjective in this position slows the

130. Cf. 5.725 and 11.633, both discussed above in this chapter.
131. On Homeric shields, see Borchhardt (1977), pp. 1-56 and illustration 8.
132. Cf. the similar use of this adjective at *Iliad* 15.308 and 20.162.

narrative and holds the focus on the relationship between the *opus* and the *animadversor*.[133] Then the clause (*hên peri men kukloi deka khalkeoi êsan*, "around which there were ten bronze circles," 33) dwells on *opus ipsum*: the verb (*êsan*, "there were") and the two adjectives (*deka, khalkeoi*, "ten, bronze") represent the surface appearance of the shield, while the naming of the material gives a hint of its manufacture. The description then continues to dwell on appearance (34-35): the repeated *en de* (and on [it]), the use of the copula (*êsan*, "there were," and *eên*, "there was"), and the adjectives of color (*leukoi*, "white," and *melanos*, "dark"), all hold the gaze on the surface of the shield.[134] The genitives of material (*kassiteroio*, "of silver," and *kuanoio*, "of blue enamel") describe appearance as well, again with a mere hint of the manufacture of the shield.

This shield is then decorated with personified abstractions (36-37), as was the *aegis* of Athena. The description of these images begins with *opus ipsum*, the physical frame within which the images are represented. It is emphasized at the beginning and the end of line 36: *têi d' epi . . . estephanôto* (upon it . . . was set around as a rim).[135] Within this frame, however, the Gorgon head is described in a way that does not hold our attention on the shield; the adjective *blosurôpis* (grim looking) draws the focus through the work and to the referent (*res ipsae*). The next line begins with the phrase *deinon derkomenê* (glancing terrifyingly); while it draws attention to the *animadversor*, it is easily read as a reaction to a Gorgon, not just to the depiction.[136]

The middle of line 36 focuses on the relationship between the viewer and the referent, not the viewer and the surface of the image; the beginning and end of the line, however, focus on the physical frame, the worked metal. The audience is encouraged to accept the world suggested by the image, but also to observe the mediating presence of the object; the ekphrasis responds to the image with enthusiasm and generosity, as it elaborates the world represented therein. The *Iliad* here again gives us not an adversarial but rather a complementary relationship between word and image: the bard elaborates the images with stories, but also dwells with interest and respect on the visual appearance of the image itself.

Around this Gorgon head are the personifications appropriate to battle (37); they are not described, but merely named in the nominative case,

---

133. See 11.18, 629, or, in the Shield of Achilles, 18.491.

134. On the repetition of *en de* as a feature of ekphrasis, see the discussion of the *aegis* of Athena in this chapter.

135. The verb *stephanôto* is a recurrent feature of Iliadic ekphrasis: See 5.739 and 18.485.

136. On the phenomenological implications of *derkesthai*, see Prier (1989), pp. 29-31.

with an unexpressed verb. But our attention still remains on the work of visual art because of the adverb *peri* (around), which gives the arrangement of the images on the shield itself.[137] Again there is a double movement of the line, toward the referent and toward the surface of the work.

The next piece of armor is not introduced as part of an action. The move to the belt is one of contiguity: the transition is effected through a pronoun referring to the shield (*tês*, "it"), which depends upon a preposition (*ex*, "from") indicating spatial arrangement:

τῆς δ' ἐξ ἀργύρεος τελαμὼν ἦν· αὐτὰρ ἐπ' αὐτοῦ
κυάνεος ἐλέλικτο δράκων, κεφαλαὶ δέ οἱ ἦσαν
τρεῖς ἀμφιστρεφέες, ἑνὸς αὐχένος ἐκπεφυῖαι.
(11.38-40)

The shield-strap was made of silver, and along it there
wound an enamel snake, with three heads growing from a
single neck and twisting this way and that.
(Hammond, p. 195)

This section opens with arrangement and appearance. The adjective *argureos* (of silver) describes material with a hint of *ars*, as above, but without attention to the *animadversor*; the noun *telamôn* (belt) is in the nominative case as subject of the copula. None of these put the object into action. The prepositional phrase *ep' autou* (upon it) keeps the focus on the material surface of *opus ipsum*. On the belt another serpent is depicted, made of blue enamel (*kuaneos*, 39); this adjective functions like *argureos* (of silver). But the verb *elelikto* (was quivering) and the noun *drakôn* (serpent) then begin to draw attention through *opus ipsum* to *res ipsae*, the referent. The next verb *êsan* (there were) and its subject (*kephalai*, "heads") continue to describe *res ipsae*, while the final participle (*ekpephuuiai*, "having grown out") brings the image to life. It describes the visible state of the serpent's heads as a result of biological growth, which belongs to the referent, not the image. The mediating quality of metals and blue glass does not prevent the bard from entering into the world of *res ipsae*. This section does not put images into action, but nevertheless brings them to life with both *elelikto* (was quivering) and *ekpephuuiai* (having grown out). It describes appearance, in detail, of both the medium and the referent; the image is described in a way that

---

137. H.L. Lorimer (1929), p. 158, suggests that there is a circle of apotropaeic masks arranged around the central Gorgon head. On the difficulty of visualizing the arrangement, see Hainsworth (1993), p. 221, note to 11.36-37.

responds to its suggestions without emphasizing any cost of visual representation.

The rest of Agamemnon's arming scene is not remarkable in its mode of mimesis:

κρατὶ δ' ἐπ' ἀμφίφαλον κυνέην θέτο τετραφάληρον
ἵππουριν· δεινὸν δὲ λόφος καθύπερθεν ἔνευεν.
εἵλετο δ' ἄλκιμα δοῦρε δύω, κεκορυθμένα χαλκῷ,
ὀξέα· τῆλε δὲ χαλκὸς ἀπ' αὐτόφιν οὐρανὸν εἴσω
λάμπ'. (11.41-45)

And on his head he placed a four-bossed helmet, set round
with horns, with a plume of horse-hair: and the crest nodded
fearfully from its top. And he took up two strong spears,
sharp-tipped with bronze, whose gleam struck bright far into
the sky. (Hammond, p. 195)

The act of arming was not mentioned in lines 32-40, hence the objects and the images upon them were named in the nominative case. As we come to the helmet (41), the description returns to the activity of arming (*theto*, "he put"); here at the end of the description, as we are about to reenter the larger narrative, the objects are again in the accusative. However, appearance is still the primary focus. The helmet's appearance is noted by the three adjectives: *amphiphalon* (two horned), *tetraphalêron* (with four bosses), and *hippourin* (crested). In contrast, the crest itself is described with reference to its movement (*eneuen*, "was nodding") and effect on the viewer (*deinon*, "terrifying").

The representations on Agamemnon's shield are those that were conventional for decorations of the age; Agamemnon's shield reminds us of a shield.[138] Its manufacture, appearance, history, effect, referents, and use are all represented in the description of these weapons. When compared to the Shield of Achilles, the major difference is that the images on Agamemnon's armor are not turned into stories. Though they are brought to life at several points, the vivification is fleeting, carried by a single participle, adjective, or verb. Agamemnon's arming scene does, however, broach several topics of poetic concern that shape our responses to Homeric description: e.g., iconicity in language; an inclination to attend, at times, to the referent as though it were not mediated by the visual representation; careful attention to the physical appearance of the work of art; admiration of visual mimesis by

138. For bibliography, see Hainsworth (1993), p. 221, note to 11. 36-37.

explicit attention to the representation; and the inclusion of the effect of the work on the describer.

The Shield of Achilles is the most magnificent work of art described in the *Iliad*. But while the Shield of Achilles is unusual, its mode of representation is familiar; its description follows the patterns established by the examples I have discussed in this chapter. In spite of its singularity, the poetics of the Shield of Achilles is like that of the proem, similes, and especially other ekphrases in the *Iliad*. This being the case, it is less useful to ask why the Shield is unusual when compared to art of the time (or of any time); it is more useful to note the many ways in which the Shield reflects and elaborates Homeric poetics.

# 5

# A THEORETICAL INTERLUDE: IMAGES WITH THOUGHT, VOICE, AND MOTION (*ILIAD* 18.417-20)

*Undying accents*
*repeated till*
*the eye and the ear lie*
*down together in the same bed.*
*- "Song," in William Carlos Williams (1986)*

Preceding the Shield of Achilles comes a scene that serves to focus several issues involved in our reading of Homeric ekphrasis; the lines encompass much of the mode of response that I discuss above in Chapter 4 and below in Part II, the commentary on the Shield of Achilles. A mere four lines (*Iliad* 18.417-20) take the audience through a remarkable range of perspectives, and their subtle blending prefigures the Shield. The lines simultaneously encourage us to accept the presence of the world depicted and remind us of the two levels of mediation (visual and verbal art), which bring this world to us and which lie between us and this world. Illusion and defamiliarization, appropriation and divestiture, lie down together in the same bed.

# Art into Life

Thetis has arrived at the palace of Hephaestus to ask him for the new arms for Achilles. After preparing to greet her, Hephaestus is joined by his attendants:

ὑπὸ δ' ἀμφίπολοι ῥώοντο ἄνακτι. (18.417)

the handmaids rushed to help their master.

The next line then begins to reveal the singularity of these servants:

χρύσειαι, ζωῇσι νεήνισιν εἰοικυῖαι. (18.418)

golden, resembling living girls.

These are not handmaids, but golden replicas that look like handmaids. The adjective *khruseiai* (golden) notes a quality that exists in the objects themselves (*opus ipsum*) and is a hint of its manufacture (*artifex et ars*); *khruseiai* draws no more than minimal attention to the observer who uses the adjective (in contrast to an adjective like *deinos* (inspiring awe), which calls much more attention to the one who makes such a judgment).

They may be beautiful statues, but what makes them wonderful is their mobility (*rhôonto*, "they rushed"). By endowing his representations with mobility, Hephaestus begins to make his replica into a more comprehensive copy of the original; he begins to turn the representation into what is represented, art into life. In the Shield of Achilles such quickening of a static image is a common response of the describer to the work of art: the description too can give motion to the image. The proximity of this scene to the Shield suggests an affinity between Hephaestus's ability to vivify works of art and the descriptive vivification of the bard in ekphrasis. The bard can give images the very qualities that Hephaestus can give. Yet, there is no suggestion in the Shield of Achilles that Hephaestus himself made the images on the shield live and move and speak; rather, the type of description that is characteristic of the *Iliad* makes the images of the Shield into stories.

# *Fingere Qui Non Visa Potest,* "Who Can Fashion Things

# Not Seen" (Horace *Satires* 1.4.84)

*You confide*
*In images in things that can be*
*Represented which is their dimension you*
*Require them to say this*
*Is real.*
- *"The Widow," in W.S. Merwin (1988)*

The next line in the account of the golden yet mobile servant girls increases the marvelous impression of Hephaestus's art. Hephaestus does not merely make robots:

τῆς ἐν μὲν νόος ἐστὶ μετὰ φρεσίν, ἐν δὲ καὶ αὐδή.
(18.419)

Within them there is mind [intelligence] in their heart, and within them there is voice.

The first attribute, *noos* (mind, intelligence, thought), adds to the portrayal (*opus ipsum*) another capacity of what is portrayed (*res ipsae*); it allows these maids to have thoughts, motives, and intentions. Later in *Iliad* 18, as the bard describes the depictions on the shield, he tells their thoughts, motives, and intentions. The language of description, like Hephaestus, gives *noos* to the image.

The presence of voice (*audê*) continues the gradual vivification of the sculptures; it (nearly) causes Hephaestus's art to erase the distinction between representation and life.[139] Hephaestus has blurred the distinction between depiction and depicted by going beyond the conventional mimesis of a visual medium, both by adding mobility and by appropriating the bard's ability to appeal to the ear (*audê*, "voice"). He is crossing "that barrier

---

139. There are many beguiling examples in literature of art coming to life; e.g., Ovid's *Metamorphoses* 10.243-97 (the making of Pygmalion) tells of a successful elimination of the distinction, as do Hesiod's descriptions of Pandora, on which see A.S. Becker (1993a). Cf. the end of Shakespeare's *A Winter's Tale* (1924), pp. 404-406, or Pope's *Imitation of Horace Epistle II.i.147-150* (1963), p. 641: "Then Marble soften'd into life grew warm, / And yielding Metal flowed to human form: / Lely on animated Canvas stole / The sleepy Eye, that spoke the melting soul." Gross (1992) is an interesting theoretical study of art coming to life.

between art, which is limited in its mode of signification, and human beings, whose speech and physical presence combine semiosis appealing to all the senses."[140] In the terminology of this essay, through the *ars et artifex, opus* nearly becomes *res ipsae*, in these marvelous creations of Hephaestus.

W.J.T. Mitchell, a theorist of both art and literature, sees the attempt to push the conventional mimetic limits of a medium as a basic impulse in representational art.[141] Language tries to gain a sense of physical presence, spatial form, and iconic representation, while the image tries to gain the symbolic and temporal narrative qualities of language. If one adds mobility to a sculpture of a handmaid, its similarity to the original is increased. By endowing the sculptures with thought and voice, the artist takes another step in the transformation of a replica into a living original. In the workshop of Hephaestus, this particular impulse of representational art is realized.

The description of the shield likewise gives voice to the visual images. But the qualities given to the golden maids (speech, motion, and thought) can all be described by the bard without going beyond the conventional limits of his own medium; epic song commonly endows its characters with speech and thought, and the temporal nature of narrative allows for motion and change. If the bard does as a matter of course what the visual arts can only achieve through a divine *artifex*, then there may seem to be a privilege given to the verbal medium. On the other hand, this could be a result of the skillful but not judgmental translation of an image into words: the change of medium changes the aspects of the referent that are emphasized. In perhaps the most famous ekphrasis in English poetry, Shakespeare describes at length a picture of the fall of Troy and Lucrece's response to it (*The Rape of Lucrece*, lines 1366-1582); it says of Lucrece, as she responds to the images: "She lends them words, and she their looks doth borrow."[142] Notice the reciprocity, as both try to take advantage of the other's strengths. Borrowing from the strengths of a different medium, the visual arts try to suggest movement, voice, and the passage of time; conversely, the verbal arts try to make the listener into a viewer.[143] One could see ekphrasis

---

140. Steiner (1982), p. 5.

141. W.J.T. Mitchell (1986), p. 98. Cf. Steiner (1982), pp. 1-18; Krieger (1967), p. 124. A fine work that argues for this assumption is Heffernan (1993).

142. Line 1498 in Shakespeare (1971).

143. See the discussion of the *progumnasmata* and the *Shield of Herakles*, above in Chapter 2. Pope (1796), volume 1, p. 6, in the preface to his *Iliad*, remarked: "the reader is hurried out of himself by the force of the Poet's imagination, and turns in one place to a hearer, in another to a spectator." One might expect that movement would be described by ancient critics as *energeia* (action, energy), while the visual qualities would be characterized as *enargeia* (vividness). Both impulses, however, are described as *enargeia* in the Scholia to the *Iliad*; the term does not just

as just such an exercise in appropriation and divestiture: an attempt to borrow, not to defeat, the capabilities of the visual arts, while supplementing them with the capabilities of the word.[144]

The final line in the description of the maids does not add a new focus, but rather expands and reinforces the suggestions of mind and motion:

καὶ σθένος, ἀθανάτων δὲ θεῶν ἄπο ἔργα ἴσασιν.
(18.420)

and [within them there is] strength; from the deathless gods they know their work.

The noun *sthenos* (strength, force, vitality) gives a name to the ability to move implied in the verb *rhôonto* (417); *sthenos* is a requisite or potential for *kinêsis* (movement).[145] Finally, the closing phrase of this line elaborates the *noos* of these golden handmaids: the handmaids do not just possess the capacity for intellect and will, but their *noos* is worthy of praise.

In the workshop of Hephaestus representations made of precious metal are endowed with *noos*, *audê*, and *sthenos*. The model that these lines offer for an interpretation of the Shield of Achilles is as follows: in the Shield these three qualities are consistently included in the description, thereby bringing the visual image to life. By so doing the ekphrasis responds to the images with imagination and sympathy, accepting and elaborating the suggested referent of the visual representation (*res ipsae*). Hephaestus's image or the bard's song can erase the difference and close the distance between *res ipsae* and *opus ipsum*, almost.

---

apply to pictorial vividness, but also to motion (e.g., Scholia T on 4.108b1, Erbse I, p. 466; Scholia bT on 15.506, Erbse IV, p. 112). The Scholia do use the term *energeia* to refer to activity and motion in a Homeric passage (e.g., Scholia bT on 12.461-70, Erbse III, p. 386, and it is so used in Aristotle's *Rhetoric* 1412a10); but it is more commonly a grammatical term indicating agency or the active voice (e.g., Scholia bT on 3.354b, Erbse I, p. 421; Scholia AbT on 19.398b, Erbse IV, p. 646).

144. On "appropriation" and "divestiture," see Chapter 2.

145. It also adds a connotation of a less tangible life force. The note in Ameis and Hentze (1965), p. 133, on 18.420 reads: "als Eigenschaft belebter Wesen, die sich betätigende Kraft, die auch die Kraft des Wollens voraussetzt."

# From Illusion to Defamiliarization

*But your eyes proclaim*
*that everything is surface. The surface is what's there*
*And nothing can exist except what's there.*
- *"Self-Portrait in a Convex Mirror," in Ashbery (1975)*

Although Hephaestus can virtually turn art into life, and so invite one to ignore the visual representation and focus on the referent, nevertheless these lines have offered a significant reminder that the lifelike image is still a replica (418): *khruseiai, zôêisi neênisin eoikuiai* (golden, resembling living girls). This line shows that the aesthetic stance of the description is by no means an exclusive emphasis on the referent, on enchantment, on perceiving art as life.[146] Through the naming of the material and the similetic comparison, the bard has assured that we remain aware of the medium (in this case, sculpted metal) as well as the message. Identity between depiction and depicted is not the goal—we are explicitly directed not to forget the mediating presence of art. The adjective *khruseiai* (golden) draws attention to the material difference between the sculptures of handmaids and the living girls they resemble. It qualifies the illusion of identity, causes one to notice the medium, and so defamiliarizes. The similetic phrase *zôêisi neênisin eoikuiai* (resembling living girls) is still more explicit in calling attention to the difference between life and art. The expression of similarity, as we would expect, presupposes difference and so checks the illusion that the representations have become what they represent.[147] Without this difference, similarity would become identity, and the simile would lose its force; the

---

146. Enchantment (*thelxis*), acceptance of the illusion of the representation, is seen as a goal of Homeric song by Walsh (1984), p. 14; cf. Ford (1992).

147. E. Cook (1986), p. 152: "all simile, any affirmation of similarity and comparison, will simultaneously be an affirmation of difference." Cf. Empson (1974), pp. 117-118; Goldhill (1986), p. 36. Expression of similarity is also a clearer exposure of the presence of an interpreter, as discussed above in this chapter. The effect on the observer, who notes the similarity, is part of the picture the description paints. Cf. Robbe-Grillet (1963), p. 116: "L' homme y est présent à chaque page, à chaque ligne, à chaque mot. Même si l' on y trouve beaucoup d'objets, et décrits avec minutie, il y a toujours et d'abord le regard qui les voit, la pensée qui les revoit, la passion qui les déforme."

simile itself, expressing the experience of the describer, reminds us of the metallic medium.[148]

Yet it is the very inclusion of such references to the mediating presence of worked gold that makes the maidens worthy of note (one could say, makes them a *thauma idesthai*, "a wonder to behold"). The handmaids are marvelous only because they are not what they seem. Although the comparison in this simile reminds the audience that art is not life, it serves to increase our admiration for the visual art; it does not to call into question the mimetic capabilities of the visual depiction. Defamiliarization, attention to the medium, increases the admiration of the audience for the mimetic capabilities of the work of art. In the *Iliad* similar attention to the verbal medium enhances the audience's trust and respect for the words of the bard (e.g., in the proem to the *Iliad*).[149] Celebration of the process, of what art can do, rather than a need for illusion or a struggle for mimetic primacy, characterizes the mode of mimesis in the *Iliad* and specifically the Shield of Achilles.

---

148. Such attention to the difference between the metallic medium and the referent could seem to devalue the mimetic capability of the image. We often think of artistic representation, especially after Plato, as a necessarily insufficient record of some original phenomenon or conception. In Greek and Roman antiquity, representation was frequently viewed, even by those who did not agree with Plato, as a somewhat deficient replica of an original. See Russell (1981), p. 100: "The whole idea of the writer as somehow creating a new world, rather than merely offering a partial image of the world of the senses, is in general alien to Greek and Roman thinking." Such a view has a varied history, and has undergone many transformations. E.g., Emerson, "Experience" (1951), p. 316: "There will be the same gulf between every me and thee, as between the original and the picture." See also the remarks of the poet Yves Bonnefoy (1990), p. 798: "But even in a poem, words formulate; they substitute signification, representation for this One, this unity faintly perceived, and therefore it is a sense of dissatisfaction that is strongest. Dissatisfaction before this fact of textuality in which the fundamental intuition vanishes, but not without leaving something glittering in its wake"; and p. 806: "written forms interpret but thereby conceal beneath the play of possibilities that each time are less than the world is." Or Kenneth Burke (1964), p. 42: "Art is a translation and every translation is a compromise (although, be it noted, a compromise which may have new virtues of its own, virtues not part of the original)." I argue here that such a sentiment is not Homeric: attention to the medium is part of the description, but that does not diminish referential capacity. See the discussion of the *aegis* of Athena in Chapter 4.

149. See the discussion of the proem in Chapter 3.

# A Model for Responding to the Shield of Achilles

Shortly after the lines portraying Hephaestus's vivified works of art the audience comes to the Shield of Achilles.[150] This ekphrasis can be considered a similar attempt to endow images with thought, voice, and motion. The bard's description fills in the cause and effect, action and reaction, motivation and intention, all of which begin to translate an image into a story.[151] Each of the three attributes—*noos*, *audê*, and *sthenos*—makes us imagine not the colors, shapes, textures, and spatial arrangement of the depicted figures, but the world represented therein. However, like the description of the handmaids, the Shield both encourages illusion and breaks that illusion by explicitly referring to the illusionistic qualities and the manufacture of the representations. Similarly, the effect is admiration (*thauma*). These lines preceding the Shield reinforce and supplement the patterns established by the descriptions of works of art throughout the *Iliad*. They continue to teach us how to read an ekphrasis. The representation of the handmaids of Hephaestus concentrates the levels of mimesis, emphasizing their simultaneous presence, and their interrelation, just as the most magnificent ekphrasis in the *Iliad* is about to begin.

---

150. See Scholia T on 18.418-20 (Erbse IV, p. 518) on the anticipation of the Shield of Achilles in these lines.

151. A good theoretical discussion of images provoking stories, with reference to Rembrandt, can be found in Bal (1991), pp. 177-215.

# PART II

# COMMENTARY ON THE SHIELD OF ACHILLES (*Iliad* 18. 462-613)

What follows is an explication of the Shield of Achilles, focusing on the levels of verbal mimesis and the representational focus in the description. Some passages, phrases, and words can be pushed more than others; some offer more to unfold and consider: hence the commentary will be at times more extensive or repetitive and at others somewhat cursory.

## The Narrative Frame

## (18.468-77)[152]

*One cannot do justice to a poem in paraphrase, but must follow it from line to line, and from word to word, in its unique order.*
*- K. Burke (1969), p. 473*

*Iliad* 18.468-77 introduces the ekphrasis, and its style of representation provides the immediate context for the Shield. Appropriately,

---

152. The corresponding part of the frame is 607-8, to be discussed below. On the ring-composition of the Shield of Achilles, see Stanley (1993), pp. 9-13.

the lines that frame the ekphrasis emphasize movement (*sthenos*), motive (*noos*), and sound (*audê*). In so doing they represent a kind of significance that lies not just in the visible, but also in the active, invisible, and aural aspects of a scene:

Ὣς εἰπὼν τὴν μὲν λίπεν αὐτοῦ, βῆ δ' ἐπὶ φύσας·
τὰς δ' ἐς πῦρ ἔτρεψε κέλευσέ τ' ἐργάζεσθαι.
φῦσαι δ' ἐν χοάνοισιν ἐείκοσι πᾶσαι ἐφύσων,      470
παντοίην εὔπρηστον ἀϋτμὴν ἐξανιεῖσαι,
ἄλλοτε μὲν σπεύδοντι παρέμμεναι, ἄλλοτε δ' αὖτε,
ὅππως Ἥφαιστός τ' ἐθέλοι καὶ ἔργον ἄνοιτο.
χαλκὸν δ' ἐν πυρὶ βάλλεν ἀτειρέα κασσίτερόν τε
καὶ χρυσὸν τιμῆντα καὶ ἄργυρον· αὐτὰρ ἔπειτα      475
θῆκεν ἐν ἀκμοθέτῳ μέγαν ἄκμονα, γέντο δὲ χειρὶ
ῥαιστῆρα κρατερήν, ἑτέρηφι δὲ γέντο πυράγρην.
(18.468-477)

So speaking he left Thetis where she was and went back to his bellows: he turned them to the fire and ordered them to set to work. There were twenty bellows in all, and they began blowing on the crucibles, sending out a good blast at every strength he needed, ready to give their help when he was busy, and ready again to blow in whatever way suited Hephaistos' wish and the progress of the work. He threw unwearying bronze on the fire, and tin, and precious gold and silver: then he set the great anvil on the anvil-block, and gripped a mighty hammer in one hand and fire-tongs in another. (Hammond, p. 320)

In the first line of this scene Hephaestus spoke (i.e., *audê*, voice), then left Thetis and went to the bellows (i.e., *sthenos*, motion). The phrase *hôs eipôn* (so saying) is a mark of a narrative transition, indicating temporal progression; the cooordination of *men* and *de* also arranges the actions in a temporal sequence. Within this described action, a difference between literary and visual mimesis is marked by the absence of Hephaestus and Thetis from the line. Their role in the scene is assured by the syntax, though neither is named: sense is derived from syntactical implication, from a peculiarly linguistic way of indicating what is unexpressed. This line (468), however, does not focus just on actions in time: *autou* (there) and *epi* (upon) note the arrangement of bodies in space, but, as Lessing enjoined, arrangement is included only to support the description of an action.[153]

The second line in the description of Hephaestus's preparations continues the focus of the first : *tas d' es pur etrepse keleuse t' ergazesthai* ("he turned them to the fire and ordered them to work," 469). Temporal succession is indicated initially by the resumptive pronoun *tas* (them) followed by the verb of action: the pronoun refers to the bellows of 468, which are now involved in a new activity. The description of this action, which presents the same object in different positions, elicits a single moving image; in contrast, the work of visual art would represent either a single moment that suggests action, or separate images representing the sequence.[154] It is not surprising that a narrative poem describes a progressive action in this way; it represents significant aspects of a scene that are more characteristic of its own medium. While a work of visual art can certainly suggest movement and voice, the difference may lie in the type of signification: the visual arts represent speech and movement primarily by what C.S. Peirce would call "iconic signs," but which also function as indexical signs. The image represents iconically the outward, visible, and physical appearances, which then act as indexical signs of speech or movement. Thus the image indicates speech and action without actually embodying them.[155] The narrative of the bard, however, with its symbolic signs sequentially arranged, represents words with words, but loses the iconicity in attempting to portray colors, textures, and bodies in space.

The line that follows involves the bellows in a third activity: *phusai d' en khoanoisin eeikosi pasai ephusôn* ("the bellows all were blowing in

---

153. Ameis and Hentze (1965), p. 137: "Mit recht ist seit Lessing Kunst des Dichters gerühmt, daß er die Rüstung und namentlich den Schild nicht fertig beschreibt, sondern in seinem einzelnen Teilen vor unsern Augen unter der Hand des Gottes entstehen läßt, die Beschreibung einzelnen Bilder aber möglichst in Erzählung umwandelt."

154. On motion and time in the visual arts of early Greece, see Hurwit (1985), pp. 169-178. See also Lorimer (1929), p. 148; Gottlieb (1958), pp. 22-33; McClain (1985), pp. 41-58.

155. For Peirce's definitions of these signs, see note 60, p. 33, in Chapter 2. The discussion of visible signs for invisible phenomena is not just a modern one. Cf. Xenophon, *Memorabilia* 3.10.1-8, in which Socrates convinces a painter and a sculptor that they can represent not only the body but also the *psukhê* (soul, mind) and its emotions by outward and visible signs. Compare the similar remarks on the visual arts depicting movement by the sweep of drapery in Lessing (1988), p. 120. (He anticipates, here and throughout the *Loakoon*, Peirce's tripartite division of signs). An image could also represent action or speech by depicting a scene in which they would easily be inferred, whether from the recognition of the referent or from the conventions of representation; an example from the Shield would be the trial scene (18.497-508), discussed below, in which the referent suggests speech and so the viewer could and would supply it.

twenty crucibles," 470). Hephaestus has approached the bellows, turned them to the fire; and now, enjoined to work, they blow. Movement and the passage of time are indicated as above; but now, by introducing a verb in the imperfect tense (*ephusôn*, "they were blowing") after the aorists of the previous lines, the ekphrasis adds another mimetic subtlety. The verb directs us to imagine a progressive, repeated action, in contrast to Hephaestus's discrete activities in his preparation. Manipulation of time by means of tense is significant only within the system of contrasts that make up the language. This contrast is not necessarily a feature of the world represented by the language: a describer can divide experience in myriad ways, depending on viewpoint, perception, interest, desire, and linguistic habit.[156] Tense becomes an important mimetic feature of the ekphrasis, as the description here emphasizes the repeated blowing of the bellows after Hephaestus's actions.

The similarity of the noun and the verb in this line (*phusai*, "bellows," and *ephusôn*, "were blowing") adds further significance. A correspondence between the words for the agency (the bellows) and the act (blowing) connects the two through physical resemblance as well as sense. When actual bellows actually blow, there is a physical contiguity of agent and action; in the description, there is a physical (aural and, for us, visual) similarity between the two. The close connection is now reflected by the relations within language. In this instance, the relationship *between the words*, rather than the relationship between a word and an object, creates a kind of linguistic iconicity.[157] The iconic drive of the line is further enhanced, in a more conventional fashion, by the pattern of aspiration (*ph, kh, ph*) and the sibilant endings (*sai, sin, si, sai, son*). The sound pattern becomes onomatopoetic, reflecting the work of the bellows; the words become iconic of the action described. The language of description here approximates some of the iconic representation that is normally associated with the visual arts, and thereby enhances its own mimesis.[158]

---

156. See José Ortega y Gassett (1983), p. 446: "La realidad es un continuo de diversidad inagotable. Para no perdernos en el tenemos que hacer en el cortes, acotaciones, apartados; en suma, establecer con carácter absoluto diferenciaciones que en realidad sólo son relativas." As translated by Elizabeth Gamble Miller in Schulte and Biguenet (1992), p. 106: "Reality is a limitless continuum of diversity. In order not to get lost in it, we have to slice it, portion it out, and separate the parts; in short, we have to allocate an absolute character to differentiations that actually are only relative." Cf. Foucault (1970), p. 9: "It is in vain that we attempt to show, by the use of images, metaphors, or similes, what we are saying; the space where they achieve their splendour is not that deployed by our eyes but that defined by the sequential elements of syntax."

157. See Conte (1986), pp. 43-45; he treats language as iconic, but iconic of previous uses of language rather than external phenomena.

158. Cf. Agamemnon's greaves (*Iliad* 11.16-18), discussed above in Chapter 4. Paul Friedländer (1912), p. 3, mentions the use of exact number (*eeikosi* in this line) as another way

The description of the bellows at work continues with a participial phrase in line 471: *pantoiên euprêston autmên exanieisai* (sending forth a varied well-blown blast). The adjective *pantoiên* (varied) indicates that the bellows blow at various strengths, a matter of motion and change and hence the passage of time. (A visual representation might represent this by depicting the twenty bellows at a variety of stages in the sequence of blowing, and so elicit the inference of this line.) The next adjective, *euprêston* (well-blown), describes not the action, but an interpretation of the action by the *animadversor*. The judgment of the perceiver is now part of the world described by the ekphrasis, and so the representation is supplemented by significant yet non-visual details.[159]

In line 472 a participial phrase continues to dwell on the bellows: *allote men speudonti paremmenai, allote d'aute* (now being at hand for [Hephaestus] hastening, now back again). The scene it suggests is vivid, but depends upon motion and time for its vividness. Spatial arrangement is indicated by *paremmenai* (being at hand); *speudonti* (hastening) then supplies activity to the arrangement. The alternating sequence of actions suggested earlier by the adjective *pantoiên* (471) continues here in the anaphoric phrases *allote men . . . allote d' aute* (now . . . now back again). Actions in time are certainly the emphasis here, with bodies in space included to represent those actions.

The final clause of the description of the bellows tells us that their alternating force responds to the wishes of Hephaestus. The thought (*noos*) of Hephaestus is now included in the description: *hoppôs Hêphaistos t' etheloi kai ergon anoito* ("whenever Hephaestus wished, and was finishing his work," 473). As with voice and motion, a visual depiction could portray the outward and visible signs of an inner state, and so provide an indexical sign of the *noos*; it could also use a symbolic sign for mind or intelligence. But here the specific intention of Hephaestus, not unexpected in the description of an action, fills out the audience's picture of his workshop.

In the first six lines of this narrative frame of the ekphrasis, the focus is not on appearance or spatial arrangement, but on mind (*noos*), voice (*audê*), and a sequence of movements (*sthenos*). Despite this emphasis, the description encourages the audience to visualize the scene. The *phanopoeia*,

---

the text enhances an audience's picture of the scene: "sondern noch mehr durch die bestimmte Zahl uns zur Fixierung des Bildes zwingen." The number twenty does indeed add precision to the image, but it is not a peculiarly verbal mode of mimesis.

159. See the description of Pandarus's bow (*Iliad* 4.105-13, discussed above in Chapter 4) for a similar use of *eu* (well) as an indication of the *animadversor*.

or "appeal to the eye,"[160] results from the nouns that identify characters or objects, as well as the adverbs, prepositions, and participles that arrange them (*en puri* "in the fire"; *epi phusas*, "to the bellows"; *es pur*, "to the fire"; *en khoanoisin*, "in the crucibles"; *autou*, "there"; *paremmenai*, "being at hand"). Of the four adjectives used (*eeikosi*, "twenty"; *pantoiên*, "varied"; *euprêston*, "well blown"; *pasai*, "all"), none describes actual physical appearance. This introductory scene focuses primarily on use and only secondarily on physical form; the frame of the Shield of Achilles emphasizes verbal, not visual, meaning. If one were to look at the passage in terms of a comparison between verbal and visual representation, one could say that, as it is about to describe a work of visual art, the poem affirms the mimetic strengths of the word. On the other hand, no such rhetorical intent need be assumed: the poem is describing an action in a fashion that is most characteristic not only of language, but specifically of Homeric language.[161]

Line 474 then takes us from *ars et artifex* to *opus ipsum*. It draws the focus much closer to the actual object to be fashioned by Hephaestus: *khalkon d'en puri ballen ateirea kassiteron te* (in the fire he threw the copper, not to be worn away, and the tin).[162] Visual appeal rests in the nouns themselves, with no fuller description of appearance. While the outward appearance of the metals may be significant, this line emphasizes their use in the process of making the shield: the materials are named in the accusative case and play their role in the sentence as part of an action. This is a common technique in the Homeric poems, as objects gain their primary significance through history, effect, and use.

The bronze is modified by the adjective *ateirea*; this quality of "not-to-be-worn-away" depends upon the passage of time, and thus describes the

---

160. Ezra Pound (1987), p. 37, and more fully p. 63; he there defines *phanopoeia* as "throwing the object (fixed or moving) on to the visual imagination." In contrast, *melopoeia* is "inducing emotional correlations by the sound and rhythm of the speech," and *logopoeia* is "inducing both of the effects by stimulating the associations (intellectual or emotional) that have remained in the receiver's consciousness in relation to the actual words or word groups employed."

161. The first verb used to describe the process of making the shield is *ergazesthai* ("to work," 469). To our ears, such a term could suggest an analogy between verbal and visual art, but in the *Iliad* it does not. Even the noun *ergon* is not commonly used to name a work of verbal art at this stage of Greek, as it is later in, e.g., the Scholia to Pindar *Pythian* 2.24; Epicurus *Sententiae Vaticanae* 45; Philodemus *Peri Poiêmatôn* 5.11; Dionysius of Halicarnassus *De compositione verborum* 25; *Anthologia Palatina* 11.354.8 (Agathias, sixth century A.D.).

162. On the questions of material and composition of Homeric shields in general, and this one in particular, see Borchhardt (1977), pp. 1-56 and illustration 8; Fittschen (1973); Liebschutz (1953), pp. 6-7; Morard (1965), pp. 348-359. On metal-working in Homer, see Gray (1954), pp. 1-15 and M. W. Edwards (1991), pp. 201-205.

viewer's experience and knowledge of bronze.[163] This quality could be inferred from the appearance of the bronze, but the type of representation in *ateirea* is further complicated by a verbal aesthetic: this adjective is commonly used with bronze in the *Iliad* (e.g., 5.292; 7.247; 14.25; 19.233; 20.108). Also the adjective is not only appropriate for bronze, but even appropriate for this spot in the line (19.233; 20.108); the language of epic has supplied its own motives for the language of description. As Achilles is swift-footed, bronze is "not-to-be-worn-away." I do not claim that the adjective does not describe bronze; it patently does. I do suggest that the adjective is significant not just for its description of the bronze, but also for its resonance within Homeric language.[164] This gives the description a more complex genesis and a more complex motivation: the ekphrasis describes not just the appearance of the materials, but also what is known or thought or said about them in epic language.

Nouns and adjectives in the accusative case continue the description: *kai khruson timênta kai arguron* ("and precious gold and silver," 475). Although there is visual appeal in the mere naming of these metals, the manner in which they are introduced emphasizes action and effect over appearance. The accusative case keeps our focus on these metals as part of an action; the adjective *timênta* (precious, honored) reflects not appearance, but the use and effect of the material. This line continues with the phrase *autar epeita* (approximately "thereupon"), taking us to a subsequent action:

αὐτὰρ ἔπειτα   475
θῆκεν ἐν ἀκμοθέτῳ μέγαν ἄκμονα, γέντο δὲ χειρὶ
ῥαιστῆρα κρατερήν, ἑτέρηφι δὲ γέντο πυράγρην.
(18.475-77)

then he set the great anvil on the anvil-block, and gripped a
mighty hammer in one hand and fire-tongs in another.
(Hammond, p. 320)

---

163. This adjective may support an analogy between song and image, if we consider the phrase *demas kai ateirea phônên* ("stature and voice not-to-be-worn-away," *Iliad* 13.45; 17.555; 22.227). Each occurrence of this phrase describes a representation or a disguise that resembles what it copies in both appearance and sound. This adjective *ateirea* could provide a bridge, albeit small, between the material of the shield and voice, then song.

164. Cf. Conte (1986), p. 44: "The poetic sign signals first to the other signs within the poetic system . . . before signaling its specific sense in a precise context." For my purposes, I would prefer to replace "first" with "also" and "before" with "as well as," to give the statement a wider appeal and a less exclusive rhetoric.

The most striking feature of line 476 is the iconicity of the language. In the action of Hephaestus, the anvil itself and the act of placing it come together on the anvil-block; in the description, the act (*thêken*, "he placed") and its object (*akmona*, "anvil") are combined in the term for the place of the action (*akmothetôi*, "anvil-block"). There would be a similar iconicity in the English "he stood the anvil on the anvil-stand," while the iconicity is lost in "he placed the anvil on the block." The relationship between the words here recapitulates relations in the action itself. This is a level of mimesis that arises from the iconic representation in language not of the objects, but of relations between objects.[165] A distinction between the verbal and visual representations can be seen if one imagines a painting of this scene. The painting might contain iconic images of Hephaestus (the agent), the anvil (the object), and the anvil-block (the scene of the action); the viewer would infer the action implied by these' images. The description, on the other hand, implies but does not depict the agent (Hephaestus), while it does name the action (*thêken*), the anvil (*akmona*), and the anvil-block (*akmothetôi*), in a way that provides an iconic connection among the three.

An example of similar verbal correspondence is used in the scholia to the *Iliad* to illustrate the mimetic primacy of verbal representation over that of painting and sculpture. Discussing a passage that repeats the verb *ballein* (to throw) in three different forms (the figure *polyptoton*), a scholiast remarks that this particular achievement of linguistic description is unrepresentable in visual arts: *amimêta de tauta kai grapheusi kai plastais* (these things are unrepresentable for both painters and sculptors).[166] Verbal play is used here by the scholiast as a weapon in a battle between the arts. An analogy and consequent rivalry were seen in the *Iliad* by these later critics, for whom a contest between the arts was more of a concern. Nevertheless, rather than reading such a figure as a triumph of verbal representation, the tenor of Homeric description suggests that enjoying the possibilities of language need not be an implicit devaluation of other media. We are encouraged merely to

---

165. Thalmann (1984), p. 24, remarks on a similar (though not identical) feature in the pseudo-Hesiodic *Shield of Herakles*: "Thus parallelism of description reproduces the pictorial composition, so that once again, as elsewhere in the poem, the construction of the passage corresponds with the scene described." For similar word-play. see the discussion of *phusai ephusôn* (18.470), above in this chapter; Agamemnon's greaves (11.16-18), above in Chapter 4; and the *hamallodotêres* ("binders of sheaves," 18.553), in the discussion of 18.550-60 in this chapter. On the importance of corresponding sounds, see Kenneth Burke's apt discussion of the "jingle dog" in a section entitled "The Five Dogs" of his essay "Mind, Body, and the Unconscious," in K. Burke (1966), pp. 63-80.

166. Scholia bT to *Iliad* 16.104-5 (Erbse IV, p. 186).

appreciate the poetic virtue of such word-play, without positing a rivalry between the shield and the Shield, between Hephaestus and Homer.

Line 476 then includes the first adjective (*megan*, "large") that names a quality readily associated with appearance. The adjective *kraterên* (powerful), used to describe the hammer in 477, does not tell us that it is large, or shining, or smooth, or grey (all of which would be features of the surface appearance); this adjective describes a feature named from experience of hammers, or by inference from visible qualities, or because this is what epic language calls a hammer.[167] Like *ateirea* and *timênta*, the adjective *kraterên* names a quality that is not iconically represented in the visual arts.[168] In the second half of line 477, *heterêphi* (in the other) returns to the pattern of appealing to the eye by noting arrangement (as in 468). The final noun of the scene (*puragrên*, "tongs") combines in itself an action and the object of that action, without referring to the agent; this noun gains what iconicity it can in a fashion similar to *akmothetôi* in the previous line.

The account of Hephaestus's preparations focuses on the significant aspects of the scene that move, speak, think, and change through time. These introductory lines show the ease with which this poem represents a scene with little emphasis on visual detail. The ekphrasis that follows includes this type of narration; but it also shows a facility and even a penchant for describing appearance in some detail and with appreciative attention to the qualites of visual representation. Such description, which often goes against Lessing's strictures, helps to create an aesthetic stance that is inclusive: *res ipsae, opus ipsum, ars et artifex*, and *animadversor* are not mutually exclusive categories, and their easy combination in the ekphrasis leads us to admire both visual and verbal representation.

---

167. The noun *rhaistêra* (hammer) is a *hapax legomenon*, occurring only here in the Homeric epics.

168. In the *Iliad*, *krateros* appears frequently in this metrical position (2.515; 3.349, 429; 5.151, 244; 6.137; 8.279; 11.410; 13.358; 15.164, 666; 16.501, 624, 645; 17.45, 559; 18.242; 21.543, 566; 24.212): this is another example of a poetic motive for the language of the description.

## The Work upon Which the Depictions Are Made

## (18.478-82)

The actions of Hephaestus (468-77) form the narrative frame of the images on the shield; the description then draws the audience closer, to an inner frame, which is the object itself. As the focus turns from Hephaestus's workshop to the shield (478-82), the description continues to represent an action in time, but now lingers longer on appearance and arrangement. These five lines include *artifex*, *opus*, and *animadversor*, and some subtle combinations of the three:

ποίει δὲ πρώτιστα σάκος μέγα τε στιβαρόν τε
πάντοσε δαιδάλλων, περὶ δ᾽ ἄντυγα βάλλε φαεινὴν
τρίπλακα μαρμαρέην, ἐκ δ᾽ ἀργύρεον τελαμῶνα. 480
πέντε δ᾽ ἄρ᾽ αὐτοῦ ἔσαν σάκεος πτύχες· αὐτὰρ ἐν
                                                  αὐτῷ
ποίει δαίδαλα πολλὰ ἰδυίῃσι πραπίδεσσιν.
(18.478-82)

First he began to make a huge and massive shield, decorating it all over. He put a triple rim round its edge, bright and gleaming, and hung a silver baldric from it. The body of the shield was made of five layers: and on its face he elaborated many designs in the cunning of his craft. (Hammond, p. 320)

The change of focus from the workshop to the work of art itself lies in the accusative noun *sakos* (shield): the direct object of the verb of action is now the shield (*opus ipsum*), not tools (as in 474-75) or metals (as in 476-77). The verb that names this action is *poiei* ("he made," 478). Though this verb has literary associations for later audiences, *poiein* does not come to be used for poetic composition (in extant texts) until centuries after Homer.[169] By

---

169. Not until Herodotus is the bard called *poiêtês* or the literary art *poiêsis* (*Histories* 2.53). A fragment from the comic poet Cratinus (fl. 453-23 B.C.) is the earliest attested use of the noun *poiêma* to refer to a work of verbal art (Fragment 198: Kassel and Austin (1983), p. 222). In the Homeric epics the work of the hand and the work of the voice are not joined by this verb or its nominal forms. There is a potentially provocative instance at *Odyssey* 2.125-26, in which *kleos* (glory through language) is the object of the verb *poieite*. In the *Odyssey*, Odysseus is the most common subject of *poiein*, while in the *Iliad* it is Hephaestus. *Poiein* referring not to song, but with words as its object does become fairly common in later Greek literature: e.g., Herodotus *Histories* 1.23; 2.53; 4.14; Aristophanes *Thesmophoriazusae* 153, 157; Plato *Symposium* 223d; Isocrates *Helen* 64; Plato *Phaedrus* 243b; *Phaedo* 60d; Pherecrates 145.10.

centering the change in the accusative nouns, the ekphrasis continues to focus not just on appearance, but also on action. (Hephaestus is still the subject, though he does not appear in the line: as above, he is represented by syntactical implication.) Line 481 provides a useful contrast to this opening phrase: *pente d' ar autou esan sakeos ptukhes* (there were five layers of the shield there). Nouns in the nominative case with the verb *esan* (there were) do not describe an activity, but rather appearance.[170]

The participle *daidallôn* ("ornamenting," 479), the next verb of making, has more rhetorical flavor; it implies skill and is a term of praise.[171] At the very beginning of the ekphrasis, before any of the images are described, the language of description thus predisposes the audience to admire the work of Hephaestus. (Such a *captatio benevolentiae* is all the more effective when the work is never seen.) This way of predisposing the audience to admire the work, before (or without) revealing it, is another peculiarly verbal level of aesthetic response.[172] Significance, the poem tells us, lies not only in action, and not only in appearance, but also in the narrator's knowledge of the skill of the *artifex*. For us this knowledge is independent of the object itself, and depends on the words of the bard.

When the phrase *iduiêisi prapidessin* ("with knowing mind," "with ingenuity," 482) is added to the verb *poiei*, the skill of the artisan is further emphasized. The phrase *iduiêisi prapidessin*, used only of Hephaestus in the Homeric epics, refers to his artistic skill in fashioning the depictions, not to his knowledge of the referent (*Iliad* 1.608; 18.380; 20.12; *Odyssey* 7.92).[173] The direct object of *poiei—daidala polla*, "many ornaments"—is the first direct reference to the images on the shield, and repeats the praise of *daidallôn*: it calls attention to the skill of Hephaestus in fashioning metal.[174] This section of the description emphasizes not only the actions of the *artifex*,

---

170. See discussions in Chapter 4 of *Iliad* 5.720-32, 738-42; 11.24, 29-30, 33-35, 39; and in Chapter 2 the opening phrases of the scenes on the *Shield of Herakles*.

171. See Morris (1992), pp. 3-4. Not until Pindar is this term used metaphorically for the verbal arts (*Nemean* 11.18; *Partheneia* 2.32; *Olympian* 1.27-30). In the Homeric epics the term is not used of verbal skill; six times in the *Iliad* the adjective *daidalos* refers to the shield of Achilles (18.479, 482; 19.13, 19, 380; 22.314) and once to Agamemnon's shield (11.32). A lyre is called *daidaleos* (9.187); but this is no evidence for an analogy with music or song, since the adjective describes the appearance of the lyre, not its sound. In the *Odyssey* this adjective most frequently modifies *ho thronos* ("chair," 1.131; 10.315, 367; 17.32), and is never used to describe song, voice, or speech.

172. *Pace* C.M. Bowra (1972), p. 142: "Homer reveals himself in the nature and quality of his creations; he does not attempt to guide our reactions to them."

173. See M.W. Edwards (1991), p. 191, on 18.380-81: "ἰδυίῃσι πραπίδεσσι is formular (4 x *Il.*, 1 x *Od.*), and used always of Hephaistos' craftsmanship."

174. Cf. the use of the term to describe metal jewelry made by Hephaestus in 18.400.

but also the quality of his *ars*. In this way, before describing the images, the ekphrasis prepares the audience to admire the (imagined) work. This response to the images, proleptic for the audience, echoes Hephaestus's final words to Thetis before he began to make this shield:

> . . . οἱ τεύχεα καλὰ παρέσσεται, οἷα τις αὖτε
> ἀνθρώπων πολέων θαυμάσσεται, ὅς κεν ἴδηται.
> (18.466-67)

> . . . there will be beautiful armor for him now, such that all
> the many men who see it will marvel at the sight.
> (Hammond, p. 320)

Hephaestus himself has assured Thetis (and the audience) that his work is to be admired: the verb *thaumassetai* (will be amazed) anticipates the reaction of the *animadversor* to the skillful work of the *artifex*.[175]

Such admiring references to *artifex et ars* enhance the audience's image of the shield. Yet lines 478-82, in their adjectives, also include more explicit visual description. In the lines describing Hephaestus's preparations (468-77) the adjectives referred to qualities that are not particularly visual: *euprêston* (well blown), *ateirea* (not-to-be-worn-away), *timênta* (honored), *kraterên* (powerful), *pantoiên* (varied). Only *megan* (large) described appearance. In contrast, the adjectives used in these first lines describing the shield refer to visible features of the nouns they modify: *mega* (large), *stibaron* (thick), *phaeinên* (shining), *marmareên* (glittering, gleaming), *argureon* (silver).[176] Size, thickness, and the play of light on a surface all designate fixed, visible qualities of *opus ipsum*. Unlike the previous passage, these lines, while describing an action, arrest that action, admiring the artistry of the *artifex* and dwelling upon the visual surface of *opus ipsum*.

Despite the focus on visible phenomena in these lines, the phrase *mega te stibaron te* ("both large and thick," 478) quietly carries a more markedly poetic significance; it is a recurring formula in this position in a hexameter line, used to describe shields (*Iliad* 3.335; 16.135; 18.609; 19.373). Highly formulaic phrases not only describe the referent, but also remind the audience of the stylized language in which the referent takes

---

175. See chapter 1 of Slatkin (1991), especially pp. 47-48, for the thematic significance of these lines within the *Iliad*.

176. *Phaeinên* is also a term that later comes to be used with song and voice: see Pindar *Pythian* 4.283 and an Orphic fragment (Kern 247). In the *Iliad* it is not used figuratively with song, voice, speech, word, or thought.

form.[177] An effect of this language, which calls attention to itself and its mediating presence, is to draw attention to the describer; it is this describer (narrator, *animadversor*) who translates the images into words, which are in turn our only access to these images. Reflexive references can increase or decrease the mimetic authority of the medium; it depends on how much the audience trusts that medium. In terms of mimesis, one could be tempted to say that such attention to mediation distracts or detracts from, or somehow problematizes, the poem's ability to represent an external referent. But in the descriptive passages already discussed, inclusion of the medium in the message enhances rather than diminishes our trust in the mimetic capability of that medium. As such it is similar to the way in which the bard's references to the medium of words and song routinely enhance the audience's sense of the authority, authenticity, and mimetic fidelity of the epic. In Homeric poetry, in contrast to much of the later tradition, attention to the window through which we see phenomena does not hinder our view of those phenomena. Contrast to this Howard Felperin's statement: "The referential value of language must, as modernist poetics is well aware, decrease in proportion to its self-referentiality."[178] Such sentiments are foreign to Homeric poetry, and foreign to the experiences of song and poetry common to many an audience. The presence of the mediator and attention to the medium is often a way of enhancing our engagement: the bard acts as an audience for the depictions in a way that serves as a model for the audience of the epic. In the *Iliad*, such attention does not make the representational capacity of the poem problematic. It fills out our picture by including the observer as well as the observed; in the *Iliad* the medium and the mediator

---

177. On the ways in which the very formularity of Homeric verse enhances its communicative power, see Thalmann (1984), p. 29: "Like the formulaic diction, then, the formal procedures were a means of communication between poet and audience. Their typicality did not drain them of significance. It was precisely what made them intelligible, gave them their expressive power." This is consistent with, but not identical to, my argument that attention to mediation enhances our trust in the medium of Homeric poetry. See also M.W. Edwards (1991), p. 192, on 18.385-86, on the rhetorical and representational usefulness of formulaic language; and K. Burke (1969b), p. 58, on a similar phenomenon he calls "formal assent." Chaucer (1987) has a characteristically witty parody of self-referential language in *The Franklin's Tale*: "Til that the brighte sonne lost his heure / For th'orisonte hath reft the sonne his light / This is as much to say as it was night." Attention is drawn to the poetic medium and its own ways of making sense, as well as to the time of day.

178. Felperin (1985) 182. Similar, though in a different context, is Quintilian 9.3.102: *ubicumque ars ostentatur veritas abesse videatur* (wherever art is displayed, truth seems to be absent).

are included in a way that encourages deeper trust in the ability of the bard's words to represent the world beyond those words.[179]

While the adjectives *mega te stibaron te* ("both large and thick," 478) begin to slow the action by focusing on appearance, the motion and narrative drive in the description are still further reduced by the lingering movement of lines 480-81. The enjambed phrase *triplaka marmareên* (threefold, glittering) arrests the progress of the narrative and holds the focus on the *antuga* (rim) of 479. The accusative case of the adjectives, however, recalls the verb *balle* ("threw," 479), which governs these words; action remains in the picture, indicated syntactically by case. With the transitional *ek d'* (and from [it]) another pair of accusatives refer to a new object. The preposition *ek* indicates a spatial, not a temporal relation; and the adjective *argureon* (silver) directs attention to the appearance of the belt. The absence of a verb keeps the action in the background, but the accusative case assures that its trace remains.

While the course of line 480 slows the narrative, line 481 brings it to a halt: *pente d' ar' autou esan sakeos ptukhes* (five were the layers of the shield there).[180] No longer do accusative nouns or adjectives appear, recalling Hephaestus's action. The verb is now existential; the focus has shifted from action to object. But, as the line comes to a close with the words *autar en autôi* (then upon it), the temporal movement of the narrative is quickly resumed; *autar* carries both an adversative and a progressive sense.[181] Hephaestus's actions, resumed with *autar*, are made explicit by the anaphoric *poiei* in 482. Here its direct object is not the folds of the shield, but the decorations upon it (*daidala polla*). The final line of this introductory description (483), as discussed above, refers to the artisan and his craft, and anticipates the images to come. To this point, the description of the shield of Achilles is like other descriptions of art in the Iliad; through line 482 there is nothing to prepare us for the length and detail of the ekphrasis that follows.

---

179. Cf. T. Hawkes (1977), p. 143: "Art represents not the mere 'embroidery' of reality, but a way of *knowing* it, of coping with it, of changing it."

180. On the problems of the layers of the shield in relation to its recurrence in *Iliad* 20. 267-72, see Liebschutz (1953), pp. 6-7; Morard (1965), pp. 348-359.

181. Denniston (1951), p. 55 (2).

## The First Representation: The Heavens

## (18.483-89)

The unparalleled elaboration of the referent in this ekphrasis (extending from 483 to 608) led the Hellenistic critic Zenodotus to consider that these lines were not part of the *Iliad* and to omit them altogether.[182] Due to the lively manner in which the scenes are described, others have claimed that they are Homeric, but do not represent an image.[183] Yet the description of these scenes is typical of, albeit more elaborate than, descriptions of objects elsewhere in the *Iliad*. The audience is asked to respond to imagined images, and they are described in ways that are consonant with the expectations established in the *Iliad*.

The first representation begins with a complex focus on both *opus* and *artifex*, but also includes *res ipsae* (the referent of the images); the ekphrasis then concentrates on naming and interpreting that referent but does not go so far as to dramatize.[184] Though it does not dramatize, the picture of the heavens interprets by adding what is known about a figure beyond what is explicitly included in that image:

ἐν μὲν γαῖαν ἔτευξ᾽, ἐν δ᾽ οὐρανόν, ἐν δὲ θάλασσαν,
ἠέλιόν τ᾽ ἀκάμαντα σελήνην τε πλήθουσαν,
ἐν δὲ τὰ τείρεα πάντα, τά τ᾽ οὐρανὸς ἐστεφάνωται,
Πληϊάδας θ᾽ Ὑάδας τε τό τε σθένος Ὠρίωνος
Ἄρκτον θ᾽, ἥν καὶ Ἄμαξιν ἐπίκλησιν καλέουσιν,
ἥ τ᾽ αὐτοῦ στρέφεται καί τ᾽ Ὠρίωνα δοκεύει,

---

182. Scholia A on 18. 483 (a), (Erbse IV, p. 527). See Pfeiffer (1968), p. 240.

183 Several readers of the Shield of Achilles base their interpretations on an unwillingness to believe that this is a way of responding to visual art, and try to explain how all these figures could be on the shield. E.g., after Madame Dacier censured this description for the impossibility of portraying all of these figures on a shield, Jean Boivin (1970/1715), pp. 234-241, accepts her premise that everything in the description must have a visible counterpart, but he postulated that the shield was decorated on both sides, much like that of the Athena Parthenos (see Pliny, *Natural Histories* 36.4). Cf. the discussions of Lessing, as well as that of Friedländer and the "Homer's mistakes" mode of criticism, above in Chapter 1.

184. Despite the frequent description of movement in the Shield, dramatization (i.e., describing the same figures performing consecutive actions) is rare in this ekphrasis, occurring only in lines 506, 520-32, and 578-86 discussed below.

οἴη δ' ἄμμορός ἐστι λοετρῶν 'Ὠκεανοῖο. (18.483-89)[185]

On it he made the earth, and sky, and sea, the weariless sun
and the moon waxing full, and all the constellations that
crown the heavens, Pleiades and Hyades, the mighty Orion
and the Bear, which men also call by the name of Wain: she
wheels round in the same place and watches for Orion, and is
the only one not to bathe in Ocean. (Hammond, p. 320)

The first line (483) introduces a triple mimetic focus, which is a feature of the
opening line of each scene on the shield (483, 490, 541, 550, 561, 573, 587,
590, 607). The preposition *en* (on) draws attention to the surface of the shield
(*opus ipsum*) on which the images are portrayed.[186] A verb of fashioning
(*eteuxe*, "he fashioned") draws attention to the action of Hephaestus (*artifex*).
The ekphrasis now, for the first time, begins to include the referent (*res
ipsae*): the accusative nouns no longer name materials (as in 474-75), tools
(as in 475-76), the shield and its parts (as in 478-81), or the decoration of the
shield (as in 482). The direct objects now extend the focus beyond the
workshop and work of Hephaestus to the world represented by these images:
*gaian* (earth), *ouranon* (sky), *thalassan* (sea). The three levels of
representation are the action (in the verb), the surface of the work (in the
preposition), and the referent (in the accusative nouns). Only the referent and
the action are named in the line; the agent and the object are indicated by
syntax and supplied through context.[187]

The nouns of the subsequent line do not change the mimetic focus,
but rather fill out a picture of the world depicted: *êelion t' akamanta selênên
te plêthousan* ("both the tireless sun and the moon waxing full," 484). While
these names and epithets keep attention on the referent, the workshop of
Hephaestus nevertheless remains in the picture, though in the background, by
virtue of the accusative case: the accusative case is a syntactical reminder of
*eteuxe*, and hence of the metal-worker and the worked metal of the image.

---

185. On cosmology in the Shield, see Hardie (1985), pp. 11-31. More from the "Homer's
mistakes" school can be found in the comments of Verdenius (1970), p. 225, on this passage:
"Such details are out of place in the description of a work of art and properly belong to a manual
of astronomy."

186. Cf. *en autôi* (on it) in line 481. This preposition is used for the same effect in the Arms
of Agamemnon (see above in Chapter 4 on 11.29, 34-35).

187. The anaphoric repetition of the preposition *en* may be the type of figure that enhances
literary mimesis. The repetition here is paratactic, without subordination or temporal
connectives; as such, it may make the language enter into a more suitable relation (*bequemes
Verhältnis*), though figurative, with a fixed referent. See Aphthonius (Spengel II.47) on the
attempt to make language fit a static referent (discussed above in Chapter 2).

The phrase used to describe the sun resonates on a poetic level as well: the virtually identical phrase *êelion d' akamanta* opens a line earlier in this book of the *Iliad* (239); there it occurs in a description of the sun itself, not a depiction.[188] In a description of a depiction of the sun (484) the same phrase is used as in a description of the actual sun (239); this congruence encourages us to imagine the sun on the shield as we would imagine the sun itself.[189] In other words the mediating presence of the metallic image is not problematic. Though the repetition of the formulaic phrase in the same metrical position may be a reflex of the poetic language, nevertheless the effect is to hold both image and referent before our attention, creating a more complex aesthetic stance.[190] This ekphrasis repeatedly describes the referent as though unmediated, but also regularly recalls both media, worked metal and epic song. There is no need to choose between illusion and defamiliarization, divestiture and appropriation. The description has both an exuberance and a deficiency of meaning when compared with the (imagined) image.[191] If one wishes to assert the primacy of the word, then one emphasizes the exuberance of the description; if one wishes to defer to the visual arts, then one emphasizes its deficiency.[192] It is more characteristic of the rhetoric of the *Iliad* to take the ekphrasis at its word, to see the description as a response to an image, and then to explore its poetics. This generous and inclusive descriptive stance of the bard encourages the audience to adopt such a response to representation.

The naming of the sun has still further resonance when one listens (or reads) with an eye (or ear) to an analogy between the arts. The adjective

---

188. The phrase is discussed in M.W. Edwards (1968), p. 274, and M. Lynn-George (1988), pp. 175-177. In the *Iliad* the adjective *akamas* is used for rivers (16.176), fighting boars (16.823), suns (18.239, 484), and fire (*akamatos*, 5.4; 15.598, 731; 16.122; 18.225). The verb *kamnein* means "to tire" or "to manufacture." Could an unsupported but perhaps suggestive pun be at work: "un-tiring" yes, but also "un-manufactured," i.e., an actual not a depicted sun?

189. For a similar phenomenon in the Tapestry of Helen, specifically *Iliad* 3.127 and 131, see Chapter 4.

190. See Redfield (1979), p. 100, on the proem: "Whether we ascribe the richness to the poet or to his tradition, it remains a poetic success." Cf. Nagy (1979), pp. 78-79, 5§19.

191. I borrow this formulation from José Ortega y Gasset (1959), pp. 1-26. On the second page of an essay that was to begin a commentary on Plato's *Symposium*, he introduces his "Axioms for a New Philology": "1. Every utterance is deficient—it says less than it wishes to say. 2. Every utterance is exuberant—it conveys more than it plans." An account of this new philology is found also in Ortega y Gasset (1957), pp. 222-257 (chapter 11, entitled "What People Say: Language. Toward a New Linguistics").

192. Several later ekphrases defer to the mimetic capabilities of the visual arts, e.g., *Carmina Anacreontea* 16, 17 (West); Lucian 43.3; Callimachus *Iambus* 6.47; Vergil *Aeneid* 8.625 (*clipei non enarrabile textum*, "the non-narratable weave of the shield"); Pausanias 1.19.6.

*akamanta* can raise a question of signs in the visual arts. A metallic image of the sun could embody "tirelessness"—its material solidity would enact the adjective. On the other hand, the language of description does not represent tirelessness with such an iconic sign, but rather names it with a symbolic sign. The adjective *akamanta*, then, names a feature of the referent that is represented effectively but differently by the word and the image.

The next verb of mimetic interest is the verb *estephanôtai* ("set as a rim," 485), which is provocative on several levels. It is rare in the *Iliad*, and used only once in a line *not* describing a work of art (15.153, of a cloud encircling Zeus's head). As used in earlier ekphrases (5.739; 11.36), it represents artistic arrangement, and thus calls attention to the *opus* and *artifex*. Its subject in these cases is the figure portrayed on the work: hence it draws in *res ipsae* as well. In this line, the *artifex* and *opus* need not be implied: the phrase *ta t'ouranos estephanôtai* (and the sky was rimmed with these [stars]) merely describes the way in which the sky is encircled by stars, without necessarily reminding us of the surface or making of the shield. But the earlier occurrences of the verb bring in a hint of the hand of Hephaestus that arranges these (metal) stars around this (metal) sky. The effect is a now familiar one: the world represented and the visual image are conflated in the language of description. While a difference between image and referent is accepted, it does not lead to distrust. It is the presence of these differences that makes both the verbal and visual representations all the more marvelous; they do not eliminate distance, nor are they the complete transformation of art into life. As in Hephaestus's golden handmaids, resemblance, in all its suggestive splendor, not identity, is the dimension in which Homeric ekphrasis admires art. The ekphrasis both appropriates and is appropriated by the work of art; it gives itself over to the suggested world of the images, without forgetting that they are images.

In the next line (486) the phrase *sthenos Oriônos* elicits a further question of verbal representation. A scholiast comments: *periphrastikôs ton Oriôna* ("Orion, periphrastically").[193] Periphrasis is a way of creating meaning that belongs to language, not to the metallic image. The noun *sthenos* is also provocative in that it is one of the qualities given to the golden maidens by Hephaestus (417-20). The poem too is able to give *sthenos* to its creations, not only by representing movement, but also figuratively as in this

---

193. Scholia A on 18.486 (Erbse IV, p. 532). On the alternate form *Oariônos*, see Pasquali (1952), p. 246. His preference for including the alpha is supported, quietly, by M.W. Edwards (1991), p. 212. See Nagy (1979), p. 202 §38 for a note on the etymology of this name. In the *Iliad* the noun *sthenos* with a genitive always occurs at the same spot in the line: 13.248; 18.607; 21.195; 23.827.

line. The proximity of the passage in which Hephaestus gives this quality to his creations makes it easy for an audience to associate the two. This is yet another effect of this periphrasis: the bard invites to his own art some of the admiration he has just given to Hephaestus. The final three lines of the description of the heavens add to the complex focus:

"Αρκτον θ', ἥν καὶ "Αμαξιν ἐπίκλησιν καλέουσιν,
ἥ τ' αὐτοῦ στρέφεται καί τ' 'Ωρίωνα δοκεύει,
οἴη δ' ἄμμορός ἐστι λοετρῶν 'Ωκεανοῖο. (18.487-89)[194]

and the Bear, which men also call by the name of Wain: she
wheels round in the same place and watches for Orion, and is
the only one not to bathe in Ocean. (Hammond, p. 320)

The clause in line 487 does not elaborate the picture, but rather elaborates the way one talks about the referent of the picture. The description has now turned from the workshop and work of Hephaestus (*artifex et ars*) and the surface appearance of the images (*opus ipsum*) to the referent itself (*res ipsae*). The describer recognizes the image, and fills in the description with knowledge provoked, but not portrayed, by the image itself. The description describes an experience of an image.

In this line, and the two that follow, the verbs underscore the change of focus: they are in the present tense, after aorists that named the actions of Hephaestus. The picture and the referent of the picture are in a nearly timeless present, while the actions in the workshop of Hephaestus are in a delimited past. In this way the ekphrasis marks a change in focus from narrative to object, and through this object to an unchanging world represented by that object.

The description further engages us in the referent rather than the depiction, by the observation that Arktos alone does not dip below the horizon: such information must be known only from the observation of the stars over time, or from the language that one inherits. A scholiast, however, suggests that the final line of this passage refers not to the constellation itself, but to the picture on the shield:

---

194. These same three lines occur at *Odyssey* 5.273-75; see Nagy (1979), pp. 201-203, and Heubeck, West, and Hainsworth (1988), pp. 276-277.

τὸ οἴη οὐκ ἔχει τὴν σύγκρισιν πρὸς ἄπαντα τὰ ζῴδια,
ἀλλὰ πρὸς μόνα τὰ ἐντετυπωμένα τῇ ἀσπίδι.[195]

The [word] "alone" is not used with reference to all the
constellations, but only to those engraved on the shield.

If one accepts the scholiast's observation, this final line would be a reminder
of the visual medium, of *opus ipsum*.[196]

So ends the first of the eight scenes described in this ekphrasis. The
type of admiration, trust, appropriation, and divestiture shown by the bard in
describing the images serves as a model for an equally generous response to
the epic from the bard's own audience. The narrator fashions for us a way of
responding to art.

## The City at Peace, I: A Wedding Procession

## (18.490-96)

*I don't paint what I see but what would enable others to see what I*
*see.*
                              - attributed to Degas in Gifford (1991), p. 24

From scene to scene this ekphrasis has gradually drawn us into the
referent of the image: we have moved from the workshop of Hephaestus
(468-77) to the shield itself (478-81), to the decoration on the shield (481-82),
to the images that made up this decoration, and to the cosmic and terrestrial
setting of the scenes to come (483-89). An object has been translated into a
narrative both by describing its manufacture (in 468-82), and by elaborating
the referent of the image with detail known not from the image itself (e.g.,
483-89). Now, the description of the city at peace (490-96) further develops
this translation of object and image into narrative. The bard describes the
action suggested by the image, complete with motion (*sthenos*), sound (*audê*),
and thought (*noos*):

---

195. Scholia bT (Erbse IV, p. 533).
196. In Aristotle *Poetics* 1461a20 this line is said to be figurative, and to refer to the referent,
not just the surface of the image: he says that "only" refers merely to the best known, not literally
to the only constellation that does not set. Cf. M.W. Edwards (1991), p. 283, on *Iliad* 18.487-89;
Heubeck, West, and Hainsworth (1988), p. 278, on *Odyssey* 5.275.

ἐν δὲ δύω ποίησε πόλεις μερόπων ἀνθρώπων    490
καλάς. ἐν τῇ μέν ῥα γάμοι τ' ἔσαν εἰλαπίναι τε,
νύμφας δ' ἐκ θαλάμων δαΐδων ὕπο λαμπομενάων
ἠγίνεον ἀνὰ ἄστυ, πολὺς δ' ὑμέναιος ὀρώρει·
κοῦροι δ' ὀρχηστῆρες ἐδίνεον, ἐν δ' ἄρα τοῖσιν
αὐλοὶ φόρμιγγές τε βοὴν ἔχον· αἱ δὲ γυναῖκες    495
ἱστάμεναι θαύμαζον ἐπὶ προθύροισιν ἑκάστη.
(18.490-96)

And on it he made two fine cities of mortal men. In one there
were marriages and feasting, and they were escorting the
brides from their houses through the streets under the light of
burning torches, and the wedding-song rose loud. The young
men were whirling in the dance, and among them reed-flutes
and lyres kept up their music, while the women all stood at
the doors of their houses and looked on admiring.
(Hammond, pp. 320-321)

The opening line again points to *ars et artifex, opus,* and *res ipsae:* the verb
(aorist again) indicates the manufacturing of the shield, the anaphoric *en de*
(and on [it]) gives spatial orientation within *opus ipsum,* and the direct object
names the referent of the images (*res ipsae*).[197] After this opening phrase, the
work and the artist are all but ignored for fifty-one lines as the poem
describes events first in a city at peace and then in a city at war.

Line 491 begins the transition from the artistry to the referent. The
adjective *kalas,* postponed as so often in the *Iliad,* slows the description. It
notes the reaction of the *animadversor*—but to what?[198] Does it hold
attention on the metalwork or on the cities? The phrase reads "cities of mortal
men, beautiful" and could thus draw attention to the referent (*res ipsae*).

197. S. Richardson (1990), p. 64: "The most remarkable pause involving movement through
time is the description of Achilleus's shield while it is being made. *Iliad* 18.478 begins the
forging, and the shield is completed at 607. Although the lines between give a full description of
each part of the shield, we are continually reminded that the action has not stopped. Every few
lines a verb of making reminds us that the narrator is describing a shield that is in the process of
being designed even as we watch." I would concur, but for a qualification: the whole action of
making the shield is narrated in past tenses, hence it is not quite "being designed even as we
watch."
198. M.W. Edwards (1991), p. 213, on 18.491-96, notes this focus on the reaction of an
observer: "καλάς: the single runover adjective is unexpected and effective, almost as if the sight
called up an exclamation."

However, the term *kalos* in the *Iliad* regularly describes arms and armor.[199] Hence, in line 491 the adjective may hold the audience's attention on the surface appearance of the shield. This adjective conflates the referent (*res ipsae*) and the representation (*opus ipsum*), as experienced by the describer (*animadversor*). The transition to *res ipsae*, the move from medium to message, is thus not fully effected by *kalas*. Here the consonance in the description of *res ipsae* and *opus ipsum* leads us, yet again, to accept that art can be admired in itself and still give us access to a world beyond art; the mediation of the image does not stand in the way of the bard's response to the represented phenomena.

The prepositional phrase that follows (*en têi*, "in one [city]") draws the focus further into the referent, now no longer lingering on the medium. The move to the referent is effected by nothing more than the gender of the pronoun: the wedding celebrations are not "on the shield" (*en tôi*, a neuter pronoun that would refer to *sakei*, "shield"), but "in one city" (*en têi*, a feminine pronoun, hence we supply *polei*, "city").[200] Despite this move into the life portrayed within the image, the verb *esan* (were) still presents a static picture: the description here merely names and arranges. Although the ekphrasis no longer describes the metallic medium, the city is not yet given the vivifying quality of movement.

The lines that follow, while apparently describing an actual scene and not a depiction, while pulling away from the workshop of Hephaestus, still do not go so far as to dramatize. The prepositional phrase *ek thalamôn* ("from the women's chambers," 492) implies motion, but it is motion that would be implied through arrangement: it does not describe the same figures in a series of actions, but is easily imagined as a series of figures. The phrase *daidôn hupo lampomenaôn* ("accompanied by shining torches," 492) still does not stray far from the imagined image. Movement then becomes part of the description as the ekphrasis continues with the verbs *êgineon* ("they were leading," 492) and *edineon* ("they were whirling," 494). Although these are verbs of motion, they still do not dramatize the image: they each describe a single progressive action, not consecutive actions of a character or characters.

While Hephaestus's manufacturing of the images was described by a verb in the aorist (*poiêse*, "he made"), events in the city at peace occur in the

---

199. *Iliad* 3.89, 328, 331; 5.621; 6.321; 7.103; 9.34; 10.472; 11.18, 33, 110, 247, 798; 12.295; 13.241, 510, 611; 15.713; 16.132; 17.91, 130, 162, 187, 760; 18.130, 137, 191, 459, 466; 19.11, 370, 380; 21.301, 317; 22.314, 323.

200. *Pace* Bowra (1972), p. 148, who claims that the focus remains on the surface appearance of the object. The shield is not referred to in the ekphrasis as *hê aspis*, so this feminine word for "shield" is unlikely to be a complicating factor. Within the Shield of Achilles, similar change of focus is effected by gender in lines 542, 548-49, and 565 (discussed below).

imperfect. The imperfect tense here could reflect the visual image: given its progressive aspect, the imperfect could represent the necessary incompleteness of a depicted action that is frozen in a metallic representation. For example, in the Homeric description of the pin of Odysseus (*Odyssey* 19.225-31), the imperfect tense describes a depicted hound as it is forever grasping a depicted deer; the action is eternally conative. And in the *Shield of Herakles* the imperfect tense describes a depicted contest that, by virtue of its status as a picture, will continue forever without resolution (305-11, especially 310-11, cf. also 176-77). In a reversal of Lessing's demand, the language here may enter into a *bequemes Verhältnis* with a motionless image.[201]

Nevertheless, in spite of this iconic drive, the imperfect implies incompleteness only in contrast to other tenses in the language. Behind the entire question of whether the description is still directing our attention to images or life, lies the system of differences that make up the language. Like the contrast between colors in the visual arts, the contrast between tenses in the verbal arts is a way of organizing and interpreting the world that is peculiar to the medium. This is, of course, to say no more than that a description uses language—an unremarkable observation. It is worthy of note only when we attend to the specific rhetoric of the ekphrasis: we ask whether the language somehow calls attention to its similarity to and difference from the visual image it represents, and charges these similarities and differences with value. Variation in the tenses of verbs does supplement the image with a specifically verbal way of representing, but it does so here in a way that tries to borrow some of the timelessness of visual representation.

The elaboration of the referent continues as sound (*audê*) joins motion (*sthenos*) in the description of the marriage celebration: *polus d' humenaios orôrei* ("a great marriage song had arisen," 493), and *auloi phormigges te boên ekhon* ("flutes and lyres were resounding," 495).[202] With these phrases the description moves more boldly into the scenes and away from the surface appearance of the depiction. It begins to turn pictures into stories. Motion and voice are then joined by thought (*noos*) in the description of the women marveling as they watch the marriage procession (495-96). The description represents the thoughts of the depicted figures as they see the wedding scene, and thus keeps our attention within *res ipsae*. Yet, note that *thauma* (wonder) characterizes both the reaction of these women to the

---

201. See Kurman (1974), p. 3 on "striving for timelessness" as a feature of ekphrasis in epic poetry. Cf. Rabkin (1977), pp. 253-254 and Krieger (1967), p. 124.

202. See Lorimer (1929), p. 151, who sees a greater sensitivity to sound than to color in the Homeric epics.

procession and an anticipated reaction of a viewer to the shield (see discussion of 18.466-67, above, p. 98): the women see the parade as a *thauma idesthai* (a wonder to behold), which is a common reaction to works of art in the *Iliad* and particularly in book 18 (lines 83, 377, 467, 549, the last two referring to the Shield of Achilles). Such a consonance gives the visual arts another similarity to the world they represent; the referent and the medium each elicit *thauma*.[203] The description has brought the virtues of Hephaestus's art to the fore: both Hephaestus and the narrator can give us images with *noos*, *sthenos*, and *audê*, and both elicit marvel or wonder (*thauma*).

## The City at Peace, II: A Lawsuit

## (18.497-508)

There is no return to Hephaestus's workshop as this new vignette opens; the scene begins fully engaged in the referent and includes thought (*noos*), motion (*sthenos*), and voice (*audê*):

λαοὶ δ' εἰν ἀγορῇ ἔσαν ἀθρόοι· ἔνθα δὲ νεῖκος
ὠρώρει, δύο δ' ἄνδρες ἐνείκεον εἵνεκα ποινῆς
ἀνδρὸς ἀποφθιμένου· ὁ μὲν εὔχετο πάντ' ἀποδοῦναι
δήμῳ πιφαύσκων, ὁ δ' ἀναίνετο μηδὲν ἑλέσθαι·     500
ἄμφω δ' ἱέσθην ἐπὶ ἴστορι πεῖραρ ἑλέσθαι.
λαοὶ δ' ἀμφοτέροισιν ἐπήπυον, ἀμφὶς ἀρωγοί·
κήρυκες δ' ἄρα λαὸν ἐρήτυον· οἱ δὲ γέροντες
ἥατ' ἐπὶ ξεστοῖσι λίθοις ἱερῷ ἐνὶ κύκλῳ,
σκῆπτρα δὲ κηρύκων ἐν χέρσ' ἔχον ἠεροφώνων·     505
τοῖσιν ἔπειτ' ἤϊσσον, ἀμοιβηδὶς δὲ δίκαζον.
κεῖτο δ' ἄρ' ἐν μέσσοισι δύω χρυσοῖο τάλαντα,
τῷ δόμεν ὃς μετὰ τοῖσι δίκην ἰθύντατα εἴποι.
(18.497-508)

The men had gathered in the market-place, where a quarrel was in progress, two men quarrelling over the blood-money for a man who had been killed: one claimed that he was

---

203. Cf. *Iliad* 3.127 and 131, in the Tapestry of Helen (discussed above in Chapter 4), and also *akamanta* in *Iliad* 18.484 (discussed in this chapter).

making full compensation, and was showing it to the people,
but the other refused to accept any payment: both were eager
to take a decision from an arbitrator. The people were taking
sides, and shouting their support for either man, while the
heralds tried to keep them in check. And the elders sat on the
polished stone seats in the sacred circle, taking the rod in
their hands as they received it from the loud-voiced heralds:
then each would stand forward with the rod, and give his
judgement in turn. And two talents of gold lay on the ground
in the middle of their circle, to be given to the one who spoke
the straightest judgment. (Hammond, p. 321)

This vignette is made up of static pictures, which are elaborated with
inferential detail, but still not dramatized. The scene is set by naming the
figures (*laoi*, "people"), by a prepositional phrase indicating spatial
arrangement (*en agorêi*, "in the meeting place"), the copula (*esan*, "were") in
a progressive imperfect tense, and an adjective also indicating arrangement
(*athrooi*, "all together"). The next clause interprets the picture further by
giving the cause of the gathering: *entha de neikos ôrôrei* (there a dispute had
arisen). In telling why the people were gathered in the agora, the description
has now switched from the imperfect (*esan*) to a pluperfect (*ôrôrei*), thereby
arranging not objects in space, but actions in time. However, the subsequent
verb in the imperfect (*eneikeon*, "they were disputing") returns the focus to
the depicted action: while these imperfects present the scene, the pluperfect
interprets.[204] The subsequent lines (498-500) further interpret the picture.
The image of the gathered people and the litigants is supplemented by the
specific dispute that precipitated this gathering, and the verbal pleas of the
parties involved.

Much has been said about the case being debated.[205] Does the one
man claim that he has paid the *poinê* ("compensation," here a blood-price)

---

204. Cf. discussion of 18.492-95, above in this chapter. The same phenomenon occurs in
Vergil's Shield of Aeneas: in the midst of imperfect verbs describing the referent, the ripping
apart of Mettus by chariots is described with a pluperfect (*Aeneid* 8.643), indicating that this
action is not represented as occurring on the shield, but is already completed and included in the
description through the interpretation of the observer.

205. The subject matter of this scene (not its mode of mimesis) has drawn more scholarly
attention than any of the other depictions of the Shield. On interpretive questions raised by this
passage, see Lowenstam (1993b), pp. 99-101; M. Lynn-George (1988), pp. 183-186; Nagy
(1990b), pp. 251-255 and Nagy (1979), pp. 109, 312; Muellner (1976), pp. 105-106; Andersen
(1976), p. 15; M.W. Edwards (1968), p. 281; Reinhardt (1961), p. 403; Leaf (1887), pp. 122-132.
For further bibliography, see M.W. Edwards (1991), pp. 214-216. The scholiasts attempt to
resolve some of the difficulties of these lines (Scholia bT on 18.499-500, Erbse IV, p. 536). On
questions of law, see Pflüger (1942), pp. 140-148; Myres (1945), p. 10; Miles (1945), pp. 92-93;

and the other deny that he has received it? Or has one man offered to pay in full and the other refused to accept any *poinê*? Recalling the remarks of Ajax (*Iliad* 9.632-36) on the compensation offered to Achilles in his dispute with Agamemnon (and the similar question at *Iliad* 13.659), the latter interpretation seems to be more appropriate to the concerns of the *Iliad*. The question would then turn to the acceptability of any price for a death. The dispute is left unresolved in this scene (as it is in *Iliad* as a whole, until the final book).[206]

The second picture of this scene is that of the elders sitting in a circle on polished stones (503-8). The description again interprets the scene, with an epithet that modifies the heralds: *êerophônôn* (loud voiced) directs attention not to the realm of the eye, but to that of the ear. This adjective reflects what a describer knows and says about heralds. The description further fills out the scene by interpreting the action portrayed therein: *toisin epeit' êisson, amoibêdis de dikazon* ("[the disputants] were rising to speak to them, and [the elders] were giving their judgments in turns," 506).[207] Although the ekphrasis here seems to dramatize the scene, it does not: it has not described the same figures performing consecutive actions. The verbs in the imperfect and the adverb *amoibêdis* (in turns) mark, rather, a plausible response to the suggestions of the images, interpreting them without turning them into stories.[208]

The next line describes two gold talents lying in the middle of the circle (507).[209] The referent is in the nominative (*talanta*, "talents"), modified by an adjective indicating number (*duô*, "two"). A prepositional phrase

---

Köstler (1946), pp. 213-227; Wolff (1946), pp. 34-49 and (1950), pp. 272-275; Hommel (1969), pp. 11-38; van den Brink (1959), pp. 199-204; Munding (1961), pp. 161-177 and (1962), pp. 60-74; Nenci (1963), pp. 1-6; Westbrook (1992), pp. 53-76.

206. See M. Lynn-George (1988), p. 183: "The commotion of the dispute within the shield echoes the broader epic question in which the shield is implicated: the price of a life and the possibility of compensation for death."

207. M.W. Edwards (1991), p. 217, on 18.506, supports the switch of subjects, from "disputants" to "elders," calling the change "abrupt but not un-Homeric."

208. For a different reading of this passage, see M.W. Edwards (1991), p. 217, on 18.501: "Presumably the dispute formed one scene on the shield, the hearing another, the litigants appearing in both." In this case, the figures would still not be put in motion by the description, but the description would be responding to consecutive panels. This would be a visual counterpart to what I call the "dramatization of the images"; it would approach the effect of narrative by a series of pictures. On such storytelling in early Greek art, see J. Carter (1972).

209. On the Homeric talent, see W. Ridgeway (1887), pp. 133-158. Philostratus the Younger, describing an image that itself was made in response to Homer's description of the shield (*Imagines* 10.8, 407K), says that he is not sure why the talents are present and included in the description.

indicates location (*en messoisi*, "in the middle"), a genitive noun indicates material (*khrusoio*, "of gold"), and a verb indicates a state, not an action (*keito*, "were lying"). In this line, appearance and arrangement are again the focus, as the words draw our gaze back to the image. Of mimetic interest is the noun *khrusoio*: it draws the referent and the metallic medium together—there can be few better instances of a *bequemes Verhältnis*. The iconicity achieved by a golden image of golden talents encourages the audience to consider again the visual representation and its seemingly natural ability to represent this scene. If the ekphrasis were implying or encouraging a rivalry between verbal and visual mimesis, it would not emphasize the particular strengths of the visual representation. Characteristically, however, the description then continues to blend levels of attention. The following line (508) moves away from appearance and arrangement and into interpretation, giving the purpose of the golden talents. Significant yet invisible aspects of the scene are emphasized. This ekphrasis moves with ease between and among the various ways to focus a description; this can be attributed to ineptitude or confusion, in the "Homer's mistakes" approach, or to a comprehensive and admiring response to imagined images.

This vignette has taken pictorial images and supplemented them by interpreting cause and effect, reason and reaction. The description has emphasized its own mimetic strengths as it translates image into word, but has left us with the impression that such elaborate description is a way of responding to a work of art, a way that allows some license for the ekphrasis without devaluing the imagined image. While these lines illustrate what Lessing would call *die Freiheit* (the "freedom") available to the verbal arts, his term *die Freiheit* implies mimetic primacy: it implies that the visual arts are deficient, not just different, in their mode and manner of mimesis.[210] In order to avoid this connotation, what Lessing calls "freedom" can be treated as the result of a describer successfully translating a visual image into a verbal medium. The changes that occur during this translation need not be seen as improvements, nor need they be seen as deficiencies; they are, rather, differences between what language does in this ekphrasis and what the layers of worked metal might do in the visual image.[211] Without claims of either primacy or deficiency, the bard (acting as an audience) goes about the business of description, sometimes remaining close to the visual surface, other times elaborating some aspect of the scene depicted.

---

210. Lessing (1988), p. 129, discussed above in Chapter 1.
211. This reciprocity is similar to Ortega y Gasset's "exuberance" and "deficiency": the image and the description are each both exuberant *and* deficient in relation to one another. See above note 191, p. 103.

# The City at War

# (18.509-40)

*In the Shield of Achilles, which encompasses, as it were, the whole universe of human life . . . war is but a single scene among many, and this placement is a form of teaching.*
- J. B. White (1984), p. 42

An image of a besieged city is likely to remind the audience of the larger story of which this ekphrasis is a small part. The place of this depiction of a city at war, as one-half of one of the scenes of the Shield, may serve to put the war at Troy into context; though it dominates this epic, war is only one part of life in the world. If we think of an actual shield and imagine that all the scenes are of equal size, then the war is but one-half of one scene. But the view that war has a minor role in this microcosm is qualified: in the ekphrasis the city at war takes up a full fourth of the ekphrasis (31 lines). War may be put within a larger context of day-to-day life, as James Boyd White rightly points out, but it is given more attention than any other scene: war looms large even in the glimpse we get of a world outside the *Iliad*. Despite this qualification, the Shield does put the war into context, and can thus be read as, in White's words, "a form of teaching."

This description of the city at war begins without a reminder of the visual medium; it is, apparently, to be in the same scene as the city at peace,[212] rather than on a new zone of the shield:

Τὴν δ' ἑτέρην πόλιν ἀμφὶ δύω στρατοὶ ἥατο λαῶν
τεύχεσι λαμπόμενοι· δίχα δέ σφισιν ἥνδανε βουλή,     510
ἠὲ διαπραθέειν ἢ ἄνδιχα πάντα δάσασθαι,
κτῆσιν ὅσην πτολίεθρον ἐπήρατον ἐντὸς ἔεργεν·
οἱ δ' οὔ πω πείθοντο, λόχῳ δ' ὑπεθωρήσσοντο.
τεῖχος μέν ῥ' ἄλοχοί τε φίλαι καὶ νήπια τέκνα
ῥύατ' ἐφεσταότες, μετὰ δ' ἀνέρες οὓς ἔχε γῆρας·     515
οἱ δ' ἴσαν· ἦρχε δ' ἄρα σφιν Ἄρης καὶ Παλλὰς Ἀθήνη,
ἄμφω χρυσείω, χρύσεια δὲ εἵματα ἕσθην,
καλὼ καὶ μεγάλω σὺν τεύχεσιν, ὥς τε θεὼ περ

---

212. Lessing (1988), p. 130, argued that this is not a new section of the shield, citing the absence of the regular introductory line that opens the other scenes (483, 490, 541, 550, 561, 573, 587, 590, and 607).

ἀμφὶς ἀριζήλω· λαοὶ δ' ὑπολίζονες ἦσαν.
οἱ δ' ὅτε δή ῥ' ἵκανον ὅθι σφίσιν εἶκε λοχῆσαι,      520
ἐν ποταμῷ, ὅθι τ' ἀρδμὸς ἔην πάντεσσι βοτοῖσιν,
ἔνθ' ἄρα τοί γ' ἵζοντ' εἰλυμένοι αἴθοπι χαλκῷ.
τοῖσι δ' ἔπειτ' ἀπάνευθε δύω σκοποὶ ἥατο λαῶν,
δέγμενοι ὁππότε μῆλα ἰδοίατο καὶ ἕλικας βοῦς.
οἱ δὲ τάχα προγένοντο, δύω δ' ἅμ' ἕποντο νομῆες      525
τερπόμενοι σύριγξι· δόλον δ' οὔ τι προνόησαν.
οἱ μὲν τὰ προϊδόντες ἐπέδραμον, ὦκα δ' ἔπειτα
τάμνοντ' ἀμφὶ βοῶν ἀγέλας καὶ πώεα καλὰ
ἀργεννέων οἰῶν, κτεῖνον δ' ἐπὶ μηλοβοτῆρας.
οἱ δ' ὡς οὖν ἐπύθοντο πολὺν κέλαδον παρὰ βουσὶν      530
εἰράων προπάροιθε καθήμενοι, αὐτίκ' ἐφ' ἵππων
βάντες ἀερσιπόδων μετεκίαθον, αἶψα δ' ἵκοντο.
στησάμενοι δ' ἐμάχοντο μάχην ποταμοῖο παρ' ὄχθας,
βάλλον δ' ἀλλήλους χαλκήρεσιν ἐγχείῃσιν.
ἐν δ' Ἔρις, ἐν δὲ Κυδοιμὸς ὁμίλεον, ἐν δ' ὀλοὴ Κήρ,      535
ἄλλον ζωὸν ἔχουσα νεούτατον, ἄλλον ἄουτον,
ἄλλον τεθνηῶτα κατὰ μόθον ἕλκε ποδοῖιν·
εἶμα δ' ἔχ' ἀμφ' ὤμοισι δαφοινεὸν αἵματι φωτῶν.
ὡμίλευν δ' ὥς τε ζωοὶ βροτοὶ ἠδ' ἐμάχοντο,
νεκρούς τ' ἀλλήλων ἔρυον κατατεθνηῶτας. (18.509-40)

The other city had two encamped armies surrounding it, their
weapons glittering. There was a debate among them, with
support for either view, whether to storm the city and sack it, or
to agree with the inhabitants a division of their property, taking
half of all the possessions contained in the lovely town. But the
defenders were not ready to yield, and had secretly armed for
an ambush. Their dear wives and young children and men
overtaken by old age stood on the walls to defend them, while
the others set out. They were led by Ares and Pallas Athene,
both shown in gold, and dressed in golden clothing, huge and
beautiful in their armour, and standing out, as gods will, clear
above the rest: and the people with them were of smaller size.
When they reached the place that suited their ambush, down by
a river, where all the cattle came to water, they took up their
position there covered in shining bronze. Then two scouts were
posted at a distance from the main body, to wait for sight of the
sheep and twist-horned cattle. Soon they appeared, and with
them two herdsmen playing their pipes, with no thought for
danger. The men in ambush saw them coming and rushed out

on them, then quickly surrounded the herds of cattle and fine
flocks of white-woolled sheep, and killed the shepherds with
them. But when the besiegers heard the great commotion
among their cattle from where they sat in their assembly-place,
they immediately mounted behind their high-stepping horses
and went in pursuit and quickly overtook them. Then they
formed for battle and fought it out by the banks of the river,
casting at each other with their bronze-tipped spears. And Strife
and Confusion were in their company, and cruel Death—she
gripped one man alive with a fresh wound in him, and another
one unwounded, and was dragging a dead man by the feet
through the shambles: the cloak on her shoulders was deep red
with men's blood. The figures closed and fought like living
men, and dragged away from each other the bodies of those
who were killed. (Hammond, pp. 321-322)

The scene of the city at war begins with vivid visual appeal, and with
attention to the content of the scenes, not the metallic surface of the shield:
spatial arrangement is emphasized (*amphi*, "around"), and the picture is set
before us without motion (*hêato*, "were sitting").[213] This arrangement is a
visible feature, but it is presented as a feature of the referent, not the image;
the visual medium remains in the background. Our focus is held on
appearance in the next line, with the phrase *teukhesi lampomenoi* (gleaming
with armor). With this phrase, however, the visual medium is more noticable:
the metal image has a *bequemes Verhältnis*, a "suitable" (i.e., iconic) relation,
to the arrangement of the armies around the city: shining armor is depicted on
shining armor.[214] Again, this ekphrasis does not just focus on its own
mimetic strengths, but also describes those areas that, by convention, are
more easily represented by the image. Such description was censured by
Lessing as a waste of time for the verbal art; but Lessing's interpretation,
albeit powerful and useful, does not always fit this epic.

---

213. The Silver Siege Rhyton, a Mycenaean work of the second half of the sixteenth century
B.C., portrays such a scene of a split army besieging a city. On a later representation of such a
scene see E.B. Harrison (1981), pp. 281-317. M.W. Edwards (1991), pp. 218-219 has further
bibilography. A written text could iconically represent spatial arrangement: e.g., the Hellenistic
*tekhnopaignia* in Gow (1952), pp. 171-185. On this type of poetry, see Fernández-Vázquez
(1983). This type of pictured poetry is not a feature of the Shield. On spatial form in literature
that is less explicit than these figure poems, see Frank (1968), pp. 3-62 and (1977), pp. 231-252,
and the responses to Frank by Holtz (1977), pp. 276-280 and Rabkin (1977), pp. 253-254.
214. Reinhardt (1961), p. 402: "Das Gegenstand entspricht das Material." Cf. Vergil *Aeneid*
8.659-62, in the Shield of Aeneas, for a similar concinnity of materials and referent.

After setting a visible scene, the ekphrasis moves to those aspects of the siege to which the word traditionally claims easier access than the eye: the deliberation among the armies concerning sack or settlement (510-13). The second half of 510 leaves the visible and proceeds to describe the *noos* of the armies: *dikha de sphisin hêndane boulê* (in two ways a plan pleased them). Appearance is supplemented by an interpretation of the referent. The scene is like other sieges in the *Iliad*, and is easily read as a description of an actual dispute. For example, a description of the siege at *Iliad* 22.120 includes the very phrase used here in 18.511: *handikha panta dasesthai* (to divide all things into two [portions]). The consonance in specific phrasing between 22.120 and 18.511, as well as the more general similarity between the description of a depicted siege and an actual siege, ultimately proves nothing. But it does indicate that the ekphrasis responds to the world suggested by the images: it describes an image as it would describe the referent. The describer treats the work of art not as a barrier between us and the world, a sign of the absence of the referent, but rather as a bridge allowing access to the world depicted therein.[215] An even deeper engagement with the referent lies in the adjective *epêraton* (charming, eliciting *eros* or affection) in 512: as many adjectives in the ekphrasis, it guides our interpretation of the images we are asked to imagine. It represents not just the physical appearance of the shield (*opus ipsum*), nor the appearance of the referent (*res ipsae*), but also the experience of the describer as pictures turn into words (*animadversor*).[216]

As the description continues, the explanation of motive ceases and the focus turns back to the arrangement of the picture (514-15). In the nouns (*teikhos* "wall," *alokhoi* "spouses," *tekna* "children") and the perfect participle (*ephestaotes*, "having stood upon [it]"), the ekphrasis draws attention to the arrangement not of the depiction itself, but that of the referent. Although a visible scene is now the focus, the ekphrasis still does not call attention explicitly to the metallic surface of the shield; focus remains on *res ipsae* not *opus ipsum*. In the adjectives *philai* (dear, beloved) and *nêpia* (young, childish), which describe the women and children, the description moves further into what is thought (or said in epic language) about them: the adjective *philos* commonly modifies *alokhos* in the *Iliad* (4.238; 5.480, 688; 6.366, 482, 495; 15.156; 17.28; 21.587; 24.710), and the phrase *nêpia tekna* occurs in this same position in the hexameter line no less than ten times in the *Iliad* (2.136, 311; 4.238; 6.95, 276, 310; 11.113; 17.223; 22.63; 24.730). We

---

215. See Poirier (1992), p. 149, quoted above in the discussion of Athena's donning the *aegis* (*Iliad* 5.736-42), p. 64, note 117.

216. Compared *eidos epêraton* in the Hesiodic description of Pandora (*Works and Days* 63), discussed in A.S. Becker (1993a), p. 288.

are encouraged by the use of these formulaic phrases to imagine the depicted wives and the depicted children much as we imagine actual wives and actual children in the rest of the *Iliad*. This consonance discourages any inclination we may have to consider the metallic picture as somehow deficient in relation to the referent.

Ares and Athena[217] then join the scene:

> ἦρχε δ' ἄρα σφιν Ἄρης καὶ Παλλὰς Ἀθήνη,
> ἄμφω χρυσείω, χρύσεια δὲ εἵματα ἕσθην,
> καλὼ καὶ μεγάλω σὺν τεύχεσιν, ὥς τε θεὼ περ
> ἀμφὶς ἀριζήλω. (18.516-9)

> They were led by Ares and Pallas Athene, both
> shown in gold, and dressed in golden clothing, huge and
> beautiful in their armour, and standing out, as gods will, clear
> above the rest. (Hammond, p. 321)

These lines point yet again to the oft-asked question: What is being described—the work of art or the world represented by the work?[218] The answer, as so often on this ekphrasis, is that these lines describe both the surface of the work and the world depicted therein. Despite the apparent focus on *res ipsae*, the mention of gold (517) assures that the surface of the shield remains in view: in the context of relief in gold, the adjective "golden" cannot help but remind one of the metallic medium. Not only is the mention of gold in this context a powerful reminder of the medium, but Athena and Ares themselves are here called "golden." Neither is golden elsewhere in the *Iliad*; the attribution is unique to this context. (In the *Iliad* Aphrodite, not Athena, is normally golden: 3.64; 9.389; 19.282; 22.470.) An effect of calling these gods "golden" in this ekphrasis is that we imagine both the gods and depictions of the gods.[219] Unlike some later ekphrastic texts (e.g., Catullus

---

217. Although the Shield has predominantly generic figures, several are named (18.486-89, 535-40, 592); none however are human beings. The Shield does not bring *kleos* (glory through language), as epic song can do.

218. Or perhaps "Of what is this a true description?" I am in this phrase using Friedländer's unfortunate formulation *echte Beschreibung*, but then appropriating it in the spirit of George Miller's "Thirteenth Maxim for the Mind": "In order to understand what another person is saying, you must assume it is true and try to imagine what it might be true of." I owe this reference to A.L. Becker and Yengoyan (1979), p. viii.

219. The large size of these divinities in relation to the people around them would recall just such a convention in visual representations of gods and humans; see the note of M.W. Edwards (1991), p. 219 on 18.517-19. On the thematic significance of Ares and Athena working together, see ibid. on 18.516.

64, Longus *Daphnis and Chloe*, and Petronius *Satyricon* 89), the Shield does not use a work of art to frame a tale, but rather continues to respond to the images throughout the description. As appropriation and divestiture blend in this ekphrasis, both media are part of the description: picture and story, metal images and words. Such attention paid to the representation itself (*opus ipsum*) does not detract from the bard's ability to respond to the referent (*res ipsae*), as indicated by such phrases as *epêraton* (eliciting *eros*), *philai alokhoi* (beloved spouses), *nêpia tekna* (childish children), and the account of Ares and Athena. To generalize this poetic stance, in the *Iliad* attention to mediation enhances our trust in representation.

The next two lines (518-19) continue this same double focus on *res ipsae* and *opus ipsum*.[220] Line 518 could describe either the referent or the surface appearance of the depiction. The final phrase of 518, *hôs te theô per*, does not necessarily recall the medium. If it meant "just as gods," then it would remind the audience that these are depictions of gods, not the gods themselves. But the more likely translation is "in as much as the two are gods," or "seeing that the two are gods"; the phrase, then, would look to the referent.

After the pause to describe the (depictions of) two gods, the tale of the city at war resumes:

οἱ δ' ὅτε δή ῥ' ἵκανον ὅθι σφίσιν εἶκε [221] λοχῆσαι,      520
ἐν ποταμῷ, ὅθι τ' ἀρδμὸς ἔην πάντεσσι βοτοῖσιν,
ἔνθ' ἄρα τοί γ' ἵζοντ' εἰλυμένοι αἴθοπι χαλκῷ.
τοῖσι δ' ἔπειτ' ἀπάνευθε δύω σκοποὶ ἥατο λαῶν,
δέγμενοι ὁππότε μῆλα ἰδοίατο καὶ ἕλικας βοῦς.
οἱ δὲ τάχα προγένοντο, δύω δ' ἅμ' ἕποντο νομῆες 525
τερπόμενοι σύριγξι· δόλον δ' οὔ τι προνόησαν.
οἱ μὲν τὰ προϊδόντες ἐπέδραμον, ὦκα δ' ἔπειτα
τάμνοντ' ἀμφὶ βοῶν ἀγέλας καὶ πώεα καλὰ

---

220. The Scholia bT (Erbse IV, p. 545) read *megalô* (great) as referring to power rather than size: *megalô: dunamei, ou megethei* (great: in force, not stature). On this reading, the word would not refer to the visual medium, but would be a more explicit interpretation of the observer. Reinhardt (1961), p. 401, remarks on the fine ambiguity of reference in these lines: "Kunst und Gegenstand sind einander gemäß: schön ist das Gold, schön sind die Götter." And on the same page: "Aber was ist hier schön, das Kunstwerk oder das, was dargestellt ist?."

221. The interpretation of *eike* (18.520) is vexed. See Ameis and Hentze (1965), p. 141: "vom Präsensstam zu *eoika* vereinzelt: es war passend oder es schien gut." Willcock (1984), p. 271, differs: "*eike*: 'there was space for' from *eikô*, 'yield.'" M.W. Edwards (1991), p. 219 on 18.520-22, concurs with the former, and finds Willcock's suggestion implausible.

ἀργεννέων οἰῶν, κτεῖνον δ' ἐπὶ μηλοβοτήρας.
(18.520-29)

When they reached the place that suited their ambush, down
by a river, where all the cattle came to water, they took up
their position there covered in shining bronze. Then two
scouts were posted at a distance from the main body, to wait
for sight of the sheep and twist-horned cattle. Soon they
appeared, and with them two herdsmen playing their pipes,
with no thought for danger. The men in ambush saw them
coming and rushed out on them, then quickly surrounded the
herds of cattle and fine flocks of white-woolled sheep, and
killed the shepherds with them. (Hammond, p. 321)

Spatial arrangement and visual appeal continue (*hothi*, "where"; *apaneuthe*,
"at a distance"; *aithopi khalkôi*, "with gleaming bronze"), but there are also
the lively characteristics of motion (*sthenos*), motivation and intention (*noos*),
and sound (*audê*).[222] Unusual here, however, is the move to full
dramatization: the story of the ambush planned in 513 is narrated in 520-29.
Once the description has established action, not a fixed image, as the focus, it
further dramatizes the picture in 530-34 by describing the same figures
performing consecutive actions:

οἱ δ' ὡς οὖν ἐπύθοντο πολὺν κέλαδον παρὰ βουσὶν
εἰράων προπάροιθε καθήμενοι, αὐτίκ' ἐφ' ἵππων
βάντες ἀερσιπόδων μετεκίαθον, αἶψα δ' ἵκοντο.
στησάμενοι δ' ἐμάχοντο μάχην ποταμοῖο παρ' ὄχθας,
βάλλον δ' ἀλλήλους χαλκήρεσιν ἐγχείῃσιν. (18.530-34)

But when the besiegers heard the great commotion among
their cattle from where they sat in their assembly-place, they
immediately mounted behind their high-stepping horses and
went in pursuit and quickly overtook them. Then they
formed for battle and fought it out by the banks of the river,
casting at each other with their bronze-tipped spears.
(Hammond, p. 321)

---

222. M.W. Edwards (1991), pp. 219-20 remarks: "the formula 'bright' bronze is not very
suitable for an ambush, and εἰλυμένοι is not used elsewhere in this position, so the poet may be
creating a new phrase to describe the craftsman's technique rather than the men's armour." Cf.
also M.W. Edwards (1968), p. 281, where he sees *argenneôn oiôn* (18.529) as an unusual

The scene is set with the participles (*kathêmenoi*, "sitting"; *stêsamenoi*, "setting themselves up") and prepositional phrases (*eiraôn proparoithe*, "before the assembling place"; *eph' hippôn*, "upon horses"; *potamoio par' okhthas*, "along the banks of the river"). This scene is then put into motion not only by the verbs, but by such temporal adverbs as *hôs* (when), *autika* (at once), and *aipsa* (quickly). The images are fully dramatized, turned into stories; Lessing would approve. In the course of these few lines a single group of men hear the din, board their chariots, give chase, arrive at the ambush, and engage in battle. Even the possibility of portraying such a sequence in the visual arts does not prevent the description from directing our attention wholly to the referent: the bard makes no mention of the way in which this scene might have been represented in separate pictures, but gives us a lively telling of the action. The ekphrasis here goes beyond interpreting images and has turned them more completely into stories. Characteristically, this first step into full dramatization in the Shield, this full engagement with *res ipsae* is preceded and followed by passages that vividly emphasize the visual medium (*opus ipsum*). The description of Ares and Athena reminded us of the material and the conventions of ancient Greek art; while in the curious scene that follows, the nature of the referent itself and a macabre simile bring *opus ipsum* to our attention.

The final lines of the city at war introduce three personified abstractions engaged in the battle (535-40). Since lines 535-38 may be interpolated, I first discuss the rhetorical effect of the passage as it stands, then explore the movement of the ekphrasis without the doubted lines:

ἐν δ' Ἔρις, ἐν δὲ Κυδοιμὸς ὁμίλεον, ἐν δ' ὀλοὴ Κήρ, 535
ἄλλον ζωὸν ἔχουσα νεούτατον, ἄλλον ἄουτον,
ἄλλον τεθνηῶτα κατὰ μόθον ἕλκε ποδοῖιν·
εἷμα δ' ἔχ' ἀμφ' ὤμοισι δαφοινεὸν αἵματι φωτῶν.
ὡμίλευν δ' ὥς τε ζωοὶ βροτοὶ ἠδ' ἐμάχοντο,
νεκρούς τ' ἀλλήλων ἔρυον κατατεθνηῶτας.
(18.535-40)

And Strife and Confusion were in their company, and cruel
Death—she gripped one man alive with a fresh wound in
him, and another one unwounded, and was dragging a dead
man by the feet through the shambles: the cloak on her
shoulders was deep red with men's blood. The figures closed

---

collocation adapted to stress color. Both would then more strongly point to the image and thus strengthen my argument for the interweaving of levels of representation.

and fought like living men, and dragged away from each
other the bodies of those who were killed.
(Hammond, pp. 321-322)

If we read the text as it now stands, the personified abstractions, being
common as shield-devices (apotropaeic figures), turn our attention to the
surface of the shield and the depictions upon it. The thrice repeated *en de*
(and in/on [it]) conflates image and referent in the following manner: we hear
(or read) *en de* and are reminded of *poiêse* (he made) or *tithei* (he placed),
which are the verbs of manufacture that commonly follow *en de* in this
ekphrasis.[223] As such, we would supply *sakei* (the shield) as the object of *en*
without difficulty. But as we come upon *Eris, Kudoimos*, and the verb
*homileon* (were coming together), we adjust our expectation, and could
understand something like *makhêi* ("battle," from 533) as the object of the
preposition. As a consequence, the action and the scene of the action, the
referent and the depictions on the surface of the shield, *res ipsae* and *opus
ipsum*, are conflated. Then we come to line 539: *hôs te zôoi brotoi* (as living
mortals), which tells us that the monsters are fighting like people. This simile
is an interpretive comment of the bard, continuing the "thick description" so
preferred by this ekphrasis.[224]

A second version of this scene begins from the assumption that lines
535-38 are interpolated, as is argued with some cogency and much authority
by Solmsen, Lynn-George, and Edwards.[225] If this be the case, then the battle
undertaken in 534 is elaborated in 539, now the subsequent line, by a simile
giving the response of the describer. This comment draws us back from the
most intense action of the shield, the dramatization of the battle, as the bard
remarks that these depictions of men were much like actual men: *hôs te zôoi
brotoi* (as living mortals). The images of Hephaestus look like actual fighting
figures.[226]

---

223. See lines 483, 485, 490, 509, 541, 550, 561, 573, 587, 590, and 607.

224. I differ from Andersen (1976), p. 10: "It is so dramatically depicted that the poet *for the
first and only time* in the Shield description comes so close to blurring the border between picture
and reality that he emphatically points to it (539)" (emphasis mine). At this point in the
ekphrasis, many lines have already blurred and pointed to the distinction.

225. These lines reappear as 156-60 of the pseudo-Hesiodic *Shield of Herakles*. Suggesting
that they are more appropriate to the *Shield of Herakles* are Solmsen (1965), pp. 1-6; M.W.
Edwards (1987), p. 282; Lorimer (1950), pp. 373 and 486. Cf. the discussion of J.M. Lynn-
George (1978), pp. 396-405. There is a good account in M.W. Edwards (1991), pp. 220-221,
note to 18.535-38.

226. Cf. *hôs te theô per* (indeed, just as [two] gods) in 518, discussed above. Remarks on
verisimilitude and illusion become common in later Greek and Latin ekphrasis; see, e.g., *Odyssey*
19.230; *Shield of Herakles* 189, 198, 209, 215, 218; Theocritus 15.81-83; Herodas 4.28-38;

The final lines of the scene (539-40), in either version, interpret but do not dramatize the images. These lines, juxtaposed to those that precede, illustrate the difference between the dramatization of an image and the recognition and interpretation of the action portrayed. To say that Strife is engaged in a battle, is covered with blood, and is dragging away bodies, remains fairly close to a fixed referent as presented in a work of visual art. To say that men heard the din of battle, sprang to their chariots, hastened to the site of the conflict, and engaged in the fray is to supplement more markedly the referent of the visual art. In the absence of any indication of a change of scene, the description becomes, in effect, a representation of action, not the representation of figures suggesting that action. Both types of description focus on the referent, but the second more emphatically translates it into a narrative.[227]

The vignette of the city at war is left incomplete, as was the lawsuit. Lynn-George relates the inconclusiveness of these scenes to the thematic movement of the *Iliad*: the epic emphasizes the difficulty of resolution and compensation in matters of death, a difficulty that is finally overcome in the last book.[228] One could also see the lack of conclusion as emphasizing the generic character of the scenes (similar to similes): a specific conclusion here would diminish the generality and make the picture tend toward the particular.[229] The inconclusiveness of the scenes could also be read as a reflection of the work of visual art. The imperfect tense was discussed above as a way of representing the ongoing yet unresolved action in a work of visual art; a more patent reflection of the incompleteness of a depicted action is to describe the action as unfinished. This scene, then, resonates not only as it relates to the imagined images, and as it relates to the themes of the *Iliad*, but also as it conforms to familiar patterns of description and narration in the

---

Statius *Thebaid* 1.546-47; Quintus of Smyrna 5.24, 40-42, 84, 90. Pollitt (1974), p. 63 classifies it as "popular criticism."

227. The description of a replica modeled on the Shield of Achilles (Philostratus the Younger *Imagines* 10.5-21, 405-410 K) provides a good illustration of the difference between dramatization and interpretation. Philostratus explains, without narrating. See Lesky (1966); Knight (1991).

228. M. Lynn-George (1988), p. 186: "Both cities are left in the unresolved dispute of death." This comment draws the timelessness and inconclusiveness of a visual depiction together with the thematic concerns of the epic. Both Andersen (1976) and Marg (1957) see in these lines a reminiscence of the fight over Patroclus's body.

229. Many similes in the *Iliad* are small scenes like these and they are often pictures of an action in progress, which is not completed: e.g, 5.499-503; 6.506-14; 9.4-7; 10.360-62; 11.67-69; 15.263-68; 16.156-63; 17.725-29. See the discussion of similes above in Chapter 3, and Lonsdale (1990a and 1990b).

*Iliad.* Ekphrasis gains significance, and trust, when it is related to the language of the epic as well as to the images described.

## The Ploughing Scene and Defamiliarization

## (18.541-49)

*Man glaubt wieder und wieder der Natur nachzufahren, aber fährt nur der Form entlang, durch die wir sie betrachten.*
                                            *- Wittgenstein (1977), I.114[230]*

A verb of fashioning introduces this third section of the shield with a return to Hephaestus's workshop:

Ἐν δ' ἐτίθει νειὸν μαλακήν, πίειραν ἄρουραν,
εὐρεῖαν τρίπολον· πολλοὶ δ' ἀροτῆρες ἐν αὐτῇ
ζεύγεα δινεύοντες ἐλάστρεον ἔνθα καὶ ἔνθα.
οἱ δ' ὁπότε στρέψαντες ἱκοίατο τέλσον ἀρούρης,
τοῖσι δ' ἔπειτ' ἐν χερσὶ δέπας μελιηδέος οἴνου      545
δόσκεν ἀνὴρ ἐπιών· τοὶ δὲ στρέψασκον ἀν' ὄγμους,
ἱέμενοι νειοῖο βαθείης τέλσον ἱκέσθαι.
ἡ δὲ μελαίνετ' ὄπισθεν, ἀρηρομένη δὲ ἐῴκει,
χρυσείη περ ἐοῦσα· τὸ δὴ περὶ θαῦμα τέτυκτο.
(18.541-49)

And he made on it a field of soft fallow, rich ploughland, broad and triple-tilled. There were many ploughmen on it, wheeling their teams and driving this way and that. Whenever they had turned and reached the headland of the field, a man would come forward and put a cup of honey-sweet wine in their hands: then they would turn back down the furrows, pressing on through the deep fallow to reach the

---

230. As translated in Wittgenstein (1968), p. 48e: "One thinks that one is tracing the outline of the thing's nature over and over again, and one is merely tracing round the frame through which we look at it."

headland again. The field darkened behind them, and looked
like earth that is ploughed, though it was made in gold. This
was the marvel of his craftsmanship. (Hammond, p. 322)[231]

In 541, as in the opening line of each previous section (483 and 490), *opus*
and *artifex* are represented, though neither is named: the shield is understood
as the object of *en* (on), while Hephaestus is understood as the subject of
*etithei* (he placed). A new verb, in contrast to *eteuxe* ("he fashioned," 483)
and *poiêse* ("he made," 490), effects a subtle shift in focus: unlike the other
verbs, *etithei* (he placed) calls less attention to the artistic fashioning of the
images. It pays less attention to the mediating quality of Hephaestus's art,
naming an action without further suggesting the manner in which that action
is performed. In other words, there is less *ars et artifex* and *opus* in the
relatively unmarked *etithei*. After the first three words of this scene, the
description settles into the world depicted. The adjectives that modify *neion*
(fallow field) quickly direct the focus of the description to the referent of the
image: *malakên* (soft) describes a feature of the earth, not metals; the
appositive phrase *pieiran arouran* (rich soil) describes a field, not the image;
the adjective *tripolon* (thrice ploughed) adds a characteristic known from
experience or inference, not from the image itself. This setting is then
peopled: *polloi d' arotêres en autêi* (and [there were] many ploughmen in it).
The pronoun *autêi* (it) is significant: its gender indicates that the (feminine)
field is the setting of this scene, not the (neuter) shield. As in the description
of the city at peace (491, *en têi*), the preposition *en* (in) has as its object a
pronoun that draws our thoughts to *res ipsae*: we are now responding to
actions as though they were not metallic depictions. Through line 547 the
focus remains on the ploughing of the field, interpreting but not dramatizing.
Motive (*noos*) and action (*sthenos*) are described, but the description does not
turn the picture into a narrative or give voice to the images.[232] Although the
movement that is described in 542-46 might appear to dramatize, the number
of ploughmen (*polloi*, "many") encourages the audience to imagine different
figures engaged in different stages of ploughing, not a single figure engaged
in consecutive actions. The verbs in the imperfect and the suggestion of
repeated action in 543-46 further enhance our image of a bustling field of
workers.

---

231. Images similar to this and to those that follow are found in art from early Greek sites,
e.g., a Phoenician bowl, c. 850 B.C., from Kerameikos grave 42: see Hurwit (1985), p. 67, figure
31.
232. Responding to the *noos* in this passage, M.W. Edwards (1991), p. 222, on 18.547,
remarks: "The sudden insight into the labourers' minds (547) is noteworthy."

This pleasant but, to this point, unremarkable ploughing scene becomes remarkable for its final two lines. The bard draws back to comment on the illusionistic qualities of the work, and draws us back to both the visual and verbal context of the scene:

ἡ δὲ μελαίνετ᾽ ὄπισθεν, ἀρηρομένῃ δὲ ἐῴκει,
χρυσείη περ ἐοῦσα· τὸ δὴ περὶ θαῦμα τέτυκτο.
(18.548-49)

The field darkened behind them, and looked like earth that is
ploughed, though it was made in gold. This was the marvel
of his craftsmanship. (Hammond, p. 322)

The clause opens with the resumptive pronoun *hê*, nominative feminine and singular. It does not refer to the neuter shield (mentioned at the outset of the ekphrasis, line 478), but rather to the feminine field (mentioned in lines 541 and 547). This pronoun (as those in 491 and 542, above, and 565 below) keeps the focus on the world of ploughing (*res ipsa*), not the metallic image (*opus ipsum*). The verb *melaineto* (was darkening) continues to describe the referent without referring to representation: a plough will, indeed, darken soil behind it, as it brings moist earth to the surface. The subsequent adverb *opisthen* (behind) indicates a spatial relationship, which is again part of the ploughing itself. The preceding lines (541-47) and the first three words of 548 draw attention to ploughing, not depicted ploughing. The description appears to have given itself over to the referential dimension of the (imagined) image, to full illusion.

In the context of a work of art, however, the verb referring to color (*melaineto* "was darkening") and an adverb indicating spatial relations (*opisthen* "behind") may act as a reminder of the surface of the shield. An ancient scholiast read in this phrase a return to the metallic surface:

κατὰ γὰρ τὴν διαβολὴν τῶν βώλων μελανοῦται ἡ
γῆ, σκιὰν οὖν εἰκὸς ἐγκεῖσθαι τῷ χρυσῷ.[233]

---

233. Scholia A on 18.548-9 (Erbse IV, p. 551). The noun *diabolên* is doubted by Erbse; its common figurative sense of "charge," "slander," or "accusation" is not possible here, and Erbse suggests *anabolê*, "that which is thrown up." If *diabolên* is accepted, it is being used in a sense that departs from the common usage and returns to a root sense. On the shading in this scene as a result of ploughing or artistry, see Monro (1897), p. 352: "The dark colour given to the gold points to the use of an enamel." So, too, Cunliffe (1963), p. 260, s.v. μελαίνω: "darkened in hue by some process of shading." In Liddell, Scott, and Jones (1940), s.v. μελαίνω I.1, the verb in this clause is read as referring to the ploughing itself, not the image: "of earth just turned up."

Due to the overturning of the lumps of soil the earth grows
dark. It is likely then that there was a shadow in the gold.

Although the emphasis of the preceding lines makes it likely that the verb
*melaineto* refers to a field being ploughed, the reading of Scholia A, that the
verb simultaneously describes the image and the referent of the image, is
credible. This reading would draw attention to the type of iconic
representation that is an aspect of the visual arts: the (imagined) image has
visible features of its own that correspond to the referent. A perceived
physical similarity between depiction and depicted serves to enhance the
audience's respect for the ability of the visual image to reproduce significant
aspects of the world. The result is an appreciation of Hephaestus's art,
brought about by close attention to the particular excellences of the visual
image, which are not part of the verbal representation.

After the first four words of line 548, the focus remains an imagined
world of ploughing (*res ipsae*), yet the reading of the scholiast suggests that
the surface appearance of the image is also being described. The second half
of the line elaborates this suggestion, and adds another level to the
description: *arêromenêi de eôikei* (and it was similar to a ploughed [field]).
As with the pronoun in the previous phrase, the feminine gender of the
participle *arêromenêi* (to a ploughed [field]) ensures that the field (*hê neios*)
is the understood noun. The expression of similarity, however, interrupts the
focus on the referent by drawing attention to the difference between the
visual representation and the world it represents. There is no longer an
acquiescence in the referential dimension of the image; *eôikei* (it was similar)
recalls the visual medium and reminds the audience that there is no darkening
earth or ploughed land, but only worked metal. Appreciation of the
verisimilitude of the image, however, calls attention to the describer's
reaction. An interpreting describer has been there throughout; here again the
latent messenger lifts the veil for the audience, and the hand that lifts the veil
is part of the picture.[234]

Line 548 directs the attention of the audience to the field being
ploughed (*res ipsae*) as though it were not represented; but the description
also attends to the surface appearance of the metallic image (*opus ipsum*) in
relation to that referent. Moreover the line reflects the interpretation of the

---

The sole other occurrence of this verb in the *Iliad* and *Odyssey* is at *Iliad* 5.354, where it
describes the bruises on the skin of Aphrodite after she has fled the attack of Diomedes. In the
Shield, then, the verb would not in itself imply that this darkness refers specifically to the
artwork of Hephaestus.

234. See the discussions of 18.418 in Chapter 5, and 18.518 and 539 in this chapter.

bard (*animadversor*), who, we are to imagine, is viewing and describing the shield. Line 549 then begins with a remark on the material: *khruseiê per eousa* (although being golden). While the gender of both the adjective and the participle makes the field (*hê neios*) the syntactical focus, the adjective *khruseiê* (golden) reminds the audience of the surface appearance of the worked metal. This phrase emphasizes the physical difference between the visual representation and the world it represents (*opus ipsum* and *res ipsae*). However, when read with the previous phrase (it was similar to a ploughed field), the words "although being golden" suggest that we admire the *difficulté vaincue* in overcoming material difference to create resemblance. Again, a result is appreciation of Hephaestus's art, based not on illusion but on admiration of the art and artistry of the representation.

Within this participial phrase, the particle *per* recalls the bard (interpreter, *animadversor*). It can be an intensive particle, or concessive (as I have taken it), or adversative: "being golden indeed," or "although being golden," or "but being golden."[235] An intensive particle would be a marked signal of the viewer's response to the image; either an adversative or a concessive sense would also call attention to the viewer. The particle, being a trace of the interpreter, guides the audience's reactions, representing, rather subtly in this case, not the appearance of the picture but the experience of the picture.[236]

The interpreter, who was implicit in the comparison of 548 and the particle *per*, comes forth more clearly in the final phrase of 549: *to dê peri thauma tetukto* (it was fashioned splendidly into a marvel).[237] The clause begins with a neuter pronoun. The previous three phrases all begin in the feminine gender, a grammatical reminder of the referent. Now the neuter resumptive pronoun *to* (it) changes the focus from the feminine field to the neuter shield. Our view turns from referent (*res ipsa*) to medium (*opus ipsum*). The emphatic noun *thauma* (marvel, wonder, cause for amazement) is

---

235. See Denniston (1951), pp. 481-490, especially p. 485. A spatial sense, drawing on this particle's relation to *peri*, is rejected in Kühner and Gerth (1966) II.2.508.1 and 3 (pp. 169-170).

236. The present participle *eousa* (being) may also be significant in a verbal representation of a visual image; the temporal movement of narrative appears suspended not by any actual suspension or slowing of our reading, as in the Hellenistic *tekhnopaignia* (figure poems), but rather by holding the description on a static referent. On suspension of the narrative and striving for timelessness as a characteristic of ekphrasis, see Kurman (1974), p. 3. On the same feature as a characteristic of poetry in general, see Krieger (1967), pp. 105 and 124-125; W.J.T. Mitchell (1986), p. 98; Felperin (1985), pp. 166, 177. Contrast Lessing (1988), pp. 119-122, where he affirms temporal movement as the particular excellence of the verbal arts.

237. On δή see Kühner and Gerth (1966) II.2.500, p. 123: "ursprünglich temporale Bedeutung." Denniston (1951), pp. 203-204 and 208, sees no temporal sense (s.v. δή I.4.v).

the cynosure of this final phrase. It is an index of the interpreter: there can be no amazement or wonder without a viewer.[238] Darkness and light, and gold, can be considered qualities of an object, but marvel or wonder can only be qualities of the relationship between the object and the viewer: the marvel expressed in *thauma* indicates the interpreter's experience of the images on the shield.[239] Appropriately, Hephaestus predicted this very reaction (*Iliad* 18.466-67, discussed above, p. 98). The correspondence between the bard's reaction to the shield and that predicted by Hephaestus reinforces the appropriateness and believability of the bard's judgment.[240] With this authority, i.e., the consonance of the bard's response here with the effect predicted by Hephaestus, the images imagined by the audience are more likely to be a *thauma* as well. A note from Scholia T suggests that we read the noun *thauma* in just this way, as enhancing credibility:

ἡ ὀπίσω τοῦ ἀρότρου γῆ ἐμελαίνετο. ἄπιστον δέ, καὶ
αὐτὸς διὰ τοῦ θαυμάζειν πιστὸν εἰργάσατο.[241]

The earth behind the plough was darkening. This is
unbelievable, and he himself [Homer] made it believable
through [his] amazement.

---

238. Its effect is much like *deinos*, "marvellously fearsome" or "terrible," which is used frequently in description of armor and weapons in the *Iliad* (3.337; 5.739, 741, 742; 6.470; 7.245, 266; 11.42; 14.385; 15.309, 481; 16.104, 138; 20.259). At 13.100 *thauma* and *deinos* are used together in description. *Deinos* is not used to describe this shield; it does not have images to frighten Achilles' opponents: since the images are for us, the audience, an apotropaeic shield is unnecessary. Contrast a describer's response to the terrible images on the baldric of Herakles (*Odyssey* 11.601-14).

239. Calling the representation a *thauma* is as close as this ekphrasis comes to the unsayable; in the *Iliad* there is little doubt that words can adequately describe the work and the world. Yet the term *thauma*, especially in the phrase *thauma idesthai*, acknowledges the untranslatability of a particular aspect of the image. On the confidence in speech and lack of concern for the ineffable in the *Iliad*, see W.G. Thalmann (1984), p. 149, speaking of early Greek hexameter poetry in general: "The attitude seems to be . . . that what cannot be described cannot be known." Grief is inexpressible in the *Iliad* (17.37, 695-96; 24.741), and there is potential aphasia at 2.488-92, but the Muses there help the bard sing the Catalogue of Ships. The *Shield of Herakles*, in contrast, often notes the inadequacy of words (145, 161, 218, 224, 230, 318). Cf. Vergil's *Aeneid* 8.625: *clipei non enarrabile textum* (the non-narratable weave of the shield).

240. On the authorizing effect of such correspondences, see Smith (1968), pp. 154-157. For a very different and disturbing response of a viewer (Thetis) to Hephaestus's art and to the images on the shield, see W.H. Auden's poem, "The Shield of Achilles," in Auden (1979).

241. Scholia T on 18.548-49 (Erbse IV, p. 551). Cf. the discussion in Aphthonius of wonder enhancing the description, above in Chapter 2.

The text calls attention to the levels of mediation between us and the world represented, to the visual medium and the interpreter; but the attention to mediation *enhances* the trust for the representation, by emphasizing the close connections between these levels. The scholiast reads Homer in the way that I wish to encourage in this essay: Homeric defamiliarization, here the explicit presence of a guiding narrator, enhances referential capacity. This is not, then, the view popular later, that attention to the medium dissolves the illusion and diminishes referential capacity.[242]

The final word in this section, *tetukto* (was fashioned), brings in the final form of attention: for the first time since the opening line of this vignette (541), we are taken back to the workshop of Hephaestus and the making of the shield. Now the relationships between the artist, the process of making the shield, and the object itself, are part of the (verbal) picture. These two paradigmatic lines encompass, explicitly or implicitly, the referent, the medium, the creation, the source, and the interpreter; they include the several forms of attention, which are blended as one reads the ekphrasis. I provide here a précis of the ways in which these lines direct our attention:

- *hê de melainet' opisthen* (and it [the earth] was darkening behind): full illusion, *res ipsae*, referent.
- *arêromenêi de eôkei / khruseiê per eousa* (it was similar to ploughed [land] / although being golden): defamiliarization of the image, *opus ipsum*, metallic medium of the shield (with a hint of *animadversor* in *eôkei* and *per*).
- *tetukto* (was fashioned): fabrication of the image, *artifex et ars*, genesis of the shield.
- *thauma* (marvel, wonder): effect of and reaction to the image, *animadversor*, the mediator and the verbal medium that gives us these images.

---

242. See the discussion of this question in relation to *Iliad* 18.478-82, above, pp. 98-100.

# The Harvest and Representation of Silence

# (18. 550-60)[243]

*aperias haec, quae verbo uno inclusa erant.*

you should uncover those things, which had been enclosed in a
single word.

*- Quintilian 8.3.68*

*Iliad* 18.550-60 blends the various levels of representation with such
ease that it further encourages us to accept such a mixture as an effective way
of describing, not a deficiency. The opening line, as we have come to expect,
points to the relationship between *opus*, *artifex*, and *res ipsae*. The
description then proceeds to focus on the referent, including motion and
emotion, *sthenos* and *noos* (550-60). However, in the midst of this scene
(lines 556-57) occurs a more subtle indication that the image is no longer the
focus and the audience is to imagine an unmediated world:

Ἐν δ' ἐτίθει τέμενος βασιλήϊον· ἔνθα δ' ἔριθοι          550
ἤμων ὀξείας δρεπάνας ἐν χερσὶν ἔχοντες.
δράγματα δ' ἄλλα μετ' ὄγμον ἐπήτριμα πῖπτον
                                                    ἔραζε,
ἄλλα δ' ἀμαλλοδετῆρες ἐν ἐλλεδανοῖσι δέοντο.
τρεῖς δ' ἄρ' ἀμαλλοδετῆρες ἐφέστασαν· αὐτὰρ ὄπισθε
παῖδες δραγμεύοντες, ἐν ἀγκαλίδεσσι φέροντες,          555
ἀσπερχὲς πάρεχον· βασιλεὺς δ' ἐν τοῖσι σιωπῇ
σκῆπτρον ἔχων ἑστήκει ἐπ' ὄγμου γηθόσυνος κῆρ.
κήρυκες δ' ἀπάνευθεν ὑπὸ δρυΐ δαῖτα πένοντο,
βοῦν δ' ἱερεύσαντες μέγαν ἄμφεπον· αἱ δὲ γυναῖκες
δεῖπνον ἐρίθοισιν λεύκ' ἄλφιτα πολλὰ πάλυνον.
(18.550-60)

And he made on it a king's estate of choice land, where

---

243. On this passage in relation to the archaic Greek land-system, see Ridgeway (1885) and
Richter (1968). See M.W. Edwards (1991), p. 223 for further bibliography.

workers were reaping the corn with sharp sickles in their
hands. The crop fell to the ground in handful after handful
along the swathe, while binders tied the cut trusses into
sheaves with twine. There were three sheaf-binders standing
ready, and boys working behind the reapers kept them
constantly supplied, gathering the cut corn and bringing it in
armfuls to them. *And among them the king holding his
sceptre stood quietly by the swathe, with delight in his heart.*
To one side his heralds were preparing a feast, busy with a
great ox they had slaughtered: and the women were pouring
out an abundance of white barley for the workers' meal.
(Hammond, p. 322, emphasis mine)

The king stands among them in silence (*siôpêi*, 556).[244] If the surface of the
shield were the focus, such mention of silence would be improbable. A
comment on the silence of the king corresponds to the attribution of sound to
images in the ekphrasis: in this case the description has moved through the
surface appearance of *opus ipsum* and is engaged in the world depicted, *res
ipsae*, to such a degree that the absence of speech is worthy of note. While the
silence of the king is the counterpart of *audê*, the description of his pleasure,
*gêthosunos kêr* (glad in his heart), adds *noos*. A scholiast remarked that this
inner, emotional state is represented by the work of visual art through
outward and visible signs.[245] But the words do not say that his bearing and
face look as though he is happy, just that he is happy. At times the ekphrasis
asks that the audience notice the visual medium; at others, as here, it keeps
the focus on the referent.

  This scene is not dramatized; figures are described in motion, but the
same figure does not perform consecutive actions. The words merely describe
the action that is suggested by the image, without turning it into a story.

---

  244. K. Reinhardt (1961), p. 402, on the silence of the king: "Weshalb schweigend? Doch
wohl, weil er genießt. Weil er der König ist. Fast ist es, als gewönne in seinem Schweigen der
Augenblick Dauer."

  245. Scholia A on 18.557c (Erbse IV, p. 553). The comment of this scholiast would better fit
the ekphrases of the Philostrati, or Ovid. Throughout their descriptions, the Philostrati explicitly
unravel visual clues, while Ovidian ekphrasis frequently tells the audience what visible stimuli
lead the narrator to his interpretations (e.g., *Metamorphoses* 2.13-14; 6.73-74, 121-22). On
explicit visual cues to interpretation in ancient Greek art, see, e.g., the amphora of the Nettos
painter, Hurwit (1985), p. 177, figure 77, dateable to c. 620-10 B.C.; the open mouth of the figure
is read as an indexical sign of speech.

# Music in the Vineyard

## (18.561-72)

*Two China men, behind them a third,*
*Are carved in lapis lazuli, . . .*
*The third, doubtless a serving-man,*
*Carries a musical instrument. . . .*
*One asks for mournful melodies;*
*accomplished fingers begin to play.*
*- "Lapis Lazuli," in Yeats (1962).*

Unusual in *Iliad* 18.561-72 is both the lingering attention to the surface of the shield and a deeper engagement in sound.[246] Previous scenes mentioned the *artifex* and *opus* in the opening line, but then proceeded to *res ipsae*. This description of the vineyard spends four lines on the materials, before moving into the referent:

Ἐν δὲ τίθει σταφυλῇσι μέγα βρίθουσαν ἀλωὴν
καλὴν χρυσείην· μέλανες δ' ἀνὰ βότρυες ἦσαν,
ἑστήκει δὲ κάμαξι διαμπερὲς ἀργυρέῃσιν.
ἀμφὶ δὲ κυανέην κάπετον, περὶ δ' ἕρκος ἔλασσε
κασσιτέρου· μία δ' οἴη ἀταρπιτὸς ἦεν ἐπ' αὐτήν,     565
τῇ νίσοντο φορῆες, ὅτε τρυγόῳεν ἀλωήν.
παρθενικαὶ δὲ καὶ ἠΐθεοι ἀταλὰ φρονέοντες
πλεκτοῖς ἐν ταλάροισι φέρον μελιηδέα καρπόν.
τοῖσιν δ' ἐν μέσσοισι πάϊς φόρμιγγι λιγείῃ
ἱμερόεν κιθάριζε, λίνον δ' ὑπὸ καλὸν ἄειδε     570
λεπταλέῃ φωνῇ· τοὶ δὲ ῥήσσοντες ἁμαρτῇ
μολπῇ τ' ἰυγμῷ τε ποσὶ σκαίροντες ἕποντο.
(18.561-72)

And he made on it a vineyard heavy with grapes, a beautiful thing made in gold: but the clusters on the vines were dark, and the rows of poles supporting them were silver: and all around the plot he set a ditch worked in blue enamel, and a fence of tin. And a single path led in to the vineyard, and

---

246. See M.W. Edwards (1991), p. 224, note to 18.561-72, on the simultaneous focus on the representation and the actual actions imagined: "Again the poet emphasizes the craftsman's skill and the happiness of the workers." Edwards's use of the conjunction "and" connects Hephaestus's workshop (*artifex et ars*) and the referent of the images (*res ipsae*) in an appropriately unproblematic manner.

along it went the pickers at the time of the grape-harvest.
Girls and young men, innocent-hearted, were carrying out
the honey-sweet crop in woven baskets. In their midst a boy
was playing a lovely tune on a clear-sounding lyre, and to it
sweetly singing the Linos-song in his delicate voice: they
followed him with singing and shouting, and danced behind
him with their feet beating time to his music.
(Hammond, p. 322)

The mimetic focus of the opening line is familiar. The movement from
metallic image to referent here begins with the naming and describing of the
teeming vineyard. The adjectives *kalên khruseiên* (beautiful, golden), which
open the next line, arrest this movement. They do so by holding our focus on
the material of which the image of the vineyard is made (*khruseiên*,
"golden"), and the evaluation of this image by the *animadversor* (*kalên*,
"beautiful"). If it were in a different context, the subsequent phrase *melanes d'
ana botrues êsan* (and there were dark bunches of grapes throughout) would
seem to describe the grapes themselves; in this context, where the focus is on
the color and the material of the manufactured image, the phrase calls
attention also to the surface appearance of *opus ipsum*. An adjective of color,
an adverb indicating spatial arrangement, and the copula suggest a vivid but
static picture.

Line 563 keeps attention on *res ipsae* until the final word,
*argureêisin* (made of silver). This adjective is another sign that a depiction
(*opus ipsum*) is being described, not an actual vineyard; the description has
not given itself over to *res ipsae*. Again in this line the referent is stationary
(*hestêkei*, "had been set up"); the material depiction has Lessing's *bequemes
Verhältnis* with the world it represents. The following clause continues to
describe the material representation, but adds an explicit reference to the
action of Hephaestus (564-5): *amphi de kuaneên kapeton, peri d' herkos
elasse / kassiterou* (on both sides he hammered out a ditch of blue enamel,
and around it a fence of silver). The adjective *kuaneên* (of blue enamel) and
genitive noun *kassiterou* (of silver) refer to *opus ipsum*, the accusative nouns
*kapeton* (ditch) and *herkos* (fence) to *res ipsae*, while the verb *elasse* (he
hammered out) returns the *artifex* to view.

A visual aesthetic is here established not only by the repeated
mention of material, but also by emphasis on the arrangement of bodies in
space. Spatial arrangement in this passage is indicated by prepositions and
adverbs (*en*, "on"; *ana*, "throughout"; *amphi*, "on both sides"; *peri*, "around";
*diamperes*, "right through"). Since the Homeric poem indicates spatial
arrangement in the same fashion whether it describes an event (e.g.,

Hephaestus's preparations at 468-77) or an image (the vineyard), these adverbial modifiers in themselves need not refer to the surface of the work of art; they can refer to the arrangement of the actions depicted or the metallic medium of the image. This consonance between the manner of describing the referent and the manner of describing the image encourages us to see an appropriate correspondence, a *bequemes Verhältnis*, between the depiction and its referent.

The description of the depiction of the vineyard becomes the description of a vineyard with the pronoun at the end of line 565: *ep' autên* (leading to it). The gender of the pronoun tells us that we are now to see the feminine vineyard, *hê aloê*, not the neuter shield, *to sakos.*[247] In line 566 the focus is drawn even further into the vineyard: *têi nisonto phorêes* (on which the carriers were accustomed to return). With *têi* the immediate locus of activity is neither the shield nor the vineyard, but the path within the vineyard. With this pronoun and the imperfect verb *nisonto* (they were accustomed to return), the ekphrasis no longer describes the arrangement of images or the actions of Hephaestus. The Homeric description is giving the figures *sthenos*, interpreting the referent. Attention to the scene represented, and not the representation of the scene, continues in the following clause: *hote trugoôien alôên* (whenever they harvested the vineyard). The mood of the verb indicates that this is an inference of the interpreter: the optative following *hote* marks an indefinite temporal clause, to be rendered "*whenever they harvested the vineyard.*" The description has generalized the depicted action into a habitual activity of the characters depicted therein. In the course of this line the referent of the description has changed from the surface of the work (*opus ipsum*) to the events suggested by the work of art (*res ipsae*).

As the description continues, the focus remains on the world evoked by the image, filling it out with the reactions of the describer. The participial phrase *atala phroneontes* (thinking the thoughts of children) describes the minds of the youths, bringing *noos* into the picture. The adjective *meliêdea* (honey sweet) adds a characteristic known from actual fruit, not its depiction. *Audê* then enters emphatically with the young lyre-player:

τοῖσιν δ' ἐν μέσσοισι πάϊς φόρμιγγι λιγείῃ
ἱμερόεν κιθάριζε, λίνον δ' ὑπὸ καλὸν ἄειδε
λεπταλέῃ φωνῇ. (18.569-71)

In their midst a boy was playing a lovely tune on a clear-

---

247. Cf. the similar transition to the referent by means of a pronoun at 18.491 and 542.

sounding lyre, and to it sweetly singing the Linos-song in his
delicate voice. (Hammond, p. 322)

The initial prepositional phrase *toisin d' en messoisi* (in their midst) arranges
the picture. The two nouns *pais* (boy) and *phormiggi* (on a lyre) populate this
picture by naming—the first step of a focus on *res ipsae*. But it is the
adjective *ligeiêi* (with a clear, sharp sound) that begins to move the
description into a fuller engagement in the referent.[248] This first step is
further enhanced by the next word: not only is the quality of sound described
by *ligeiêi*, but the adverb *himeroen* (appealingly) describes the skillful
playing of the lyre player. This adverb reflects not just a quality thought to be
in the imagined sound, but also the effect of that sound on an *animadversor*—
in this case, no longer a viewer but a listener.[249] The describer is engaged in
the referent to such a degree that this ekphrasis includes not only the
attribution of sound, but an apreciative response to that (imagined) sound. In
an appealing and suggestive fashion, these lines correspond to the levels of
ekphrastic description I have proposed above in Chapter 3, but here the whole
paradigm is shifted in the following way: in these few words the description
represents the material (the lyre and its clear sound, corresponding to *opus
ipsum*), an artist in the act of fashioning his work (the boy playing the lyre,
corresponding to *ars et artifex*), and a reaction of the audience (the adverb
*himeroen*, corresponding to *animadversor*). Song in the *Iliad* is described in a
manner commensurate with the way the Shield of Achilles is described. Such
a consonance gives me further confidence that the aesthetic I am here
exploring is an Homeric one, and lends weight to the correspondence
between our response to Homeric poetry and the bard's response to visual art.

The description of the boy's singing continues to show the same
engagement in the referent and the same similarity to the levels of ekphrasis:
*linon d' hupo kalon aeide / leptaleêi phônêi* (and he sang the Linos-song
beautifully to the accompaniment of [the lyre] with a delicate voice). The
verb *aeide* (he sang) denotes the making of the song (*ars et artifex*); *leptaleêi
phônêi* (with a delicate voice) is an aesthetic judgment of that making by an
*animadversor*; *linon* (Linos [song]) names this *opus ipsum*. *Kalon* can be
adjectival (beautiful) or adverbial (beautifully). If adverbial it is another
reaction to the singing, and if adjectival it is a reaction to the song itself;
either would draw attention to the *animadversor*. Only an elaboration of the

248. The formula *phormiggi ligeiêi* (on a lyre with a clear, sharp sound) occurs once earlier
in the *Iliad*: at 9.186 Achilles is playing as the embassy from Agamemnon arrives.
249. Cf. the similar use of *himertous* in Hesiod *Theogony* 577, discussed in A.S. Becker
(1993a), p. 284.

referent, i.e., the subject of the song, is omitted.[250] The same poetics of Homeric ekphrasis appear, whether of a represented song or of a described image; further support thus accrues to a reading of the ekphrasis as a *mise en abîme* for the poetics of the *Iliad*—specifically, the audience's response to the *Iliad*.

The early lines of this scene demonstrate a willingness to mingle the description of the work of art (*opus*), its manufacture (*artifex*), its referent (*res ipsae*), and the evaluation of the viewer (*animadversor*). But after the first word of line 565, the ekphrasis gives itself over to the referent to such a degree that the quality of the boy's music is praised in the description. The vignette then concludes with the dancing of the children (571-72), which once again sets the picture in motion (giving it *sthenos*).

## Violence in the Bower and Dramatization of Images

## (18.573-86)

*It was her nature to be blind and sighted at one time, to leap off the cliff and to stand there watching herself fly down through the air, and I was learning that credulousness and detachment even when I was still spending much of my time on the floor. In effect, of course, she was being an artist.*
*- Arthur Miller (1987), p. 8, describing his mother*

The tendency to combine medium and referent in the description is here taken still further. Juxtaposed are sound, movement, metals, the actions of Hephaestus, and a sequence of actions performed by the depicted figures, now fully dramatized by the description:[251]

Ἐν δ' ἀγέλην ποίησε βοῶν ὀρθοκραιράων·
αἱ δὲ βόες χρυσοῖο τετεύχατο κασσιτέρου τε,

---

250. On the Linos-song see the Scholia AbT on 18.570 (Erbse IV, pp. 555-558). For bibliography and discussion, see M. Lynn-George (1988), pp. 191-192, and M.W. Edwards (1991), p. 225 on 18.569-70.

251. Similar, though not enlivened to the same degree, is the description of the snakes on Agamemnon's armor at 11.26-28, 38-40 (discussed in Chapter 4).

μυκηθμῷ δ᾽ ἀπὸ κόπρου ἐπεσσεύοντο νομόνδε        575
πὰρ ποταμὸν κελάδοντα, παρὰ ῥοδανὸν δονακῆα.
χρύσειοι δὲ νομῆες ἅμ᾽ ἐστιχόωντο βόεσσι
τέσσαρες, ἐννέα δέ σφι κύνες πόδας ἀργοὶ ἕποντο.
σμερδαλέω δὲ λέοντε δύ᾽ ἐν πρώτῃσι βόεσσι
ταῦρον ἐρύγμηλον ἐχέτην· ὁ δὲ μακρὰ μεμυκὼς        580
ἕλκετο· τὸν δὲ κύνες μετεκίαθον ἠδ᾽ αἰζηοί.
τὼ μὲν ἀναρρήξαντε βοὸς μεγάλοιο βοείην
ἔγκατα καὶ μέλαν αἷμα λαφύσσετον· οἱ δὲ νομῆες
αὔτως ἐνδίεσαν ταχέας κύνας ὀτρύνοντες.
οἱ δ᾽ ἤτοι δακέειν μὲν ἀπετρωπῶντο λεόντων,        585
ἱστάμενοι δὲ μάλ᾽ ἐγγὺς ὑλάκτεον ἔκ τ᾽ ἀλέοντο.
(18.573-86):

And he made on it a herd of straight-horned cattle. The cows
were fashioned in gold and tin, and were mooing as they
hurried from the farmyard to their pasture by a purling river,
beside the beds of swaying reeds. Four herdsmen in gold
walked along with the cattle, and there were nine quick-
footed dogs accompanying them. But at the head of the cattle
two fearsome lions had caught a bellowing bull, and he was
dragged away roaring loud. The dogs and the young men
went after him. The lions had broken open the great ox's hide
and were gulping its inwards and black blood. The herdsmen
could only set their quick dogs at them and urge them on.
The dogs would always turn back before biting the lions, but
they stood close and barked at them, while keeping clear.
(Hammond, p. 322-323)

The preposition of the first line (*en*, "on [it]") reminds us, again, of the
surface of the shield. As expected, an accusative noun *agelên* (herd) names
the referent of the image. The verb *poiêse* (he made) returns us to the *ars et
artifex* in the manner of line 490, after the three previous scenes were
introduced by [*e*]*tithei* (he placed). A genitive phrase follows, *boôn
orthokraipaôn* (of straight horned cattle), which modifies and specifies the
noun *agelên*. This is the familiar matrix of relations between *artifex*, *opus*,
and *res ipsae*, which marks opening lines throughout the Shield. The next line
retains the complex focus, adding a new level of specificity: the referent and
the materials are named, while the verb of fashioning is in the pluperfect
(*teteukhato*, "he had fashioned"), indicating a completed action; the
*animadversor* thus notes the sequence of actions in making this image. In the
following lines (575-76) the cows bellow (*audê*) and move (*sthenos*),

proceeding along a resounding river with waving reeds. These lines, now focusing on *res ipsae*, have moved from naming to interpretation. The referent has taken hold, and the audience, with the other scenes in mind, has every expectation that the description will continue to elaborate the world suggested by the depictions.[252] The opening word of 577, however, interrupts the movement into the referent by bringing the material surface pointedly back into the picture; the line mingles the mediating quality of the worked metal (*khruseioi*, "golden") with the motion of the herdsmen (*estikhoônto*, "were proceeding"). This shows the degree to which this description can hold medium and referent together, without asking us to choose between life and art: illusion and defamiliarization can "lie down together in the same bed."[253] Here attention to the status of these images *qua* images does nothing to detract from their referential value: despite attention to the medium, the line accepts, recognizes, and interprets the world suggested by the image: golden herdsmen move and golden cows bellow.

One could draw on the description of Hephaestus's handmaids (417-20) to say that Hephaestus's art can do such magical things. But this ekphrasis directs us differently: the description does not suggest that the metal cowherds actually move along the surface of the shield as Achilles goes into battle; it does not ask us to imagine that these are gold and tin robots that can move and moo. They are wonderful images that are given a response that honors their wonder; the art of Hephaestus, we are asked to imagine, elicits this reaction from the describer. In this Homeric line there is no dissonance, and the apparent paradox is only apparent: depictions can low and move in the describer's experience of the images, which is what is being described by this ekphrasis. It draws together the various relations between the images, their referents, their making, and their audience. There is no cost of representation, no failure of one or another kind of mimesis, and no rivalry between the arts. Such vivification of an image, without forgetting that it is all the while an image, encourages a way of reading a work of visual art: to return to the terms of Paul Ricoeur, both appropriation and divestiture constitute the bard's reaction to the images. Similarly, as a *mise en abîme*, the ekphrasis teaches us a way of responding to the epic, patterning ourselves after the bard in his ekphrastic role as audience, with the wisdom and valor

---

252. The alliteration and assonance of line 576 has long been thought to be onomatopoetic; if so, it would be a feature of verbal mimesis that makes the language iconic, not just symbolic. See M.W. Edwards (1991), pp. 58 and 226 on 18.573-76.

253. For the context of this phrase from William Carlos Williams's "Song," see the beginning of Chapter 5.

and generosity necessary for both appropriation and divestiture.[254] Common Homeric patterns of description fill scenes with *noos*, *sthenos*, and *audê*, just as Hephaestus can do with his golden handmaids. The analogy is then encouraged between the bard and Hephaestus, between the Shield and the *Iliad*, between the describer's response to the Shield and the audience's response to the *Iliad*. This ekphrasis continues to accept the suggestions of the image. The bard *qua* audience shows us just this way of responding to art, filling in and filling out, all the while following the representations with care and attention.

To return to the ekphrasis, the adjective *khruseioi* ("golden," 577) is the last reference to the medium in this scene; the lines that follow dramatize an attack by lions; complete with bellowing and barking, the lions, men, and dogs appear performing consecutive actions: *nomêes ham' estikhoônto boessi* (the herdsmen were proceeding along with the cows), *kunes heponto* (the dogs were following), *leonte tauron ekhetên* (two lions were grasping a bull), *ho de helketo* (it was being dragged), *kunes metekiathon* (the dogs were pursuing), *tô men anarrêxante boeiên egkata laphusseton* (the two [lions] once they ripped the hide were gulping down the entrails), *nomêes endiesan kunes* (the herdsmen were setting the dogs on), *apetrôpônto leontôn* ([the dogs] were turning themselves away from the lions), *ek t' aleonto* ([the dogs] were keeping out of the way). Picture becomes story, and is fully dramatized. Within this story, the adjective *smerdaleô* ("dreadful," 579) represents the reaction of an *animadversor*; but it is a reaction to the (imagined) lions, not to an (imagined) image.[255] The bard's response here plays down the mediating quality of the image and allows the referent to have its effect.

The ekphrasis encourages us to react to art as life, almost; it simultaneously reacts to the world and to a depiction of that world, as it translates visible phenomena into language. The levels of mediation between us and the world depicted act not as barriers, but as bridges: they bring that world to us, and this ekphrasis emphasizes the bridge, not the deficiencies, differences, or costs of mimesis. As mentioned above, later theoretical discourse argues that explicit attention to the medium (or media) decreases a

---

254. I borrow the phrase "wisdom and valor and generosity" from Thoreau (1983), p. 145, in the chapter entitled "Reading": "we must laboriously seek the meaning of each word and line, conjecturing a larger sense than common use permits, out of what wisdom and valor and generosity we have."

255. Lions, common in similes, are also common in art of the age. See Hampe (1952), pp. 32-33; M. W. Edwards (1987), p. 283; Lonsdale (1990b). This may explain the a note in Scholia T (Erbse IV, p. 563): this most dramatized, and hence, in one sense, least pictorial scene of the ekphrasis elicits the remark *graphikôs edeixe to pan* ([he] set it all out pictorially).

work's ability to represent.[256] This assumes that the medium must be transparent for successful mimesis. Such a view is based on a Lessing-like belief that representation should aim only at illusion (*die Täuschung*), the illusion that the medium is not there; anything that detracts from illusion then detracts from representation. In the Shield of Achilles, and in the *Iliad*, moments of explicitly guided interpretation do not create distance or alienation, but rather share an experience of the narrator.[257] The Shield of Achilles does not pretend that there is no describer, that there is no description, nor pretend that there is no image, between us and the represented events. Mediation, appreciated, is part of what makes it wondrous.

# The Sheepfold

# (18.587-89)

These lines have no *sthenos*, *noos*, or *audê*; as such they are anomalous on the shield:

Ἐν δὲ νομὸν ποίησε περικλυτὸς ἀμφιγυήεις
ἐν καλῇ βήσσῃ μέγαν οἰῶν ἀργεννάων,
σταθμούς τε κλισίας τε κατηρεφέας ἰδὲ σηκούς.
(18.587-89)

And the famous lame god made on it a great pasture-ground
for white-woolled sheep in a beautiful valley, with steadings
and covered huts and sheepfolds. (Hammond, p. 323)

The opening phrase is deceptively familiar, but with a significant difference. The preposition (*en*), particle (*de*), direct object (*nomon*, "pasture"), and verb (*poiêse*, "he made") all fit the familiar paradigm for the introductory line of a scene. The novelty here is the naming of Hephaestus (through epithets). In

---

256. See above pp. 98-100 and pp.129-130.
257. Cf. Trypanis (1977), p. 65: "With a few brush strokes the rhapsode brings an object, a person, or a scene to life before our eyes, leaving the listener to fill in the blanks in the picture from his own imagination. In this way the listener has a creative share in the artistic experience."

the lines that opened each previous scene, the referent was elaborated after the central caesura: in line 490 the prepositional phrase and the verb of fashioning are joined by the direct object (*poleis*, "cities") and a genitive phrase describing these cities; 541 is similar, but an adjective and an appositive phrase follow the direct object *neion* (fallow field); similarly in 550 the *temenos* (precinct) is modified by an adjective, and followed by a clause detailing the figures in it; in 561 the direct object (*alôên*, "vineyard"), which again names the referent but is here postponed to the end of the line, is filled out with the phrase *staphulêisi mega brithousan* (greatly laden with clusters); in 573 *agelên* (herd), like *poleis* in 490, is given a modifying phrase in the genitive. In each case the first line represents *opus* and *artifex* by implication alone, but explicitly names and elaborates the referent of the image. The opening line of the description of the sheepfold breaks this pattern by naming the *artifex* (Hephaestus) through his epithets.

The pair of lines that follow also refrain from elaborating *res ipsae*: 588 describes the appearance of the referent without giving it life, while 589 merely names the images. In the first book of the *Iliad* occurs a scene useful for comparison. Following the banquet, the gods retire to bed, and here are their bedchambers:

ἧχι ἑκάστῳ δῶμα περικλυτὸς ἀμφιγυήεις
Ἥφαιστος ποίησεν ἰδυίῃσι πραπίδεσσι. (1.607-8)

in the houses made for them in the cunning of his craft by the
famous lame god Hephaistos. (Hammond, p. 64)

The lines do not tell what the chambers looked like; the only guide for the audience's image of this palace is the praise of the artisan (*iduiêsi prapidessi*).[258] His skill is noted, and only in this way is the audience's visualization of the bedchambers influenced by the description. The ekphrasis is able to elicit admiration for the work of art through praise of its maker, a particularly linguistic level of representation, and one which is not confined to the Shield of Achilles. The three lines describing the sheepfold (587-9) are not unlike description elsewhere in the *Iliad*, although they are remarkably spare in this context of elaborate interpretation.

---

258. Two phrases from this pair of lines recur in the Shield of Achilles: at *Iliad* 18.482, Hephaestus made the images *iduiêsi prapidessi* and at 587 he is *periklutos amphiguêeis*. The second phrase identifies the artisan; the first notes his skill as an artist.

# The Dance Floor and the Dance

## (18.590-606)

*Rhythm is a form cut into TIME, as a design is determined SPACE.*
*- Ezra Pound (1987), p. 198.*[259]

The initial noun (*khoron*) of this final vignette is mimetically appealing. Does it mean "dance floor," "dance," or "band of dancers"? Accordingly, is this a description of Pound's design or rhythm? The scholiasts wish the reference of the noun to be fixed on the first option, and the lines immediately following show that this must be true.[260] But the noun *khoros* allows and even encourages the conflation of the decorated floor with both the action that occurs there and those who perform this action. So, too, this ekphrasis, which mingles the image, the agent, and the action there proposed:

Ἐν δὲ χορὸν ποίκιλλε περικλυτὸς ἀμφιγυήεις,          590
τῷ ἴκελον οἷόν ποτ' ἐνὶ Κνωσῷ εὐρείῃ
Δαίδαλος ἤσκησεν καλλιπλοκάμῳ Ἀριάδνῃ.
ἔνθα μὲν ἠίθεοι καὶ παρθένοι ἀλφεσίβοιαι
ὠρχεῦντ', ἀλλήλων ἐπὶ καρπῷ χεῖρας ἔχοντες.
τῶν δ' αἱ μὲν λεπτὰς ὀθόνας ἔχον, οἱ δὲ χιτῶνας     595
εἵατ' ἐϋννήτους, ἦκα στίλβοντας ἐλαίῳ·
καί ῥ' αἱ μὲν καλὰς στεφάνας ἔχον, οἱ δὲ μαχαίρας
εἶχον χρυσείας ἐξ ἀργυρέων τελαμώνων.
οἱ δ' ὀτὲ μὲν θρέξασκον ἐπισταμένοισι πόδεσσι
ῥεῖα μάλ', ὡς ὅτε τις τροχὸν ἄρμενον ἐν παλάμῃσιν    600
ἑζόμενος κεραμεὺς πειρήσεται, αἴ κε θέῃσιν·
ἄλλοτε δ' αὖ θρέξασκον ἐπὶ στίχας ἀλλήλοισι.
πολλὸς δ' ἱμερόεντα χορὸν περιίσταθ' ὅμιλος
τερπόμενοι· [μετὰ δέ σφιν ἐμέλπετο θεῖος ἀοιδὸς
φορμίζων·] δοιὼ δὲ κυβιστητῆρε κατ' αὐτοὺς          605
μολπῆς ἐξάρχοντες ἐδίνευον κατὰ μέσσους. (18.590-606)

---

259. Cf. Marvin Bell, "Quilt, Dutch China Plate" in Pack, Lea, and Parini (1985), p. 14: "What is to be done with such an object, / which says beautifully that design is the motion a shape makes?"

260. Scholia Α on 18.590a (Erbse IV, p. 564): *ton topon khoron eirēken, ou to sustēma tōn khoreuontōn* (He called the *place* the chorus, *not* the band of dancers). A dance floor is a common subject for the representational arts—see M. W. Edwards (1987), p. 283—hence the word *khoron* may draw us to imagine the surface of a shield (*opus ipsum*).

And the famous lame god elaborated a dancing-floor on it, like
the dancing-floor which once Daidalos built in the broad space
of Knosos for lovely-haired Ariadne. On it there were dancing
young men and girls whose marriage would win many oxen,
holding each other's hands at the wrist. The girls wore dresses
of fine linen, and the men closely-woven tunics with a light
sheen of olive oil: and the girls had beautiful garlands on their
heads, and the men wore golden daggers hanging from belts of
silver. At times they would run round on their skillful feet very
lightly, as when a potter sits to a wheel that fits comfortably in
his hands and tries it, to see if it will spin smoothly: and then
they would form lines and run to meet each other. A large
crowd stood round enjoying the sight of the lovely dance: and
two acrobats among the performers led their dancing, whirling
and tumbling at the centre. (Hammond, p. 323)

Again, the preposition *en* (on) gives us *opus ipsum*, an accusative noun
*khoron* names *res ipsae*, and a verb of making gives us *ars et artifex*. The
verb differs from the familiar verbs in the opening lines of previous scenes:
*poikille* (he made with skillful art, adorned, embroidered) implies the
dappling work of the artist, and so points more specifically to the visual arts,
more emphatically to the *artifex* and the resulting *opus*, than do the unmarked
*poiêse* (he made) or the still less marked *etithei* (he placed).[261] Here also,
continuing this increased attention to *ars et artifex*, Hephaestus is named. As
in 587, the second half of the opening line does not elaborate the referent, but
rather holds attention on the maker. The focus stays on Hephaestus's work.

The simile of the following lines (591-92) directs attention to the
interpreting words of the *animadversor*, the bard who provides our only
access to these pictures.[262] The appearance of this depiction is not described;
the describer provides a simile to provoke the audience to imagine it. If the
dance floor were "shining" or "wide," then the interpreter would remain in the
background; description by simile, however, gives a reaction of the observer
to help the audience visualize the dance floor. The describer is sharing or
eliciting an experience of seeing. A comment of a scholiast is of interest here;
it has been charged, report Scholia A, that the comparison of the work of a

261. See M.W. Edwards (1991), p. 228, on 18.590-92, responding to the implication in
*poikille*: "Possibly the word hints that this picture is more in the nature of a decorative frieze, like
the rows of identical figures on Geometric vases, than a real life episode like the others on the
shield." The term *poikilos* and its congeners are not used metaphorically for the verbal arts until
Pindar (*Pythian* 9.77; *Olympian* 1.29, 6.87; *Nemean* 4.14). On *ta poikila* see Bolling (1958), pp.
275-282, and B.H. Fowler (1984), pp. 119-149, especially p. 147.

262. For more on Daedalus and ancient Greek art, see Morris (1992).

god to that of a mortal is blasphemous: it makes Hephaestus an imitator (*mimêtês*) of Daedalus. Not so, says the scholiast. The comparison is a way for the text to represent effectively and convincingly an (unseen) visual image to the audience; it has both a rhetorical and referential purpose, and accomplishes them with success.[263] The scholiast goes on to say that the comparison with Daedalus's work enhances the audience's visualization of the referent: it does turn us into viewers, yet it does so not by describing the surface appearance of the image, but by associating an as yet undescribed and unseen image with an image presumed to be already familiar to the audience. To view this dance floor, one must look over the shoulder of the bard and share an *experience* of images; the artist is more than normally apparent in the work. It is consistent with the poetics of this ekphrasis that the presence of the bard enhances, as the scholiast says, rather than detracts from the mimetic force of the text.

From lines 593 to 598 the bard names and interprets figures on the dance floor and their actions, still without dramatizing.[264] The words can easily be read as an active response interpreting a visual image: e.g., of the young women, *alphesiboiai* (bringing in many oxen [as a bride-price]) or of the tunics *eunnêtous, êka stilbontas elaiôi* (finely spun, softly glistening with oil). The final line (598) of this section that sets the scene brings the materials back into the picture (*khruseias*, "of gold"; *argureôn*, "of silver"); but they are the materials of both the referent, and the image.[265] Thus the language of description creates another *bequemes Verhältnis*, an iconic concinnity, between the visual representation and what it represents. In spite of Lessing's observations to the contrary, Homeric ekphrasis readily describes visual appearance, accenting the virtues of visual representation, even as it translates the image into its own forms of representation.

A useful illustration of just such translation follows, when the description begins to focus on movement, i.e., *sthenos*:

οἱ δ' ὁτὲ μὲν θρέξασκον ἐπισταμένοισι πόδεσσι
ῥεῖα μάλ', ὡς ὅτε τις τροχὸν ἄρμενον ἐν παλάμῃσιν
ἑζόμενος κεραμεὺς πειρήσεται, αἴ κε θέῃσιν·
ἄλλοτε δ' αὖ θρέξασκον ἐπὶ στίχας ἀλλήλοισι.
(18.599-602)

---

263. Scholia A on 18.591-2a (Erbse IV, p. 565).

264. On the clothing and accessories of the dancers, see Lorimer (1950), pp. 387 and 390 note 3. Cf. M.W. Edwards (1991), pp. 229-230, notes on 18.595-96 and 597-98.

265. See M. W. Edwards (1991), p. 230, note on 18. 597-8: "The gold and silver remind us again of the craftsman's technique."

At times they would run round on their skillful feet very
lightly, as when a potter sits to a wheel that fits comfortably
in his hands and tries it, to see if it will spin smoothly: and
then they would form lines and run to meet each other.
(Hammond, p. 323)

The point of the comparison in this simile is swift controlled motion.[266] No
longer is the description concerned with the image (*opus*), or with the
workshop of Hephaestus (*artifex* and *ars*), but it is now fully engaged in the
referent. This engagement is enhanced by the interpreting adjective
*epistamenoisi* (skillful) and the adverbial phrase *rheia mal'* (very easily). The
bard here comments on the skillful and graceful way in which this motion is
being performed; as in the praise for the singing boy (569-71), attention is
drawn fully into *res ipsae*, the world evoked by the image. This ekphrasis
does not direct us to imagine that the figures on the shield are whirling about
as Achilles enters the battle. The movement of these dancers is a reflex of the
revery of response that describes, in reaction to visual representations, a
world of flesh and blood, of voice, thoughts, and motion. The description
does not leave the work behind, but rather uses it both as a stimulus and as a
touchstone. This scene emphasizes the *artifex* in the opening line, uses the
interpretation of the *animadversor* to draw attention to the referent, and then
begins to describe the scene. Thereafter, the mediation of the visual image is
no longer of concern: the bard (*animadversor*) comes forth to interpret the
referent of the image with the simile of the potter's wheel. This is Homeric
description: admiration of the visual art, but equal pleasure in the language
that describes the experience of a work of visual art.

This scene concludes with lines full of *noos*, perhaps with *audê* (if
the bracketed clause belongs),[267] and finally *sthenos*:

πολλὸς δ' ἱμερόεντα χορὸν περιίσταθ' ὅμιλος
τερπόμενοι· [μετὰ δέ σφιν ἐμέλπετο θεῖος ἀοιδὸς
φορμίζων·] δοιὼ δὲ κυβιστητῆρε κατ' αὐτοὺς        605
μολπῆς ἐξάρχοντες ἐδίνευον κατὰ μέσσους. (18.602-6)

---

266. As noted in Scholia T on 18.600-1a.1 (Erbse IV, p. 567).

267. The bracketed clause brings a singer to the scene. This clause is omitted in Monro and
Allen's text (1920) and in Hammond's translation. Evidence is set out in a note on 18.604-6 in
Erbse's apparatus (Erbse IV, p. 569). For a discussion of the question, see Forderer (1965), pp.
23-27. For opinions see Taplin (1980), p. 9, and note 27; Reinhardt (1961), p. 402. See also
M.W. Edwards (1991), pp. 230-231 on 18.604-6; Janko (1992), p. 28.

A large crowd stood round enjoying the sight of the lovely
dance: and two acrobats among the performers led their
dancing, whirling and tumbling at the centre.
(Hammond, p. 323)[268]

The adjective *himeroenta* (eliciting desire, delightful, charming) gives us the
effect of the dance on a viewer (cf. *himeroen* in 570, discussed above); the
participle *terpomenoi* (filled with pleasure, enjoying) gives us the response of
viewers within the picture (as in 18.495-96 with *thaumazon,*"were amazed").
Both the adjective and the participle give us *noos*. The bracketed words
contain the singer and his singing, while the final line sets the picture in
motion again (*sthenos*), with the verb *edineuon*, "they were whirling," which
was used earlier in the description of the dancers in the City at Peace (494).
The entire scene shows a great degree of engagement in the pleasures of art
and skill, be it that of Daedalus, that of dancers, that of a potter, the joy of the
audience, perhaps the singing of a bard, and the tumbling of an acrobat.

# A Return to the Frame

# (18.607-8)

There is no change in the language of description that would indicate
that this is the final depiction to be described; we are, however, given some
hints of closure. The indications of closure lie in the referent alone:

Ἐν δὲ τίθει ποταμοῖο μέγα σθένος Ὠκεανοῖο
ἄντυγα πὰρ πυμάτην σάκεος πύκα ποιητοῖο.
(18.607-8)

And he made on it the mighty river of Ocean, running on the

---

268. The phrase in brackets can be translated: "among them a god-like singer was
performing, playing the lyre."

rim round the edge of the strong-built shield.
(Hammond, p. 323)

The first three words form a familiar introduction to a scene. Then the periphrasis of *sthenos* with a genitive noun recalls the opening scene of the Shield (*sthenos Ôriônos*, 486). As in the opening scene, the periphrasis shows that the language is representing a way of thinking (or speaking) about the river Ocean.[269] The return of a phrase used in the early stages of the ekphrasis can reinforce a closural sense, but is not enough on its own to signal that we have come to the end of the description of the shield. Such a closural sense may be indicated by what is here portrayed: in a microcosmic description of the world, the ring of Ocean forms a natural boundary that may suggest to the audience that this is the end. On this line M.W. Edwards says: "Okeanos . . . surrounds the pictures on the shield as he surrounds the flat disc of the earth on which men and women work out their lives."[270] The image is again iconic, as the shield corresponds to the world. But the description is also iconic, as the ring-composition creates a correspondence between the ekphrasis and the shield it describes.[271]

As the next line (608) begins, the hints of closure in 607 are made more secure; we are oriented explicitly on the shield now, not just in the world, by the word *antuga* ("rim," recurring here from 479). The correspondence between the outer ring of the shield and the river that encircles the earth establishes a strong iconicity between the world represented and the depiction of that world on the shield. This line describes what the image can embody.

# The Rest of the Armor

## (18. 609-13, and later in the *Iliad*)

Αὐτὰρ ἐπεὶ δὴ τεῦξε σάκος μέγα τε στιβαρόν τε,
τεῦξ᾽ ἄρα οἱ θώρηκα φαεινότερον πυρὸς αὐγῆς,    610

---

269. On Ocean, see Romm (1992), pp. 179-183.

270. M.W. Edwards (1991), p. 231.

271. On the ring-composition of the Shield, see Stanley (1993), pp. 9-13. Cf. Thalmann (1984), p. 10, on the *Shield of Herakles*: "Once again there is a correspondence between poetic pattern and the physical object described, for the whole account of the shield is enclosed by ring composition."

τεῦξε δέ οἱ κόρυθα βριαρὴν κροτάφοις ἀραρυῖαν,
καλὴν δαιδαλέην, ἐπὶ δὲ χρύσεον λόφον ἧκε,
τεῦξε δέ οἱ κνημῖδας ἑανοῦ κασσιτέροιο. (18.609-13)

Then when he had finished the huge and massive shield, he
made him a corselet brighter than the light of burning fire,
and he made him a heavy helmet to fit close round his
temples, a beautiful finely-worked thing, and he added a
golden crest on top, and he made him greaves of fine-beaten
tin. (Hammond, p. 323)

The phrase *mega te stibaron te* (both large and thick) recalls the
opening of the ekphrasis (478), and hence brings us back to where we started
this long description. Such ring-composition could here also be seen as
iconic, in that the edges of the description are approximating the rim of the
shield: the phrase *sakos mega te stibaron te* (a shield both large and thick)
encircles the Shield, as the depiction of Oceanus encircled the shield. The rest
of the armor is then dispensed with quickly and with little variation; these
lines reflect a familiar pattern of describing objects in the *Iliad*. A new piece
is introduced in each line but for 612, and the verb of fashioning is *teuxe* (he
fashioned); the first three pieces are described by a reaction of the
*animadversor*: *mega te stibaron te* (609), *phainoteron puros augês* ("shining
more than the gleam of fire," 610), *kalên daidaleên* ("beautiful, ornamented,"
612). The two lines that follow emphasize the material: *khruseon* ("golden,"
612), *heanou kassiteroio* ("of pliant tin," 613). Here, as in most of the
descriptions of art in the *Iliad*, there is no representation to be described. The
audience's attention is focused on *artifex* and *opus ipsum*, while both are
colored by the reactions of the *animadversor*.

As the next book opens, Thetis merely says that the arms are
singular and beautiful (19.10-11). They are called *daidala* ("ornaments,"
19.13), too bright for others to look at but they strike fire into Achilles' eyes
(19.14-17). Achilles' reacts with *kholos* ("anger," 16) and *terpsis* ("pleasure,"
19.18 and 19), demonstrating precisely the ability to respond to *both* the
referent *and* the medium, for which I argue in this essay.[272] The shield then

---

272. Cf. Stanley (1993), p. 25 (cf. also p. 3), who sees Achilles' pleasure as his response to
the artistry and his anger here being provoked by the scenes on the shield: " In this context the
*Shield* is less a reminder of human mortality or of the cost of war than of Achilleus' relationship
to the world of Agamemnon: an ambivalence he has expressed to the Embassy of Greeks in Book
9 and again to Patroklos in Book 16 but has yet to resolve as he returns to battle with the Shield,
divided between resurgent anger and an admiration for Hephaistos' artistry in portraying this
world."

appears at 19.373-80, where it gives rise to a marvelous simile: it gives off a shine (*selas*) like the moon and like a watchfire to one out at sea, driven away from his loved ones by the storm. Then in its final appearance, Aeneas's spear cannot break through the shield (20. 267-72).

Thetis does not pause to look at the shield. Nor does Achilles, nor Hector, when each sees the arms, make any note of the depictions. The depictions on the shield are there for us, not for the characters in the epic. The ekphrasis gives us an aesthetic at work, and that aesthetic emerges as the narrator of the *Iliad* becomes an audience for another's work of art.

# EPILOGUE: A WAY OF
# RESPONDING

*I refer to a way of reading things which Emerson induces in us,
rather than to any ideas or attitudes abstracted from a reading of
him.*

        *- Poirier (1987), p. 192, on our early American bard*

If one responds to the Shield of Achilles with an eye to verbal
representation, noticing the often elusive movement of the language of
description, an inclusive rhetoric emerges.[273] With its attention to the
relations between the referent, the artist, the object, and the perceiver, the
Shield is a lesson in responding to works of art, be they songs or reliefs in
metal. In responding to representations, the Shield encourages us to respect
the particular and peculiar virtues of the image; it enters the illusion of the
image, but at the same time admires its mediating qualities. The Shield,
however, also makes the image its own, translating the image into its own
particular and peculiar virtues. This is analogous to the larger process of the
reader's being appropriated by the *Iliad* (learning to respond to its world and
its ways of understanding that world), and appropriating the *Iliad* (bringing it
into one's own world and one's own ways of understanding).

---

273. This is reading with the help of more than one mode of interpretation: Ricoeur,
rhetoricians, Scholia, Lessing, Edmund Burke, Kenneth Burke, similes and ekphrases from the
*Iliad* and other early Greek poetry, and the levels of description I have developed from the
Shield. Cf. Geertz on Wittgenstein and multiple frames, as quoted in Gunn (1990), p. 102: "What
he said . . . was that the limits of my language are the limits of my world, which implies not that
the reach of our minds, of what we can say, think, appreciate, and judge, is trapped within the
borders of our society, our country, our class, or our time, but that the reach of our minds, the
range of signs we can manage somehow to interpret, is what defines the intellectual, emotional,
and moral space within which we live."

The Shield appropriates visual images by translating them into stories. The translation includes motion, thought, motive, cause and effect, prior and subsequent action, and sound. These emphasize the peculiar virtues of verbal representation; the poem represents the significant, yet invisible and transitory aspects of a scene. The poem can turn an image into a story by describing Hephaestus's creation of these depictions in metal (*ars et artifex*), or by making a story of the referent of the image (*res ipsae*). In these ways the bard has appropriated the images, made them his own. Yet the focus on *res ipsae* can also be read as the ability of the bard to be appropriated by the image. When the description turns to the referent of the visual art and represents it as though it were not a depiction, the description has given itself over to the illusion of the image. In this way the focus on *res ipsae* can be read as respect for the illusionistic qualities or the evocative powers of the work of visual art.[274]

The focus on *res ipsae* in the Shield also attends to color, shape, texture, size, spatial arrangement, and the play of light and dark. These are the peculiar virtues of the visual representation, the areas in which the image enters into a *bequemes Verhältnis*, an iconic relationship, with its referent. The ways in which these features are included in the ekphrasis show respect for the ability of the images to capture significant visible aspects of the world. Such a focus on the world beyond the work celebrates the visual arts in just those areas where they differ from the verbal.

While the Shield makes images into stories, it does not let us forget that they are images; the metallic medium (*opus ipsum*) is part of the picture. This attention to the modality of the visual arts is also respectful; we are not told of the distance between the hard, still metals and the life captured therein, but rather of the exquisite results of the attempt to bridge that distance.[275] Such a focus on the material surface of the shield defamiliarizes

---

274. Cf. the remarks of Yves Bonnefoy (1990), p. 798, *mutatis mutandis*: "Poetry is what descends from level to level in its own ever-changing text, going down to the point where, lost in a land without name or road, it decides to go no further . . .. The text is not poetry's true place; it is only the path it followed a moment earlier, its past. — And if, under these circumstances, someone reads a poem without feeling he [*sic*] must be bound to its text, does this mean that he has betrayed it? Hasn't he rather . . . been faithful to its most specific concern?" So, too, response to a work of representational art, as the images on the shield.

275. This reading of Homeric poetics is similar to that of Poirier (1992), p. 150, quoted above in Chapter 4, in the discussion of the *aegis* of Athena, but worth quoting again: "One virtue of the sound I am describing is, then, that it can create spaces or gaps in ascertained structures of meaning and that it can do so in such a way as simultaneously to create trust and reassurance instead of human separation." And ibid. p. 149: "A deconstructionist argues that when a word is used as the sign of a thing it create's a sense of the thing's absence more than of its presence. This means . . . that the word is not the thing it represents. Language, so the argument goes, can create

the visual medium in a way that emphasizes our respect for its mimetic capability.

For the audience this effect depends upon the viewer, who is the describer, who mediates both the image and the story. This *animadversor* comments on the two levels of mediation between the audience and the world represented on the shield, and so completes the defamiliarization. But this too does not estrange the audience or diminish its ability to be appropriated by the representations. Attention to the medium and the mediator can, in some texts, remind the audience of the absence of the referent, thereby breaking the illusion; but attention to the medium and mediator can also serve to guide the audience, to act as its Vergil to our Dante: the one through whom the audience gains access to the referent. Defamiliarization in the Shield calls attention not to the chasm that separates, but rather the bridges that connect the audience and the represented world.

A complex matrix of ways to respond to an image is not confusion or naive limitation; just as in the first two lines of the *Iliad*, it reveals a rhetoric of inclusion. The audience is brought to consider and admire the relations between each level of mediation represented (and their relations to the audience). Thus the referent is represented, as is the medium, as is the creation and creator of that medium, as is the song of the bard, as is the bard himself, who is both creator (for the audience) and audience (for the artistry and art of Hephaestus). An effect of this is trust in the ability of visual or verbal art to teach us a way of comprehending its or our world.

---

an abyss—a Frostean gap with a vengeance—and writing is constructed on that abyss. Emersonian pragmatists like Frost or Stevens scarcely deny this, but for them the evidence of a gap or an abyss is an invitation simply to get moving and keep moving, to make a transition."

# Bibliography

Ackerman, Diane. 1990. *A Natural History of the Senses*. New York: Random House.

Allen, T.W. 1924. *Homer: The Origins and Transmission*. Oxford: Clarendon Press.

Ameis, K. F., and Hentze, C. 1965 (1908). *Homers* Ilias *fur den Schulgebrauch II.2: Gesang XVI-XVIII. Vierte Berichtigte Auflage*. Amsterdam: Hakkert.

Andersen, Øivind. 1976. Some Thoughts on the Shield of Achilles. *Symbolae Osloenses* 51: 5-18.

Arnheim, Rudolf. 1980. A Plea for Visual Thinking. In *The Language of Images*, ed. W.J.T. Mitchell, pp. 171-179. Chicago and London: University of Chicago Press.

—. 1978. A Stricture on Space and Time. *Critical Inquiry* 4: 645-655.

—. 1976. The Unity of the Arts: Time, Space, and Distance. *Yearbook of Comparative and General Literature* 25: 7-12.

Armstrong, James I. 1958. The Arming Motif in the *Iliad. American Journal of Philology* 79: 337-354.

Arrigon, Robert L. 1960. Symbolism in the Shield of Achilles. *Classical Bulletin* 36: 49-50.

Ashbery, John. 1975. *Self-portrait in a Convex Mirror: Poems*. New York: Viking Press.

Atchity, K.J. 1978. *Homer's* Iliad: *The Shield of Memory*. Carbondale: Southern Illinois Press.

—. 1975. The Power of Words in the *Iliad*. *Classical Outlook* 53: 5-6.

—. 1973. Achilles' Sidonian Bowl. *Classical Outlook* 51: 25-26.

Athanassakis, A.N. 1983. *Hesiod:* Theogony, Works and Days, Shield. Baltimore and London: Johns Hopkins University Press.

Auden, W.H. 1979. *Selected Poems*. Ed. E. Mendelson. New York: Vintage Books.

Auerbach, Eric. 1953 (1946). *Mimesis: The Representation of Reality in Western Literature*. Trans. Willard R. Trask. Princeton, N.J.: Princeton University Press.

Austin, Norman. 1975. *Archery at the Dark of the Moon*. Berkeley, Los Angeles, and London: University of California Press.

—. 1966. The Function of Digressions in the *Iliad. Greek, Roman, and Byzantine Studies* 7: 295-312.

Bakhtin, M.M. 1981. *The Dialogic Imagination: Four Essays*. Ed. M. Holquist; trans. M. Holquist and C. Emerson. Austin: University of Texas Press.

Bal, Mieke. 1991. *Reading Rembrandt: Beyond the Word-Image Opposition*. Cambridge, U.K.: Cambridge University Press.

Barnes, Hazel. 1979. Enjambement and Oral Composition. *Transactions of the American Philological Association* 109: 1-10.

Bartsch, S. . 1989. *Decoding the Ancient Novel: The Reader and the Role of Description in Heliodorus and Achilles Tatius*. Princeton, N.J.: Princeton University Press.

Bassett, Samuel E. 1938. *The Poetry of Homer*. Berkeley, Los Angeles, and London: University of California Press.

—. 1922. The Three Threads of the Plot of the *Iliad. Transactions of the American Philological Association* 53: 52-61.

Baxandall, Michael. 1972. *Painting and Experience in Fifteenth Century Italy*. Oxford: Oxford University Press.

Becker, A.L. 1995. *Beyond Translation: Essays Toward a Modern Philology*. Ann Arbor: University of Michigan Press. (forthcoming)

—. 1992. Silence across Languages: An Essay. In *Text and Context: Cross-disciplinary Perspectives on Language Study*, eds. Claire Kramsch and Sally McConnell-Ginet, pp. 115-123. Lexington, Mass. and Toronto: D.C. Heath.

—. 1991. A Short Essay on Languaging. In *Research and Reflexivity*, ed. Frederick Steier, pp. 226-234. London, U.K., Newbury Park, Calif., and New Delhi, India: Sage Publications.

—. 1989. Aridharma: Framing an Old Javanese Tale. In *Writing on the Tongue*. Michigan Papers on South and Southeast Asia No. 33, ed. A.L. Becker, pp. 281-320. Ann Arbor: Center for South and Southeast Asian Studies, University of Michigan.

—. 1988. Language in Particular: A Lecture. In *Linguistics in Context: Connecting Observation and Understanding*, ed. Deborah Tannen, pp. 17-35. Norwood, N.J.: Ablex Press.

—. 1982. Beyond Translation: Esthetics and Language Description. In *Georgetown University Round Table on Languages and Linguistics '82*, ed. H. Byrnes, pp. 124-138.

—. 1981. On Emerson on Language. In *Georgetown University Round Table on Languages and Linguistics '81*, ed. Deborah Tannen, pp. 1-11.

Becker, A.L., and Yengoyan, A.A., eds. 1979. *The Imagination of Reality: Essays in South East Asian Coherence Systems.* Norwood, N. J.: Ablex Press.

Becker, A. S. 1993a. Sculpture and Language in Early Greek Ekphrasis: Lessing's *Loakoon*, Burke's *Enquiry*, and the Hesiodic Descriptions of Pandora. *Arethusa* 26: 277-293.

—. 1993b. A Short Essay on Plato's *Ion. Electronic Antiquity* 4: 1-8.

—. 1992. Reading Poetry through a Distant Lens: Ecphrasis, Ancient Greek Rhetoricians, and the pseudo-Hesiodic *Shield of Herakles. American Journal of Philology* 113: 5-24.

—. 1992b. Review of L.M. Slatkin, *The Power of Thetis: Allusion and Interpretation in the* Iliad. *Bryn Mawr Classical Review* 3.3: 217-220.

—. 1991. Review of R.A. Prier *The Phenomenology of Sight and Appearance in Archaic Greek. American Journal of Philology* 112: 395-399.

—. 1990. The Shield of Achilles and the Poetics of Homeric Description. *American Journal of Philology* 111: 139-153.

Becker, C. 1964. Der Schild des Aeneas. *Wiener Studien* 77: 111-127.

Becker, Judith O. 1993. *Gamelan Stories: Tantrism, Islam and Aesthetics in Central Java.* Tempe, Ariz.: Arizona State University Press.

—. ed. 1984. *Karawitan: Source Readings in Javanese Gamelan and Vocal Music*, Volume 1. Ann Arbor: Center for South and Southeast Asian Studies, University of Michigan.

—. 1980. *Traditional Music in Modern Java: Gamelan in a Changing Society.* Honolulu: University Press of Hawaii.

Benedetti, M. 1980. Osservasioni su om. σάκος. *Studi i Saggi linguistici*, supplement to *L'Italia Dialettale* 20: 115-162.

Benson, J.L. 1970. *Horse, Bird, and Man: The Origins of Greek Painting.* Amherst: University of Massachusetts Press.

Bergmann, Emilie L. 1979. *Art Inscribed: Essays on Ecphrasis in Spanish Golden Age Poetry.* Harvard Studies in Romance Languages No. 35. Cambridge, Mass., and London: Harvard University Press.

Bergren, Ann. 1979-80. Helen's Web: Time and Tableau in the *Iliad. Helios* 7.1: 19-34.

Beye, Charles R. 1966. *The* Iliad, *the* Odyssey, *and the Epic Tradition.* Garden City, N. Y.: Doubleday.

Bienkowski, P. 1981. Lo scudo di Achille. *Mitteilungen des deutschen archaeologischen Instituts. Romische Abteilung* 6: 183-207.

Bloom, H., ed. 1986. *Homer: Modern Critical Views.* New York: Chelsea House.

Bogan, James. 1992. Virtuous Amusements and Wicked Demons. Unpublished manuscript.

Boivin, Jean. 1970 (1715). *Apologie d'Homere et bouclier d'Achille.* Paris: Francois Jouenne. (Geneva: Slatkine Reprints.)

Boland, Eavan. 1990. *Outside History: Selected Poems 1980-1990.* New York and London: W.W. Norton.

Bolling, G.M. 1958. ΠΟΙΚΙΛΟΣ and ΘΡUΝΑ. *American Journal of Philology* 79: 275-282.

—. 1950. *Ilias Atheniensium: The Athenian* Iliad *of the Sixth Century B.C.* APA and LSA Special Publications. Lancaster, Pa: Lancaster Press.

—. 1944. *The Athetized Lines of the* Iliad. Baltimore: Waverly Press.

Bonnefoy, Yves. 1990. Lifting Our Eyes from the Page. *Critical Inquiry* 16: 794-806.

Borchhardt, H. 1977. Frühe griechische Schildformen. In *Kriegswesen.* Archaeologia Homerica No. I.E.1, eds. H.G. Buchholz and J. Wiesner, pp. 1-56. Göttingen: Vandenhoeck & Ruprecht.

Boulding, Kenneth. 1956. *The Image: Knowledge in Life and Society.* Ann Arbor: University of Michigan Press.

Bowra, C.M. 1972. *Homer.* New York: Charles Scribner's and Sons.

——. 1930. *Tradition and Design in the* Iliad. Oxford: Clarendon Press.

Boyd, Barbara Weiden. 1992. Virgil's Camilla and the Traditions of Catalogue and Ecphrasis (*Aeneid* 7.803-17). *American Journal of Philology* 113: 213-234.

Buchholz, H.-G., and Wiesner, J., eds. 1977. *Kriegswesen.* Archaeologia Homerica No. I.E.1. Göttingen: Vandenhoeck & Ruprecht.

Buhler, W. 1960. *Die Europa des Moschos.* Hermes Einzelschriften No. 13. Wiesbaden: Franz Steiner.

Burke, Edmund. 1968 (1757). *A Philosophical Enquiry into the Origins of Our Ideas of the Sublime and the Beautiful.* Ed. J.T. Boulton. Notre Dame, Ind.: Notre Dame University Press.

Burke, Kenneth. 1973 (1957). *The Philosophy of Literary Form: Studies in Symbolic Action.* Berkeley, Los Angeles, and London: University of California Press.

——. 1969a (1945) *A Grammar of Motives.* Berkeley, Los Angeles, and London: University of California Press.

——. 1969b (1950). *A Rhetoric of Motives.* Berkeley, Los Angeles, and London: University of California Press.

——. 1966. *Language as Symbolic Action: Essays on Life, Literature, and Method.* Berkeley, Los Angeles, and London: University of California Press.

——. 1964. *Perspectives by Incongruity.* Ed. S.E. Hyman. Bloomington: Indiana University Press.

Burkert, Walter. 1992. *The Orientalizing Revolution: Near Eastern Influence on Greek Culture in the Early Archaic Age.* Trans. Margaret E. Pinder and Walter Burkert. Cambridge, Mass., and London: Harvard University Press.

——. 1985. *Greek Religion.* Trans. John Raffan. Cambridge, Mass., and London: Harvard University Press.

Byre, Calvin. 1992. Narration, Description, and Theme in the Shield of Achilles. *Classical Journal* 88: 33-42.

Carter, J. 1972. The Beginning of Narrative Art in the Greek Geometric Period. *Annual of the British School at Athens* 67: 25-58.

Carter, R. and Todorov, T. 1982. *French Literary Theory Today: A Reader.* Cambridge, U.K.: Cambridge University Press.

160   *Bibliography*

Catling, H.W. 1977. Beinschienen. In *Kriegswesen.* Archaeologia Homerica No. I.E.1, eds. H.G. Buchholz and J. Wiesner, pp. 143-161. Göttingen: Vandenhoeck & Ruprecht.

Chantraine, P. 1968-80. *Dictionnnaire étymologique de la langue grecque.* Paris: Klincksieck.

Chaucer, Geoffrey. 1987. *The Riverside Chaucer,* 3rd ed. Ed. L.D. Benson. Boston, Mass.: Houghton Mifflin.

Cheyns, A. 1980. La notion de *phrenes* dans l'*Iliade* et l'*Odyssée,* I. *Cahiers de l' Institut de linguistique de Louvain* 6, 3-4: 121-202.

Coffey, Michael. 1957. The Homeric Simile. *American Journal of Philology* 78: 113-132.

Coleridge. S.T. 1965. *Biographia literaria.* Ed. J.T. Shawcross. London: Oxford University Press.

—. 1956. *Collected Letters of Samuel Taylor Coleridge,* Volume 1. Ed. E.L. Griggs. Oxford: Clarendon Press.

Conte, Gian Biagio. 1986. *The Rhetoric of Imitation: Genre and Poetic Memory in Virgil and Other Latin Poets.* Ithaca, N.Y., and London: Cornell University Press.

Cook, A. 1984. Visual Aspects of the Homeric Simile in Indo-European Context. *Quaderni Urbinati di Cultura Classica* 46, n.s. 17: 39-59.

Cook, E. . 1986. *Seeing through Words: The Scope of Late Renaissance Poetry.* New Haven, Conn., and London: Yale University Press.

Cook, R.M. 1937. The Date of the Hesiodic *Shield. Classical Quarterly* 31: 204-214.

cummings, e.e. 1923. *One Hundred Selected Poems.* New York: Grove Press.

Cunliffe, R.J. 1963. *A Lexicon to the Homeric Dialect.* Norman: Oklahoma University Press.

Dällenbach, L. 1989. *The Mirror in the Text.* Trans. J. Whiteley and E. Hughes. Chicago and London: University of Chicago Press.

da Vinci, Leonardo. 1956. *Treatise on Painting,* volume 1. Trans. A.P. McMahon. Princeton, N.J.: Princeton University Press.

de Jong, I.J.F. 1991. Narratology and Oral Poetry: The Case of Homer. *Poetics Today* 12: 405-423.

—. 1987. *Narrators and Focalizers: The Presentation of the Story in the* Iliad. Amsterdam: Benjamins.

de Jonge, P., ed. 1955. *Ut Pictura Poesis: Studia Latina P.I. Enk Septuagenario Oblata.* Leiden: E.J. Brill.

Denniston, J.D. 1951. *The Greek Particles*, 2nd ed. Oxford: Clarendon Press.

Dewey, John. 1980 (1934). *Art as Experience.* New York: Perigee Books.

Dio Chrysostom. 1992. *Orations VII, XII, XXXVI.* Ed. D.A. Russell. Cambridge, U.K.: Cambridge University Press.

Doherty, Lillian Eileen. 1992. Gender and Internal Audiences in the *Odyssey. American Journal of Philology* 113: 161-177.

—. 1991. The Internal and Implied Audiences of *Odyssey* 11. *Arethusa* 24: 145-176.

Dolders, Arno. 1983. Ut Pictura Poesis: A Selective, Annotated Bibliography of Books and Articles, Published between 1900 and 1980, on the Inter-relation of Literature and Painting from 1400 to 1800. *Yearbook of Comparative and General Literature* 32: 105-124.

Donahue, A.A. 1988. *Xoana and the Origins of Greek Sculpture.* American Classical Studies No. 15. Atlanta: Scholars Press.

Downey, G. 1959. Ekphrasis. In *Reallexicon fur Antike und Christentum: Sachworterbuch zur Auseinandersetzung des Christentums mit der Antiken Welt*, Volume 4, ed. Theodor Krauser, columns 922-944. Stuttgart: Anton Hiersemann.

Drury, Maurice O'C. 1984. Some Notes on Conversations with Wittgenstein. In *Recollections of Wittgenstein*, ed. Rush Rhees. Oxford: Oxford University Press.

du Bos, Jean Baptiste . 1755. *Réflexions critiques sur la poèsie et sur la peinture.* Paris: Pissot. (First published anonymously in 1719).

DuBois, P. 1982. *History, Rhetorical Description, and the Epic.* Cambridge, U.K.: Cambridge University Press.

Duethorn, Guenter. 1962. *Achilles' Shield and the Structure of the* Iliad. Amherst, Mass.: Amherst College Press.

Dundas, Judith. 1993. *Pencils Rhetorique: Renaissance Poets and the Art of Painting.* Newark: University of Delaware Press.

Durante, M. 1960. Richerche sulla preistorica della lingua poetica greca. La terminologie relativa alla creazione poetica. *Rendiconti dell' Academia dei Lincei, classe di scienze morali, storiche et filologiche* 15: 238-244.

Easterling, P.E. 1989. Agamemnon's *Skêptron* in the *Iliad.* In *Images of Authority: Papers Presented to Joyce Reynolds on the Occasion of Her Seventieth*

*Birthday*, eds. M.M. Mackenzie and C. Roueché, pp. 104-121. Cambridge, U.K.: Cambridge University Press.

Easterling, P.E., and Knox, B.M.W. 1985. *The Cambridge History of Classical Literature, Volume 1: Greek Literature.* Cambridge, U.K.: Cambridge University Press.

Edgecombe, Rodney Stenning. 1993. A Typology of Ecphrases. *Classical and Modern Literature* 13.2: 103-116.

Edwards, Mark W. 1991. *The* Iliad*: A Commentary*, Volume V, books 17-20. Cambridge, U.K.: Cambridge University Press.

—. 1987. *Homer, Poet of the* Iliad. Baltimore and London: Johns Hopkins University Press.

—. 1968. Some Stylistic Notes on *Iliad* XVIII. *American Journal of Philology* 89: 257-283.

—. 1966. Some Features of Homeric Craftsmanship. *Transactions of the American Philological Association* 97: 115-179.

Edwards, R. 1989. *The Dream of Chaucer: Representation and Reflection in the Early Narratives.* Durham, N.C., and London: Duke University Press.

Emerson, Ralph Waldo. 1951. *Emerson's Essays: First and Second Series Complete in One Volume.* Introduction by Irwin Edman. New York: Harper and Row.

Empson, William. 1974. *Some Versions of the Pastoral.* New York: New Directions.

Erbse, H., ed. 1969-1988. *Scholia Graeca in Homeri* Iliadem *(Scholia Vetera).* Volumes 1-7. Berlin: Walter de Gruyter.

Eustathius. 1976. *Eustathii Archiepiscopi Thessalonicensis Commentarii ad Homeri* Iliadem *Pertinentes.* Ed. Marchinus Van Der Valk. Leiden: E.J.Brill.

Evelyn-White, H.G. 1914. *Hesiod, the Homeric Hymns, and Homerica.* Cambridge, Mass., and London: Harvard University Press.

Evett, D. 1991. *Literature and the Visual Arts in Tudor England.* Athens, Ga.: University of Georgia Press.

Feldman, B. 1968. Homers andere Welt: Der Schild des Akhilleus. *Antaios* 10: 76-90.

Felperin, Howard. 1985. *Beyond Deconstruction: The Uses and Abuses of Literary Theory.* Oxford: Clarendon Press.

Fenik, B.C. 1968. *Typical Battle Scenes in the* Iliad. Wiesbaden: Franz Steiner.

Fernández-Vázquez, Antonio A. 1983. The Ekphrastic Principle and Transubstantiation in Paz's "Custodia." *Critica Hispanica* 5,1: 1-11.

Fish, S. 1972. *Self-consuming Artifacts: The Experience of Seventeenth Century Literature.* Berkeley, Los Angeles, and London: University of California Press.

Fittschen, Klaus. 1973. *Der Schild des Achilleus.* Archaeologia Homerica No. II.N.1. Göttingen: Vandenhoeck & Ruprecht.

Ford, Andrew. 1992. *Homer: The Poetry of the Past.* Ithaca, N.Y., and London: Cornell University Press.

Forderer, M. 1965. Der Sanger in der homerischen Schildbeschreibung. In *Synousia: Festgabe fur W. Schadewaldt zum 15 Marz 1965,* eds. H. Flashar and K. Gaiser, pp. 23-27. Pfulligen: Gunther Neske.

—. 1955. Der Schild des Achilleus und der Lobgesang im Feuerofen. *Studium Generale* 8: 294-301.

Foucault, M. 1970. *The Order of Things: An Archaeology of the Human Sciences.* New York: Random House.

Fowler, Barbara H. 1984. The Archaic Aesthetic. *American Journal of Philology* 105: 119-149.

Fowler, D.P. 1991. Narrate and Describe: The Problem of Ekphrasis. *Journal of Roman Studies* 81: 25-35.

—. 1990. Deviant Focalisation in Virgil's *Aeneid. Proceedings of the Cambridge Philological Society* 216, n.s. 36: 42-63.

Frank, Joseph. 1977. Spatial Form: An Answer to Critics. *Critical Inquiry* 4: 231-252.

—. 1968. *The Widening Gyre: Crisis and Mastery in Modern Literature.* Bloomington: Indiana University Press.

Fränkel, Hermann. 1975. *Early Greek Poetry and Philosophy.* Trans. M. Hadas and J. Willis. Oxford: Basil Blackwell.

—. 1921. *Die homerische Gleichnisse.* Göttingen: Vandenhoeck & Ruprecht.

Friedländer, Paul. 1912. *Johannes von Gaza, Paulus Silentiarius, und Kunstbeschreibungen justinianischer Zeit.* Leipzig: Teubner.

Furbank, P.N. 1991. Diderot's Dream. *Raritan* 11,1: 1-9.

Gärtner, H.A. 1976. Beobachtungen zum Schild des Achilleus. In *Studien zum antiken Epos.* Beiträge zur klassischen Philologie No. 72, eds. H. Görgemanns and E.A. Schmidt, pp. 46-65. Meisenheim am Glan: Hain.

Geertz, Clifford. 1988. *Works and Lives: The Anthropologist as Author*. Stanford, Calif.: Stanford University Press.

———. 1983. *Local Knowledge: Further Essays in Interpretive Anthropology*. New York: Basic Books.

———. 1973. *The Interpretation of Cultures*. New York: Basic Books.

Gentili, Bruno. 1988. *Poetry and Its Public in Ancient Greece from Homer to the Fifth Century*. Trans. and with intro. by A. Thomas Cole. Baltimore and London: Johns Hopkins University Press.

Gide, André. 1947. *Prétextes: réflexions sur quelques points de littérature et de morale*. Paris: Mercure de France.

Gifford, Don. 1991. *The Farther Shore: A Natural History of Perception, 1798-1984*. New York: Vintage.

Givón, Talmy. 1979. *On Understanding Grammar*. New York: Academic Press.

Goff, Barbara. 1988. Euripides' *Ion* 1132-1165: The Tent. *Proceedings of the Cambridge Philological Society* 214, n.s. 34: 42-54.

Goldhill, Simon. 1986. Framing and Polyphony: Readings in Hellenistic Poetry. *Proceedings of the Cambridge Philological Society* 212, n.s. 32: 25-52.

Gottlieb, Carla. 1958. Movement in Painting. *Journal of Aesthetics and Art Criticism* 17: 22-33.

Gow, A.S.F., ed. 1952. *Bucolici Graeci*. Oxford: Clarendon Press.

Graff, G. 1987. *A Dictionary of Narratology*. Norman, Okla., and London: University of Oklahoma Press.

Gray, D.H. 1954. Metal-working in Homer. *Journal of Hellenic Studies* 74: 1-15.

Graz, Louis. 1965. *Le feu dans l'Iliade et l'Odyssée*. Paris: Klincksieck.

Gregory, Horace. 1970 (1944). *The Shield of Achilles: Essays on Beliefs in Poetry*. Westport, Conn.: Greenwood Press.

Griffin, Jasper. 1980. *Homer on Life and Death*. Oxford: Clarendon Press.

Gross, Kenneth. 1992. *The Dream of the Moving Statue*. Ithaca, N.Y., and London: Cornell University Press.

———. 1989. Moving Statues, Talking Statues. *Raritan* 9,2: 1-25.

Gunn, Giles. 1990. Rorty's *Novum Organum*. *Raritan* 10,1: 80-103.

Hagstrum, Jean H. 1958. *The Sister Arts: The Tradition of Literary Pictorialism and English Poetry from Dryden to Gray.* Chicago and London: University of Chicago Press.

Hainsworth, Bryan. 1993. *The* Iliad: *A Commentary,*Volume 3, books 9-12. Cambridge, U.K.: Cambridge University Press.

Halbfas, Franz. 1910. Theorie und Praxis in der Geschichtsschreibung bei Dionys von Halikarnass. Westfälischen Wilhelms-Universität Ph.D. dissertation.

Hall, Aimée. 1992. Unpublished poems.

Halm, C. 1964 (1863). *Rhetores Latini Minores.* Dubuque, Iowa: Wm. C. Brown.

Hammond, Mason. 1987. *Homer. The* Iliad: *A New Prose Translation.* New York: Penguin Books.

Hammond, N.G.L., and Scullard, H.H. 1970. *The Oxford Classical Dictionary,* 2nd ed. Oxford: Clarendon Press.

Hamon, P. 1981. *Introduction à l'analyse du descriptif.* Paris: Hachette.

—. 1972. Qu'est-ce qu'une description? *Poétique* 12: 465-485, translated in *French Literary theory Today: A Reader,* eds. R. Carter and T. Todorov, pp. 147-178. Cambridge, U.K.: Cambridge University Press, 1982.

Hampe, R. 1952. *Die Gleichnisse Homers und die Bildkunst seiner Zeit.* Tübingen: Max Niemeyer Verlag.

Hardie, P.R. 1985. Imago Mundi: Cosmological and Theological Aspects of the Shield of Achilles. *Journal of Hellenic Studies* 105: 11-31.

Harlan, Eva C. 1965. The Description of Painting as a Literary Device and Its Application in Achilles Tatius. Columbia University Ph.D. Dissertation.

Harrison, E.B. 1981. Motifs of the City-Siege on the Shield of Athena Parthenos. *American Journal of Archaeology* 85: 281-317.

Havelock, Eric A. 1986. *The Muse Learns to Write: Reflections on Orality and Literacy from Antiquity to the Present.* New Haven, Conn., and London: Yale University Press.

Hawkes, Terence. 1977. *Structuralism and Semiotics.* Berkeley, Los Angeles, and London: University of California Press.

Hawthorne, Nathaniel. 1981 (1851). *The House of the Seven Gables.* New York: Bantam Books.

Heaney, Seamus. 1991. *Seeing Things.* New York: Farrar, Strauss, and Giroux.

Heath, Malcolm. 1989. *Unity in Greek Poetics*. Oxford: Clarendon Press.

Heffernan, James A.W. 1993. *Museum of Words: The Poetics of Ekphrasis from Homer to Ashbery*. Chicago and London: University of Chicago Press.

—, ed. 1987. *Space, Time, Image Sign: Essays on Literature and the Visual Arts*. New York, Bern, Frankfurt am Main, Paris: Peter Lang.

—. 1984. *The Re-creation of Landscape: A Study of Wordsworth, Coleridge, Constable, and Turner*. Hanover, N.H., and London: University Press of New England.

—. 1979. Reflections on Reflections in English Romantic Poetry and Painting. In *The Arts and Their Interrelations*., ed. Harry R. Garvin. Lewisburg, Pa.: Bucknell University Press.

Herodas. 1922. *The Mimes and Fragments*. With notes by Walter Headlam; ed. A.D. Knox. Cambridge, U.K.: Cambridge University Press. (Reprinted, New York: Arno Press., 1979.)

Heubeck, A., and Hoekstra, A. 1989. *A Commentary on Homer's* Odyssey, Volume 2, books 9-16. Oxford: Clarendon Press.

Heubeck, A., West, S., and Hainsworth, J.B. 1988. *A Commentary on Homer's* Odyssey, Volume 1, introduction and books 1-8. Oxford: Clarendon Press.

Higbie, Carolyn. 1990. *Measure and Music: Enjambement and Sentence Structure in the* Iliad. Oxford: Clarendon Press.

Holtz, William. 1977. Spatial Form in Modern Literature: A Reconsideration. *Critical Inquiry* 4: 276-280.

Holub, Robert C. 1984. *Reception Theory: A Critical Introduction*. London and New York: Metheun.

Hommel, H. 1969. *Politeia und Res Publica: Beiträge zum Verständnis von Politik, Recht, und Staat in der Antike*, ed. P. Steinmetz, pp. 11-38. Wiesbaden: Franz Steiner.

Howatson, M.C. 1989. *The Oxford Companion to Classical Literature*, 2nd ed. Oxford: Oxford University Press.

Howe, T.P. 1954. The Origin and Function of the Gorgon-Head. *American Journal of Archaeology* 58: 209-221.

Hubbard, T.K. 1992. Nature and Art in the Shield of Achilles. *Arion* 2: 16-41.

Hurwit, Jeffrey M. 1985. *The Art and Culture of Early Greece 1100-480*. Ithaca, N.Y., and London: Cornell University Press.

Irwin, Eleanor. 1974. *Colour Terms in Greek Poetry*. Toronto: A.M. Hakkert.

Iser, W. 1974. *The Implied Reader*. Baltimore and London: Johns Hopkins University Press.

Janko, Richard. 1992. *The Iliad: A Commentary*, Volume 4, books 13-16. Cambridge, U.K.: Cambridge University Press.

—. 1986. The Shield of Herakles and the Legend of Cycnus. *Classical Quarterly* 36: 38-59.

—. 1982. *Homer, Hesiod, and the Hymns*. Cambridge, U.K.: Cambridge University Press.

Johansen, K. Friis. 1967. *The Iliad in Early Greek Art*. Copenhagen: Munksgaard.

Johnson, Michael L. 1989. *Ecphrases: Poems as Interpretations of the Other Arts*. Topeka, Kans.: Woodley Press.

Kahane, Ahuvia. 1992. The First Word of the *Odyssey*. *Transactions of the American Philological Association* 122: 115-131.

Kakrides, J. Th. 1971. Imagined Ecphrases: Homer Revisited. *Publications of the New Society of Letters at Lund* 64: 108-124.

Kakridis, P.J. 1961. Achilleus Rustung. *Hermes* 89: 288-297.

Kannicht, Richard. 1982. Poetry and Art: Homer and the Monuments Afresh. *Classical Antiquity* 1: 70-86.

Kassel, R. and Austin, C., eds. 1983. *Poetae Comici Graeci*, Volume 4: *Aristophon - Crobylus*. Berlin and New York: Walter de Gruyter.

Katz, Marilyn A. 1991. *Penelope's Renown: Meaning and Indeterminacy in the* Odyssey. Princeton, N.J.: Princeton University Press.

Kennedy, George A., ed. 1989a. *The Cambridge History of Literary Criticism*, Volume 1: *Classical Criticism*. Cambridge, U.K.: Cambridge University Press.

—. 1989b Ancient Antecedents of Modern Literary Theory. *American Journal of Philology* 110: 492-498.

—. 1986. Helen's Web Unraveled. *Arethusa* 19: 5-14.

—. 1983. *Greek Rhetoric under Christian Emperors*. Princeton, N.J.: Princeton Unversity Press.

Kermode, Frank. 1985. *Forms of Attention*. Chicago and London: University of Chicago Press

Kirk, G.S. 1990. *The* Iliad: *A Commentary*, Volume 2, books 5-8. Cambridge, U.K.: Cambridge University Press.

——. 1985. *The* Iliad: *A Commentary,*Volume 1, books 1-4. Cambridge, U.K.: Cambridge University Press.

——. 1966. Verse-Structure and Sentence-Structure in Homer. *Yale Classical Studies* 20: 75-152.

Knight, Virginia. 1991. The Depiction of Scenes from Epic in the *Eikones* of the Younger Philostratus. Unpublished manuscript.

Köstler, R. 1946. Die Gerichtsszene auf dem Achilleusschild. *Anzeiger der Osterreichischen Akademie der Wissenschaften in Wien* 83: 213-227.

Kramer, O.C. 1976. Speech and Silence in the *Iliad. Classical Journal* 71: 300-304.

Krieger, Murray. 1992. *Ekphrasis: The Illusion of the Natural Sign.* Baltimore and London: Johns Hopkins University Press.

——. 1967. *The Play and the Place of Criticism.* Baltimore and London: Johns Hopkins University Press.

Kriegler, Helga. 1969. *Untersuchungen zu der optischen und akustischen Daten der bacchylideischen Dichtung.* Vienna: Verlag Notring.

Kühner, R., and Gerth, B. 1966 (1904). *Ausführliche Grammatik der griechischen Sprache.* Darmstadt: Wissenschaftliche Buchgesellschaft.

Kurman, G. 1974. Ecphrasis in Epic Poetry. *Comparative Literature* 26: 1-13.

Langer, Suzanne. 1957. *Problems of Art.* New York: Scribners.

Lanham, R. 1976. *The Motives of Eloquence: Literary Rhetoric in the Renaissance.* New Haven, Conn., and London: Yale University Press.

Leach, E.W. 1988. *The Rhetoric of Space: Literary and Artistic Representations of Landscape in Republican and Augustan Rome.* Princeton, N.J.: Princeton University Press.

Leaf, Walter. 1887. The Trial Scene in *Iliad* XVIII. *Journal of Hellenic Studies* 8: 122-132.

Lee, D. J. N. 1964. *The Similes of the* Iliad *and the* Odyssey *Compared.* Melbourne, Australia: Melbourne University Press.

Lee, R.W. 1940. *Ut Pictura Poesis*: The Humanistic Theory of Painting. *Art Bulletin* 22: 197-269.

Lentricchia, F. and McLaughlin, T. 1990. *Critical Terms for Literary Study*. Chicago and London: University of Chicago Press.

Lesky, Albin. 1966. Bildwerk und Deutung bei Philostrat und Homer. In *Gesammelte Schriften: Aufsatze und Reden zu Antiker und Deutscher Dichtung und Kultur*, ed. Walter Kraus, pp. 11-25. Berne and Muncher: A. Francke.

Lessing, G.E. 1988 (1766). *Laokoon: oder über die Grenzen der Malerei und Poesie*. Ed. Kurt Wölfel. Frankfurt am Main: Insel Verlag.

—. 1984. Laokoon: *On the Limits of Painting and Poetry*. Trans. E.A. McCormick. Baltimore and London: Johns Hopkins University Press.

Liddell, H., Scott, R., and Jones, H.S. 1940. *A Greek-English Lexicon*, 9th ed. Oxford: Clarendon Press.

Liebschutz, P. 1953. La contexture du Bouclier d'Achille dans l'*Iliade. Bulletin de l'Association Guillaume Budé* 2: 6-7.

"Longinus." 1964. *On the Sublime*. Ed. with intro. and comm. by D.A. Russell. Oxford: Clarendon Press.

Lonsdale, S.H. 1990a. Simile and Ecphrasis in Homer and Virgil: The Poet as Craftsman and Choreographer. *Vergilius* 36: 7-30.

—. 1990b. *Lion, Herding, and Hunting Similes in the* Iliad. Stuttgart: B.G. Teubner.

Lord, A.B. 1960. *The Singer of Tales*. Cambridge, Mass.: Harvard University Press.

Lorimer, H.L. 1950. *Homer and the Monuments*. London: MacMillan.

—. 1929. Homer's Use of the Past. *Journal of Hellenic Studies* 49: 145-159.

Lowenstam, Steven. 1993a. The Pictures on Juno's Temple in the *Aeneid. Classical World* 87: 37-49.

—. 1993b. *The Scepter and the Spear: Studies on Forms of Repetition in the Homeric Poems*. Lanham, Md: Rowman & Littlefield.

—. 1992. The Uses of Vase-Depictions in Homeric Studies. *Transactions of the American Philological Association* 122: 165-198.

Lukacs, Georg. 1962. To Narrate or Describe. In *Homer: A Collection of Critical Essays*, eds. George Steiner and Robert Fagles, pp. 86-89. Englewood Cliffs, N.J.: Prentice Hall.

Lynn-George, J.M. 1978. The Relationship of Σ 535-540 and *Scutum* 156-160 Re-examined. *Hermes* 106: 396-405.

Lynn-George, Michael. 1988. *Epos: Word, Narrative and the* Iliad. London: Macmillan.

McClain, Jeoraldean. 1985. Time in the Visual Arts: Lessing and Modern Criticism. *Journal of Aesthetics and Art Criticism* 44: 41-58.

McClatchy, J.D. 1990. The Shield of Herakles. *Raritan* 9,3: 24-26.

Macleod, Colin. 1983. *Collected Essays*. Oxford: Clarendon Press.

Maguire, Henry. 1981. *Art and Eloquence in Byzantium*. Princeton, N.J.: Princeton University Press.

Manakidou, Flora. 1993. *Beschreibung von Kunstwerken in der hellenistischen Dichtung*. Stuttgart and Leipzig: B.G. Teubner.

Marg, Walter. 1957. *Homer über die Dichtung*. Orbis Antiquus No. 11. Münster: Aschendorffsche Verlagsbuchhandlung.

Marinatos, Spyridon. 1967. *Kleidung, Haar- und Barttracht*. Archaeologia Homerica No. I.A and B. Göttingen: Vandenhoeck & Ruprecht.

Markoe, G. 1985. *Phoenician Bronze and Silver Bowls from Cyprus and the Mediterranean*. Berkeley, Los Angeles, and London: University of California Press.

Mason, Jeff. 1989. *Philosophical Rhetoric: the Function of Indirection in Philosophical Writing*. London and New York: Routledge.

Meijering, Roos. 1987. *Literary and Rhetorical Theories in Greek Scholia*. Gröningen: Egbert Forsten.

Meltzer, F. 1987. *Salome and the Dance of Writing*. Chicago and London: University of Chicago Press.

Melville, Herman. 1992 (1851). *Moby-Dick*. Rutland, VT. and London: Charles E. Tuttle and J.M. Dent.

Merwin, W.S. 1988. *Selected Poems*. New York: Atheneum.

Miles, J.C. 1945. A Note on *Iliad* XVIII, 497-508. *Hermathena* 65: 92-93.

Miller, Arthur. 1987. *Timebends: A Life*. New York: Grove Press.

Miller, G. and Johnson-Laird, P.N. 1976. *Language and Perception*. Cambridge, Mass., and London: Harvard University Press.

Mitchell, W.J.T. 1986. *Iconology: Image, Text, Ideology*. Chicago and London: University of Chicago Press.

—, ed. 1980. *The Language of Images*. Chicago and London: University of Chicago Press.

Monro, D.B. 1897. *Homer* Iliad: *Books XIII-XXIV*, 4th ed. Oxford: Clarendon Press.

Monro, D.B., and Allen, T.W. 1920. *Homeri Opera I and II*, 3rd ed. Oxford: Clarendon Press

Moon, Warren G., ed. 1983. *Ancient Greek Art and Iconography*. Madison: University of Wisconsin Press.

Moran, R. 1989. Seeing and Believing: Metaphor, Image, and Force. *Critical Inquiry* 16: 87-112.

Morard, A. 1965. Le bouclier d'Achille. *Bulletin de l'Association Guillaume Budé* 3: 348-359.

Morris, Sarah P. 1992. *Daidalos and the Origins of Greek Art*. Princeton, N.J.: Princeton University Press.

Morrison, Toni. 1992. *Playing in the Dark: Whiteness and the Literary Imagination*. New York: Vintage Books.

Moulton, Carroll. 1977. *Similes in the Homeric Poems*. Hypomnemata No. 49. Göttingen: Vandenhoeck & Ruprecht.

Muellner, L. 1976. *The Meaning of Homeric* Euxomai *through Its Formulas*. Innsbruck: Innsbrucker Beiträge zur Sprachwissenschaft.

Munding, H. 1961-62. Die Bewertung der Rechtsidee in der *Ilias*. *Philologus* 105: 161-177 and 106: 60-74.

Myres, J.L. 1945. Blood-fued and Justice in Homer and Aeschylus. *Classical Review* 59: 10.

—. 1941. Hesiod's *Shield of Herakles*: Its Structure and Workmanship. *Journal of Hellenic Studies* 61: 17-30.

—. 1930. *Who Were the Greeks?* Sather Classical Lectures VI. Berkeley, Los Angeles, and London: University of California Press.

Nagy, Gregory. 1992. Homeric Questions. *Transactions of the American Philological Association* 122: 17-60.

—. 1990a. *Greek Mythology and Poetics*. Ithaca, N.Y., and London: Cornell University Press.

—. 1990b. *Pindar's Homer: The Lyric Possession of an Epic Past*. Baltimore and London: Johns Hopkins University Press.

—. 1979. *The Best of the Achaeans: Concepts of the Hero in Archaic Greek Poetry.* Baltimore and London: Johns Hopkins University Press.

Nemerov, Howard. 1972-73. The Painter Dreaming in the Scholar's House. *The Structurist* 12: 38

Nenci, G. 1963. Il guidice nei poemi omerici. *Giustizia e Societa* 1963: 1-6.

Nicosia, Salvatore. 1968. *Teocrito e l'Arte Figurata.* Quaderni Dell'Istituto Di Filologia Greca Della Universita di Palermo No. 5.

Niemirska-Pliszczynska, J. 1964. Quid scutum in *Iliade* atque *Aeneide* descriptum valeat. *Eos* 54: 217-224.

Notopoulos, J.A. 1957. Homer and Geometric Art. *Athena* 61: 65-93.

O'Malley, Glenn. 1957. Literary Synaesthesia. *Journal of Aesthetics and Art Criticism* 15: 391-411.

Ong, Walter J., S.J. 1982. *Orality and Literacy: The Technologizing of the Word.* London and New York: Methuen.

—. 1977. *Interfaces of the Word.* Ithaca, N.Y., and London: Cornell University Press.

—. 1967. *The Presence of the Word.* New Haven, Conn., and London: Yale University Press.

Onians, J. 1980. Abstraction and Imagination in Late Antiquity. *Art History* 3: 1-23.

Ortega y Gasset, José. 1983. Miseria y Esplendor de la Traduccion. *Obras Completas,* Volume 5, pp. 431-452. Madrid: Alianza Editorial. (Translated in *Theories of Translation: An Anthology of Essays from Dryden to Derrida*, eds. Rainer Schulte and John Biguenet, pp. 93-112. Chicago and London: University of Chicago Press, 1992.

—. 1968. *The Dehumanization of Art and Other Essays on Art, Culture, and Literature.* Princeton, N.J.: Princeton University Press.

—. 1959. The Difficulty of Reading. *Diogenes* 28: 1-17.

—. 1957. *Man and People.* Trans. Willard R. Trask. London and New York: W.W. Norton.

Pack, R., Lea, S., and Parini, J., eds. 1985. *The Breadloaf Anthology of Contemporary American Poetry.* Hanover, N.H., and London: University Press of New England.

Pallis, A. 1930. *The "Σ" Rhapsody.* Oxford: Oxford University Press.

Palm, J. 1965-66. Bemerkungen zur Ekphrase in der griechischen Literatur. *Kungliga Humanistika Vetenskapssamfundet i Uppsala, Årsbok*, pp. 109-211.

Papillon, T.L. 1989. Text and Context in Pindar's *Isthmian* 8.70. *American Journal of Philology* 110: 1-9.

Papini, M. 1983. Lo scudo di Achilleus: Appunti per una nuova interpretazione. *Annali della Facoltà di Lettere e Filosofia dell' Università di Siena* 4: 261-273.

Pasquali, Giorgio. 1952. *Storia della tradizione e critica del testo*. Florence: Felice Le Monnier.

Peabody, Berkeley. 1975. *The Winged Word: A Study of the Technique of Ancient Greek Oral Composition as Seen Principally through Hesiod's* Works and Days. Albany: State University of New York Press.

Peirce, Charles Sanders. 1931-58. *Collected Works*. Ed. C. Hartshorn and P. Weiss. Cambridge, Mass.: Harvard University Press.

Peradotto, John. 1990. *Man in the Middle Voice: Name and Narration in the* Odyssey. Princeton, N.J.: Princeton University Press.

Perutelli, Alessandro. 1978. L'inversione speculare: per una retorica dell' ekphrasis. *Materiali e Discussioni per l'analisi dei testi classici* 1: 87-98.

Pfeiffer, Rudolf. 1968. *History of Classical Scholarship from the Beginnings to the End of the Hellenistic Age*. Oxford: Clarendon Press.

Pflüger, H.H. 1942. Die Gerichtsszene auf dem Schilde des Achilleus. *Hermes* 77: 140-148.

Poirier, Richard. 1992. *Poetry and Pragmatism*. Cambridge, Mass.: Harvard University Press.

—. 1987. *The Renewal of Literature: Emersonian Reflections*. New Haven, Conn., and London: Yale Unversity Press.

Pollitt, J.J. 1974. *The Ancient View of Greek Art*. New Haven, Conn., and London: Yale University Press.

Pope, Alexander. 1963. The Poems of Alexander Pope. Ed. John Butt. New Haven: Yale University Press.

—. trans. 1796. *The* Iliad *of Homer*. Ed. G. Wakefield. London: Baldwin Press.

Pound, Ezra. 1987 (1934). *ABC of Reading*. New York: New Direction Press.

Praz, M. 1970. *Mnemosyne: The Parallel between Literature and the Visual Arts*. Princeton, N.J.: Princeton University Press.

Preminger, A., and Brogan, T.V.F., eds. 1993. *The New Princeton Encyclopedia of Poetry and Poetics.* Princeton, N.J.: Princeton University Press.

Prier, R.A. 1989. *Thauma Idesthai: The Phenomenology of Sight and Appearance in Archaic Greek.* Tallahassee: Florida State University Press.

Pucci, Pietro. 1987. *Odysseus Polutropos: Intertextual Readings in the* Odyssey *and* Iliad. Ithaca, N.Y., and London: Cornell University Press.

Rabel, R.J. 1989. The Shield of Achilleus and the Death of Hector. *Eranos* 87: 81-90.

Rabkin, Eric S. 1977. Spatial Form and Plot. *Critical Inquiry* 4: 253-254.

Redfield, James. 1979. The Proem of the *Iliad:* Homer's Art. *Classical Philology* 74: 95-110.

Reinhardt, Karl. 1961. *Die Ilias und ihr Dichter.* Göttingen: Vandenhoek & Ruprecht.

Richardson, Nicholas. 1993. *The* Iliad: *A Commentary,* Volume 6, books 21-24. Cambridge, U.K.: Cambridge University Press.

Richardson, Scott. 1990. *The Homeric Narrator.* Nashville: Vanderbilt University Press.

Richter, W. 1968. *Die Landwirtschaft im homerischen Zeitalter.* Archaeologia Homerica No. II.H. Göttingen: Vandenhoeck & Ruprecht.

Ricoeur, P. 1981. *Hermeneutics and the Human Sciences: Essays on language, action, and interpretation.* Cambridge, U.K.: Cambridge University Press.

Ridgeway, W. 1885. The Homeric Land System. *Journal of Hellenic Studies* 6: 319-339.

—. 1887. The Homeric Talent: Its Origin, Value, and Affinities. *Journal of Hellenic Studies* 8: 133-158.

Riffaterre, Michael. 1986. Textuality: W.H. Auden's "Musée des Beaux Arts." In *Textual Analysis: Some Readers Reading,* ed. Mary Ann Caws, pp. 1-13. New York: Modern Languages Association of America.

Ritoók, Z. 1989. The Views of Early Greek Epic on Poetry and Art. *Mnemosyne* 42: 331-348

Robbe-Grillet, Alain. 1983. *Dans le labyrinthe.* Ed. with an intro. and notes by David Meakin. Oxford: Basil Blackwell.

—. 1963. *Pour un nouveau roman.* Paris: Les éditions de minuit.

Roberts, M. 1989. *The Jeweled Style: Poetry and Poetics in Late Antiquity.* Ithaca, N.Y., and London: Cornell University Press.

Roisman, Hanna M., and Roisman, Joseph, eds. 1993. Essays on Homeric Epic. *Colby Quarterly 29,3.*

Romm, James S. 1992. *The Ends of the Earth in Ancient Thought.* Princeton, N.J.: Princeton University Press.

Rosand, D. 1990. Ekphrasis and the Generation of Images. *Arion* 1: 61-105.

Rosenmeyer, T.G. 1988. *Deina Ta Polla: A Classicist's Checklist of Twenty Literary-Critical Positions.* Arethusa Monographs No. 12. Buffalo, N.Y.: Department of Classics, SUNY Buffalo.

Ross, Haj (John Robert). 1985. Languages as Poems. *Georgetown University Round Table on Languages and Linguistics '85,* eds. Deborah Tannen and J.E. Alatis, pp. 180-204.

—. 1982. Human Linguistics. *Georgetown University Round Table on Languages and Linguistics '82,* ed. H. Byrnes, pp. 1-30.

Roston, M. 1990. *Changing Perspectives in Literature and the Visual Arts 1650-1820.* Princeton, N.J.: Princeton University Press.

Rowell, Henry T. 1947. The Original Form of Naevius' *Bellum Punicum. American Journal of Philology* 68: 21-46.

Russell, D.A. 1981. *Criticism in Antiquity.* Berkeley, Los Angeles, and London: University of California Press.

Russell, D.A., and Winterbottom, M. 1972. *Ancient Literary Criticism: The Principal Texts in New Translations.* Oxford: Clarendon Press.

Russo, Carlo F. 1950. *Hesiodi Scutum.* Biblioteca di Studi Superiori No. 9, Filologia Graeca. Firenze: "La Nuova Italia" Editrice.

Russo, Joseph. 1976. How and What Does Homer Communicate? The Medium and Message of Homeric Verse. *Classical Journal* 71: 289-299.

Russo, Joseph, Fernandez-Galiano, M., and Heubeck, A. 1992. *A Commentary on Homer's* Odyssey, Volume 3, books 17-24. Oxford: Clarendon Press.

Rutherford, R. B. 1992. *Homer:* Odyssey *Books XIX and XX.* Cambridge, U.K.: Cambridge University Press.

Ruthven, K.K. 1979. *Critical Assumptions.* Cambridge, U.K.: Cambridge University Press.

Samona, G.A. 1984. *Gli itinerari sacri dell'aedo. Ricerca storico-religiosa sui cantori omerici.* Rome: Bulzoni Editore.

—. 1983. Lo scudo, la cetra, e l'arco. L' aedo metieta na costo nell' *Iliade* e la Moira di Achille. *Studi e materiali di storia delle religioni* 1983: 161-182.

Schadewaldt, Wolfgang. 1966. *Iliasstudien.* Berlin: Akademie-Verlag.

—. 1944. *Von Homers Welt und Werk: Aufsatze und Auslegungen zur Homerischen Frage.* Leipzig: Koehler & Amelang.

Schefold, K. 1975. *Wort und Bild: Studien zur Gegenwart der Antike.* Basel: Archäologischer Verlag.

—. 1964. Transcendensia de la poesia para les artes plasticas en la Grecia primitiva. *Folia Humanistica* 2,18: 535-545.

Schein, S. 1984. *The Mortal Hero: An Introduction to Homer's* Iliad. Berkeley, Los Angeles, and London: University of California Press.

Schmeling, G. 1974. *Chariton.* New York: Twayne.

Schrade, Hubert. 1952. *Gotter und Menschen Homers.* Stuttgart: W. Kohlhammer.

Schulte, Rainer, and Biguenet, John, eds. 1992. *Theories of Translation: An Anthology of Essays from Dryden to Derrida.* Chicago and London: University of Chicago Press.

Scott, William C. 1974. *The Oral Nature of Homeric Simile.* Mnemosyne Supplement No. 28. Leiden: E.J. Brill.

Severyns, A. 1946. Simples remarques sur les comparaisons homériques. *Bulletin de Correspondance Hellénique*, pp. 540-547.

Shakespeare, William. 1971. *The Rape of Lucrece.* Ed. J.W. Lever. New York: Penguin Books.

—. 1924. *The Complete Works of William Shakespeare.* Ed. W.J. Craig. Oxford: Oxford University Press.

Shannon, R.S. 1975. *The Arms of Achilles and Homeric Compositional Technique.* Mnemosyne Supplement No. 36. Leiden: E.J. Brill.

Shapiro, H.A. 1980. Jason's Cloak. *Transactions of the American Philological Association* 110: 263-286.

—. 1984. Herakles and Kyknos. *American Journal of Archaeology* 88: 523-529.

Shapiro, M. 1990. Ecphrasis in Vergil and Dante. *Comparative Literature* 42: 97-114.

Sheppard, J. T. 1922. *The Pattern of the* Iliad. London: Methuen.

Shipp, G.P. 1953. *Studies in the Language of Homer.* Cambridge, U.K.: Cambridge University Press.

Sidney, Sir Philip. 1951 (1595). *Apologie for Poetrie.* Ed. E.S. Shuckburgh. Cambridge, U.K.: Cambridge University Press.

Slatkin, Laura. 1991. *The Power of Thetis: Allusion and Interpretation in the* Iliad. Berkeley, Los Angeles, and London: University of California Press.

Smith, Barbara Herrnstein. 1968. *Poetic Closure: A Study of How Poems End.* Chicago and London: University of Chicago Press.

Snodgrass, A.M. 1980. Towards the Interpretation of Geometric Figure Scenes. *Mitteilungen des deutschen archaeologischen Instituts, Athenische Abteilung* 95: 51-58.

—. 1979. Poet and Painter in Eighth-Century Greece. *Proceedings of the Cambridge Philological Society* 205, n.s. 25: 118-130.

—. 1974. An Historical Homeric Society. *Journal of Hellenic Studies* 94: 114-125.

Snyder, J.M. 1981. The Web of Song: Weaving Imagery in Homer and the Lyric Poets. *Classical Journal* 76: 193-196.

Solmsen, Friedrich. 1965. *Ilias* Σ 535-540. *Hermes* 93: 1-6.

Spengel, Leonardus. 1854. *Rhetores Graeci.* Leipzig: B.G.Teubner. (Reprinted 1966, Frankfurt am Main: Minerva GmbH.)

Sperduti, Alice. 1950. The Divine Nature of Poetry in Antiquity. *Transactions of the American Philological Association* 81: 209-240.

Spitzer, Leo. 1967. The "Ode on a Grecian Urn," or Content vs. Metagrammar. In *Essays on English and American Literature*, ed. Anna Hatcher, pp. 67-97. Princeton, N.J.: Princeton University Press.

Stacy, R.H. 1977. *Defamiliarization in Language and Literature.* Syracuse, N.Y.: Syracuse University Press.

Stanley, Keith. 1993. *The Shield of Homer: Narrative Structure in the* Iliad. Princeton, N.J.: Princeton University Press.

Steiner, Wendy. 1988. *Pictures of Romance: Form against Content in Painting and Poetry.* Chicago and London: University of Chicago Press.

—. 1982. *The Colors of Rhetoric: Problems in the Relation between Modern Literature and Painting.* Chicago and London: University of Chicago Press.

Stevens, Wallace. 1972. *The Palm at the End of the Mind. Selected Poems and a Play.* Ed. Holly Stevens. New York: Vintage Books.

—. 1942. The Relations between Poetry and Painting. In *The Necessary Angel: Essays on Reality and the Imagination*, pp. 157-176. New York: Vintage Books.

Stewart, Douglas J. 1966. Ekphrasis: A Friendly Communication. *Arion* 5: 554-555.

Tannen, Deborah. 1988. Hearing Voices in Conversation, Fiction, and Mixed Genres. In *Linguistics in Context: Connecting Observation and Understanding*. Advances in Discourse Processes No. 29, ed. Deborah Tannen, pp. 89-113. Norwood, N.J.: Ablex Press.

Taplin, Oliver. 1992. *Homeric Soundings: The Shaping of the* Iliad. Oxford: Clarendon Press.

—. 1980. The Shield of Achilles within the *Iliad. Greece and Rome* 27: 1-21.

Tashiro, Tom T. 1965. Three Passages in Homer and the Homeric Legacy. *Antioch Review* 25: 63-89.

Tatarkiewicz, W. 1963. The Classification of the Arts in Antiquity. *Journal of the History of Ideas* 24: 231-240.

Thalmann, William G. 1984. *Conventions of Form and Thought in Early Greek Epic Poetry*. Baltimore: Johns Hopkins University Press.

Thomas, Richard. 1983. Virgil's Ecphrastic Centerpieces. *Harvard Studies in Classical Philology* 87: 175-184.

Thoreau, Henry David. 1983 (1854). *Walden and Civil Disobedience*. Introduction by Michael Meyer. New York: Viking Penguin.

Trimpi, Wesley. 1978. Horace's *Ut pictura poesis*: The Argument for Stylistic Decorum. *Traditio* 34: 29-73.

—. 1973. The Meaning of Horace's *Ut Pictura Poesis. Journal of the Warburg and Courtauld Institutes* 36: 1-34.

Trypanis, C. 1977. *The Homeric Epics*. Warminster: Aris & Phillips.

Tyler, S. 1978. *The Said and the Unsaid: Mind, Meaning, and Culture*. New York: Academic Press.

van den Brink, H. 1959. *Ilias* Σ 497-508. *Hermeneus* 30: 199-204.

Vanderlinden, E. 1980. Le Bouclier d' Achille. *Les Études Classiques* 48: 105-115.

van Groningen, B.A. 1958. *La composition littéraire archaïque grecque*. Amsterdam: North Holland Publishing.

van Ooteghem, J. 1950. La danse minoenne dans l'*Iliade* XVIII 590-606. *Les Études Classiques* 18: 323-333.

Verdenius, W.J. 1970. Homer, The Educator of the Greeks. In *Mededelingen der Koningklijke Nederlandse Akademie van Wetenschappen*, Afd. Letterkunde Niewe Reeks, Deel 33 no. 5, pp. 205-232. Amsterdam: North-Holland Publishing.

——. 1960. L'Association des idées comme principe de composition dans Homère, Hesiode, Theognis. *Revue des Études Grecques* 73: 345-361.

Vessey, D. W. T. 1975. Silius Italicus: The Shield of Hannibal. *American Journal of Philology* 96: 391-405.

von Fritz, Kurt. 1943. *Noos* and *Noein* in the Homeric Poems. *Classical Philology* 38: 79-93.

Walsh, George B. 1984. *The Varieties of Enchantment: Early Greek Views of the Nature and Function of Poetry.* Chapel Hill, N.C., and London: University of North Carolina Press.

Webster, T.B.L. 1956. Greek Archaeology and Literature (1951-1955). *Lustrum* 1: 87-118.

——. 1939. Greek Theories of Art and Literature Down to 400 B.C. *Classical Quarterly* 33: 106-149.

West, D.A. 1975-76. *Cernere erat*: The Shield of Aeneas. *Proceedings of the Virgil Society* 15: 1-6.

West, M.L. 1985. *The Hesiodic Catalogue of Women.* Oxford: Clarendon Press.

——. 1981. The Singing of Homer and the Modes of Early Greek Music. *Journal of Hellenic Studies* 101: 113-129.

Westbrook, Raymond. 1992. The Trial Scene in the *Iliad. Harvard Studies in Classical Philologie* 94: 53-76.

White, James Boyd. 1987. Thinking about Our Language. *Yale Law Journal* 96: 1956-1987.

——. 1984. *When Words Lose Their Meaning.* Chicago and London: University of Chicago Press.

Whitman, Cedric. 1958. *Homer and the Heroic Tradition.* Cambridge, Mass., and London: Harvard University Press.

Willcock, M.M., ed. 1984. *The* Iliad *of Homer XIII-XXIV.* London: St. Martin's Press.

Williams, R.D. 1981. The Shield of Aeneas. *Vergilius* 27: 8-11.

——. 1960. The Pictures on Dido's Temple. *Classical Quarterly* n.s. 10: 145-151.

Williams, William Carlos. 1986. *The Collected Poems of William Carlos Williams,* Volume 1: 1909-1939. Ed. A.W. Litz and C. MacGowan. New York: New Directions.

Wittgenstein, Ludwig. 1977 (1958). *Philosophische Untersuchungen.* Frankfurt am Main: Suhrkamp Verlag.

—. 1968. *Philosophical Investigations: The English Text of the Third Edition.* Trans. G.E.M. Anscombe. New York: MacMillan.

Wolff, H.J. 1950. Nochmals zum Schild des Achilles. *Jura* 1: 272-275.

—. 1946. The Origin of Judicial Litigation Among the Greeks. *Traditio* 4: 31-87.

Yeats, William Butler. 1962. *Selected Poems and Two Plays of William Butler Yeats.* Ed. and with intro. by M.L. Rosenthal. New York: Collier.

Yoshida, Atsuhiko. 1964. La structure de l'illustration du bouclier d'Achille. *Revue Belge de Philologie et d'Histoire* 42: 5-15.

Zanker, Graham. 1987. *Realism in Alexandrian Poetry: A Literature and Its Audience.* London: Croom Helm.

—. 1981. *Enargeia* in the Ancient Criticism of Poetry. *Rheinisches Museum* 124: 297-311.

Zeitlin, Froma I. 1982. *Under the Sign of the Shield: Semiotics and Aeschylus' Seven against Thebes.* Rome: Edizioni dell'Ateneo, s.p.a.

Zuckerkandl, Victor. 1956. *Sound and Symbol: Music and the External World.* New York: Pantheon.

# INDEX

## General Index

Achilles, 1, 45, 47, 52-54, 80, 93,
129 n.238, 136 n.248, 141, 146,
149 n.272, 150
aesthetic, Homeric, 11, 64, 67, 84,
93, 97, 103, 136, 150
*aegis*, of Athena, 61-65, 74; of
Zeus, 71 n.128
*aeide* (sing), 45, 46 n.84, 47-48,
136
Agamemnon, 112, 136 n.248, 149
n.272; arms of, 63 n.114, 67-77,
97 n.171; scepter of, 14, 19
n.33, 52-54
Ameis, K. and Hentze, C., 83
n.145, 89 n.153, 119 n.221
analogy between arts, 4, 5-7, 38,
55 n.99, 57, 92 n.161, 93 n.163,
94, 97 n.171, 103, 140, 151; *see
also* rivalry
anaphora, 63, 91, 100, 102 n.187,
107
*animadversor*, *see* levels of
representation
Andersen, Ø., 5 n.9, 111 n.205,
122 n.224, 123 n.228
appropriation, *see* Ricoeur

Ares, 34, 55, 118-19, 121
Arnheim, R., 12 n.20
*ars et artifex*, *see* levels of
representation
Ashbery, John, 3, 84
*aspis* (shield), 108 n.200
Atchity, K., 4 n.7
Athena, 18, 57, 101 n.183, 118-
19, 121; *see also aegis*
*audê* (voice), 81, 83, 86, 88, 91,
106, 109, 110, 120, 132, 135,
138, 140, 141, 146
Auden, W.H., 3, 129 n.240
audience, bard as model for, 4-5,
101, 108, 151-153
Auerbach, E., 58 n.104
Austin, N., 5 n.9, 55 n.99
Bal, M., 86 n.151
Barnes, H., 69 n.123
Bartsch, S., 31 n.53
Bassett, S., 5 n.9
Baxandall, M., 5 n.11, 51 n.94
Becker, A.L., 39 n.73, 118 n.218
Becker, A.S., 13 n.23, 34 n.64, 46
n.86, 81 n.139, 117 n.216, 136
n.249

# Index of Ancient Authors and Passages

# About the Author

Andrew Sprague Becker is an Associate Professor of Classics at Virginia Polytechnic Institute and State University. He was born in Burma (Myanmar), and studied traditional Javanese dance and theater while living in Indonesia. He received his degrees in Classics from the University of Michigan, Cambridge University, and the University of North Carolina at Chapel Hill. His scholarship includes articles on Homer, Hesiod, ancient rhetoric and modern literary theories, Dio Chrysostom, and Plato. He is an award winning teacher, and lives in Blacksburg with his wife, also a classicist, and three children.

14773718R00115

Printed in Great Britain
by Amazon.co.uk, Ltd.,
Marston Gate.